WHOSE DOG ARE YOU?

THE ANIMAL TURN

Series Editor
Linda Kalof

Series Advisory Board
Marc Bekoff and Nigel Rothfels

WHOSE DOG ARE YOU?

*The Technology of Dog Breeds
and the Aesthetics of Modern
Human-Canine Relations*

Martin Wallen

Michigan State University Press
East Lansing

∞ The paper used in this publication meets the minimum requirements of ANSI/NISO Z39.48-1992 (R 1997) (Permanence of Paper).

 Michigan State University Press
East Lansing, Michigan 48823-5245

Printed and bound in the United States of America.

26 25 24 23 22 21 20 19 18 17   1 2 3 4 5 6 7 8 9 10

LIBRARY OF CONGRESS CATALOGING-IN-PUBLICATION
Names: Wallen, Martin, author.
Title: Whose dog are you? : the technology of dog breeds and the aesthetics of modern human-canine relations / Martin Wallen.
Description: East Lansing : Michigan State University Press, 2017. | Series: The animal turn | Includes bibliographical references and index.
Identifiers: LCCN 2016057844 | ISBN 9781611862584 (cloth : alk. paper) | ISBN 9781609175405 (pdf) | ISBN 9781628953091 (epub) | ISBN 9781628963090 (kindle)
Subjects: LCSH: Dogs—Breeding. | Dog breeds. | Human-animal relationships. | Foxhounds.
Classification: LCC SF427.2 .W354 2017 | DDC 636.7/1—dc23
LC record available at https://lccn.loc.gov/2016057844

Book design by Scribe Inc. (www.scribenet.com)
Cover design by Erin Kirk New.
Cover image: J. M. W. Turner, *Dawn after the Wreck*, 1841. © Samuel Courtauld Trust, The Courtauld Gallery, London, UK/Bridgeman Images. Used with permission.

green press INITIATIVE Michigan State University Press is a member of the Green Press Initiative and is committed to developing and encouraging ecologically responsible publishing practices. For more information about the Green Press Initiative and the use of recycled paper in book publishing, please visit www.greenpressinitiative.org.

For Linda
and
Bounce
O Rare!

Contents

Acknowledgments

When I first began thinking about this project, I had just gotten a puppy. For some time I had been wondering about a way to write about the relation between a human and a horse, a relation that—in the parlance of riding—works all the better for being "quiet." Could there ever be a writing that recounts the kind of questioning-by-giving-way that horse lovers always and continually have to learn in order to engage with these sensitive and powerful creatures? That question I have yet to answer. The dog I had brought home turned my attention canine-ward, leading me to recall with delight the claims by seventeenth-century sportsmen that dogs possessed tails simply to display their own pleasure in hunting. In one way of thinking, that explanation makes perfect sense; after all, a horse's tail works well to swish away flies—and to show displeasure—so why should a dog's tail *not* display pleasure, especially given how much joy it brings to humans? This project as a whole grows from that joy, found in the cynosure of possibility, of what a tail means to a dog wagging it. The limitless questions that arise from the simple fact that there are dogs in the world would seem to be due to the limitless variety of dogs, to their apparent insistence on distinguishing themselves from one another in all their diverse challenges to imposed limits. The dogs seen from afar, and the one dog whose long life (but not long enough) has become a poignant memory, warrant far more questions than I have posed here, and more possibilities for posing their own questions than we now allow.

Research for chapter 2 was generously supported by a John H. Daniels Fellowship at the National Sporting Library and Museum in Middleburg, Virginia. The staff at this delightful research facility made certain that I had access to virtually all the literature a dog lover could ever hope to dig up. Liz Tobey, in particular, went out of her way to make certain the month I spent there was productive and enlightening. Liz has since shown herself to be a true friend, one I cherish. I am also thankful to the staff at the Chapin-Horowitz Dog Book Collection of William and Mary University for making time to guide me through their vast holdings.

Parts of chapters 2 and 3 appeared, in an early form, as "Foxhounds, Curs, and the Dawn of Breeding: The Discourse of Modern Human-Canine Relations," in *Cultural Critique* 79 (2011): 125–41.

Part of chapter 4 appeared in *World Picture* 11, as "Biting the Philosopher's Hand: Other People's Dogs, Other Responses."

Brian Price kindly read large chunks of the work in progress, multiple times, and his comments always compelled me to refine my thinking, to read more, to take up further inquiry. Excellent host, fellow imbiber, and challenging intellectual, Brian remains a valued colleague and friend from afar, though how he can bear a life without a dog I cannot understand. Other people who offered support in many, many ways include Kevin Jackson, Claire Preston, Chris Page, Anne Dunan, Carol Moder, along with my fellow panelists at the ACLA conferences where I read versions of drafts. Special recognition is due to Otto M. Austin. Linda Kalof has proven to be the kind of editor one can only dream of.

And most of all, Linda Austin has set aside her own work, time and again, to read through yet another draft, to offer her advice, to give me her support, and to share my love of dogs.

Introduction

I am his Highness' dog at Kew,
Pray tell me Sir, whose Dog are You?

—EPIGRAM ENGRAVED ON THE COLLAR OF A DOG PRESENTED
TO THE PRINCE, BY ALEXANDER POPE, *MINOR POEMS*

WHEN THE INEVITABLE QUESTION CAME UP, IN THE EARLY DAYS OF THE OBAMA administration, about what breed the first family would have as their White House Dog, the new president (still able to show sparks of wit) commented that he would prefer to have a dog from a shelter, and stated that "a lot of shelter dogs are mutts," adding the charming comparison, "like me." The parallel that the president drew referred to his own mixed-race heritage, and led to the predictable responses, ranging from those happy with his comfort in talking about sensitive race issues to those offended that he should refer to mixed-race people as mutts.[1] President Obama's joke says as much about the way people in the twenty-first century think about dogs as it does about the way Americans view race, and there is much in that small statement that bears thinking about.[2] To follow the analogy—perhaps in a backward order—Obama's racial heritage makes him a mutt because, as we are reminded, it consists of an African, or black, father and an American, or white, mother, and the "muttness" refers to the mixture of races as much if not more than to that of national or regional identities. Neither Ann Dunham, the president's mother, nor Barack Obama Sr. has been described as a mutt or as belonging to mixed ethnicities, even though the Dunham family tradition contains rumors of Cherokee blood.[3] In this line of thinking, neither of the president's parents was a mutt, only he is, and only because he represents the mixture of white and black races.

For a dog to be a mutt like Mr. Obama, then, would mean that it is a mixed breed. And that is the point that holds interest for me, as it is quite a bit different from saying that this dog is of no breed. A mutt, a mongrel, a Heinz are terms that can only have meaning through the reference to breed identity, and they persist in framing the single dog in terms of type. Such framing in terms of breed has become almost inevitable, and holds consequences that most of us would rather avoid facing up to, for they make our happy relations with dogs into something of an uncomfortable paradox.

On the one hand, in this era we profess to care deeply for our animal companions—a care that Alice Kuzniar, as well as anyone, has shown makes for intensely close relations.[4] And, on the other hand, we continue to condone breeding practices that subject animals to questionable treatment, that effectively reduce animals to breeding machines to produce offspring conforming as closely as possible to a breed ideal. The beautiful and sweet dogs we care for deeply have been molded both physically and temperamentally to predetermine their capacity for one kind of relationship or another. This paradox has come to seem to me inescapable, for as I think about the care for animals that we value—that I personally value—I cannot help but question what such care is in itself when it entails selecting a canine companion for qualities that have been preprogrammed: what do I in fact care for, this individual who is sharing a world and experiences with me in unrepeatable ways, or a type, of which a potentially infinite series of individuals are merely representatives? This book has grown out of my effort to understand this paradox governing the treatment of dogs in the modern era, which in dog years can be delineated as spanning the time of the death of Alexander Pope's dog Bounce to the present. The attempt to confront this paradox has led me to try to understand the two principal figures involved in this modern relation of caring that at some point depends upon uncaring. At the basis of this study, therefore, lie these questions: how has the modern human-canine relationship come to take on the quality of this paradox? Are other possibilities, less troubled by this or equivalent paradoxes, available to us? What would it mean, after all, to see our dogs without regard to breed—as neither purebred nor mutt; what would it mean for us as well as for the dogs?

Even while playing a prominent role in the relations people in the West have with dogs, breed has remained largely unexamined apart from such observations of historians like Harriet Ritvo that the number of recognized breeds proliferated, beginning in Britain, after the Napoleonic Wars.[5] As I shall argue, breed developed as a discourse in the eighteenth century, and as a discourse, breed is more than a historic detail, as it determines the point where we can begin critically examining modern human-dog relations. Further, as a discourse, breed carries with it many cultural forces contributing to concepts of the human and the animal. One of the primary forces can be found in the modern view of nature, the view that I shall characterize—following the critical thinking of Martin Heidegger, Jacques Derrida, and others—as technology. My reference is to the view of the natural world as a field of raw materials to be used, developed, and regulated, and the view that privileges human interventions—and a particular kind of human intervention—in the world above all others. This is more than any one scientific endeavor, but the mode of knowing that has made such endeavors possible and that has shaped much of the relations that humans in the technologized era look forward to having with dogs and other nonhumans. This mode privileges particular human interventions because it begins with the claim that nature is a system. And if nature is a system, then simply by determining the laws—the grammar, if you will—governing the functions in the system, such knowledge gains mastery over the entirety. This knowing that characterizes the modern view of nature is *technē*, and its multifarious interventions in the world constitute modern technology in the singular.

The reason I refer to technology here, and throughout this study, in this singular overarching sense is that it has not only led to the creation of dog breeds, but has affected the modern attitude toward dogs, animals, and the natural world. Its prominence can be seen directly in the effects it has had on modern dogs through regulated breeding strategies, changing "dog" from the being that pre-nineteenth-century commentators described mostly in terms of variability and adaptable utility to the being that modern dog lovers describe in terms of distinct breeds with their own inherent characteristics. In fact, the proliferation of breeds that Ritvo comments on can be traced back to the technological success in the second half of the eighteenth century in creating one particular dog with specific characteristics sustainable over generations: this is the Foxhound, who epitomizes both the modern dog in itself and emblematizes the modern view that people hold toward dogs. The success of this hound spurred breeders in the early nineteenth century to create more new breeds, extending and reinforcing the belief that technology does indeed possess the capacity to know the world comprehensively, and in a way that warrants manipulating beings so that they serve human desires more directly.

A quibble might be raised here that technology entails artistic inventiveness as much as it does the regulative inventions of "improvement." This claim depends on the view—deeply ingrained in Western and modern thought—that knowledge is singular, so that inventiveness is likewise singular. In this view, knowledge is governed primarily by objective science, and secondarily by certain branches of philosophy. A major theme of this study begins, however, with the possibility that knowledge is anything but singular, that a challenge we modern humans must begin to engage lies in accepting different modes of knowledge. As humans seek to live responsively with other beings in the world, we have to accept not only that animals respond and feel, but also that they know the world around them, and in modes utterly different from the one sanctioned by science. Technology in its modern form has attained its dominance in part by transmuting all modes of knowledge and engagement to versions of itself and then privileging itself as the comprehensive management of all others. A modern breed dog carries his technological character bodily in his conformation to a breed standard, and discursively in the breed history through which we anticipate his character. A good dog affirms our expectations by not suggesting any other possibility, while a bad dog disrupts our expectations by raising unanticipated possibilities for engagement. In approaching dogs through their breeds—even if we refer to them as mutts—we delimit the possibilities for friendship by objectifying our dogs categorically into beings known in advance. And in this way we reinforce the modern technological insistence on a singular knowledge.

Certainly technology does drive inventiveness, as exemplified in the beautiful Foxhound and the proliferating number of other breed dogs that followed the creation of that one dog. And certainly previous ages have engaged in various forms of technological creativeness. But the modern form of technology—particularly in the area of human-canine relations—has turned much of its potential for inventiveness into a force of exploitation and regulation. In this regard it functions along the lines described by Michel Foucault as power undergoing "a very profound transformation" into biopower that disciplines the bodies of dogs, optimizing and extorting their capabilities, while also managing the populations of dogs (as well as their human companions) through a "series of interventions and *regulatory controls: a biopolitics of the population.*"[6] It is in this sense that modern technology operates in the political sphere through both legislative actions and the discourse normalizing dogs and their relations with humans.

Throughout my discussion I shall refer to the "landscape," by which I have in mind not merely "nature," as anything like "bare life," but the world framed into an objective realm of aesthetic judgment and technological manipulation. The landscape, as I shall show in detail, represents "nature"; it provides the framed, delimited system of significations of a primordial "nature," that innocent and naive pastoral that only existed in its own disappearance. The framing is of key importance, for it is the delimitation that makes possible the comprehension of nature as system and as a unified whole that can be described in codified aesthetic terms as well as conventionalized scientific terms. By turning away from references to "nature" or the "natural world" and instead to the landscape, I hope to underscore the point made by others that the world in which we encounter other beings—among them dogs—has always already been technologized in the sense of what Derrida calls "writing," in which "nature" as a so-called "proper name" appears as the trace of its loss.[7] Not only can we not return to a pre-technological, pre-landscaped, "natural" state, but the desire for such a return is a powerful part of the discursive framing of the world into a landscape, as will become evident in my discussion of the originary narratives grounding dog breeds. It is thus no accident that a good part of modern aesthetic discourse relies on the world viewed in terms of a landscape painting—an analogy that warrants further consideration.

Cary Wolfe has argued that the "full force of animal studies . . . is that it fundamentally unsettles and reconfigures the question of the knowing subject and the disciplinary paradigms and procedures that take for granted its form and reproduce it."[8] This knowing subject took on its recognizably modern form during the eighteenth century, and through two convergent discourses that I shall examine in this introduction. The first, which I have just described as technology, organizes the world discursively into a systemic field of resources to be developed, regulated, and improved upon. The interventions of technology might be broken down into the various *dispositifs* that regulate human-canine relations, that establish and enforce the norms for canine appearance and behavior biologically and socially (through breed clubs, for example), among others. The second discourse can be found in the aesthetic doctrines that gained prominence in Britain and Germany in the eighteenth century around a subject privileged both by the capacity to frame the natural world into a landscape comprehensible as a totality, and by landownership (which also conferred legislative power). The privilege of this proprietary aesthetic subject is also at work in the discourse of technology, which frames the landscape as necessitating human intervention. It is this aesthetic subject that I turn to first, to identify the discursive elements generating it and its distinctive capacity for judgment, and how those same elements have contributed to technological knowledge and to the prominence of breed in human-dog relations.

In regard to modern human-dog relations, the convergence of aesthetics and technology is especially important to consider, for the privileged subject that took shape in this time also shaped the dogs on whose loyal companionship it has based much of its belief in its own responsiveness to animals. Aesthetic doctrine of the eighteenth century allowed a narrow version of dogs to enter the ordered landscape because of their role in hunting, which had long been legally restricted to landowners; and with this inclusion, aesthetic doctrine enforced the law of privileged normality.[9] This same doctrine grounded the taxonomic divisions that divided dogs and humans analogously into breeds and races as reflections of regional origin, an alignment whose self-serving artificiality I hope to make apparent. And at the same time, the aesthetic discourse complemented the technological discourse in ways that obscured the violence done to animals and the landscape in the name of "improvement" and "preservation." In regard to dogs, the violence can be seen in the breeding programs geared toward creating a particular kind of dog to serve a particular end, and in the multiple laws that officially distinguished good dogs from bad dogs; these, the most obvious of violent acts, led to dogs being killed or maimed to ensure that "dog" held as predictable and normative a meaning as possible. It is such violence that aesthetic discourse made appear natural—or at least beneficial—and continues to do so today: as I shall show in the final chapter, twenty-first-century ethical claims to forge new and more caring relations with dogs continue to rehearse the aesthetic terms of judging a dog to be beautiful or good according to breed conformation. And so, although at the risk of giving a reductionist view of eighteenth-century aesthetics, which was by no means a single, unified doctrine, I wish to identify as plainly as possible the functions that privileged a particular view of dogs to make breed enforcement appear to be a necessary element in the human engagement with primordial nature; for dogs themselves constituted increasingly prominent thematic elements in the aestheticized and regulated landscape, earning value and significance from the judgment of beauty as an experience of union with the nonhuman world. I shall consider in turn each of these components of eighteenth-century aesthetics—privilege, the framed prospect, judgment—in regard to the development of modern human relations with dogs.

In order to emphasize the particularity of modern human-dog relations, the fact that they have been confined to one genre among other possibilities, I shall first look to a set of writings about dogs from a prominent dog lover just prior to the modern era. These writings are by the acerbic satirist Alexander Pope, who happened to express an affection for dogs—most famously with Bounce—in terms that are not easily recognizable from within the modern discourse, and that also stand utterly apart from the dominant mode of human-canine relations of the time, hunting; these writings do not belong to the modern genre, and thus challenge our ability to read them. Pope liked dogs. He kept them throughout his life, but because of his physical disability, he was incapable of hunting, and further, because of his religion, politics, and class, he was not legally qualified to hunt or even to own a large dog. He kept dogs, then, solely as companions—as pets—and his comments on dogs should be understood in this context, for he was among the few non-aristocratic Englishmen of the eighteenth century to write about dogs from the perspective of friendship rather than of hunting. Because Pope preceded the aesthetics of both subjectivity and sensibility, his accounts of friendship can seem void of care and attentiveness when set alongside modern accounts, or even those of his contemporaries, such as the ladies who loved their lapdogs. The fact that he described those associations in terms markedly different from what later dog lovers would recognize as expressive of affection, knowledge, or simple closeness compels us to consider the conventions governing what it means "to know" or to be friends with a dog.

For the purposes of providing an example of human-canine relations apart from breed discourse and the modern version of affection, I will examine an early letter—from 1709—in which Pope takes up what he calls his "Discourse on Dogs," and where he identifies some of the essential qualities of his own relations to dogs and of the most exemplary human-canine partnerships. My question concerns what elements Pope's friendships with dogs might contain that were dropped from the later mode of human-dog friendship, or vice versa. Since the rest of this study will delineate this later mode, a glance at Pope's premodern, non-hunting friendship can provide a measure against which to examine the friendships we take to exemplify care and loyalty. By no means do I wish to posit Pope's friendships as a lost standard we should try to recover, or as engagements unfettered by technology or occurring in a world the modern landscape might aim to represent. Pope worked in a different landscape—no less technologized, representational, than our own, but in an utterly different way. What makes the dog-loving Pope interesting is not any primordial quality we might return to, but rather the fact that his expressions of friendship should seem virtually unrecognizable as such today. In our landscape, Pope's canine friendships do not signify anything like an origin or exemplum for modern friendships; they only signify non-friendships. The example of Pope as a dog lover reminds us that other possibilities than what seems natural, genuine, normal today have existed. And other landscapes have presented the "natural" in ways that now seem anything but.

A brief word on Pope's aesthetics will therefore help us approach his friendships. The aesthetics of organic unity fostered by Kant and the Romantics gained prominence only after

Jonathan Richardson, *Alexander Pope and His Dog Bounce*, c. 1718. Private Collection/Bridgeman Images.

Pope; a governing principle of his aesthetics is discontinuity, which is reflected in his friendships. The relations to which he refers, thus, do not foreground similitude or reconciliation of differences. Instead particulars are aligned contiguously without subordination.[10] His poetry in particular works apart from the detailed descriptions prominent in modern poetry and narrative, in which characters develop their meaning within a setting unified through a visualizing rhetoric. Naturally enough, though Pope had several dogs over the span of his life, none of his references to them delineate what we today would see as an individual character. Pope names very few of the dogs in his poems (Bounce, Fop, Shock, and Argus), nor does he describe them, or address them directly to their face (apart from his plaintive question, "Ah Bounce! ah gentle Beast! why wouldst thou dye?");[11] nowhere does he describe any dog objectively as a being present before him. The dogs instead acquire an emblematic quality, which means the references generate cultural allusions—either expected or surprising—and which in this case refer to Pope's understanding of friendship. Claims that Bounce was actually multiple dogs underscore the notion that even as a singular name a dog served an emblematic function for Pope—as, say, the large dog defiantly kept by the Catholic poet at Twickenham.[12]

In Pope's nondescriptive, emblematic landscape, the contiguous relations among the particular figures, such as dogs and humans, disallow any comprehensive overview that would situate every detail in a subordinate relation to the organic whole. Thus, in comparing Pope's landscape to that in John Denham's *Cooper's Hill*, Robert Cummings draws the pertinent distinction with succinctness: "Denham . . . looks outward and downward from a height . . . [while] Pope is insufficiently attentive to facts of any kind."[13] This apt comparison focuses on the very point that separates Pope's landscape, aesthetics, and engagement with dogs from Denham in particular, and from the descriptive georgic mode more broadly. Unease with the lack of visual description in *Windsor Forest* leads Cummings to argue that the poem should not be read as a georgic at all, but as a *silva*, characterized as "a poem of discontinuous arguments, one whose parts do not relate to each other."[14] Riled by the "looseness" of the poem, Cummings asserts that it "has no business to claim the generic protection of the descriptive poem; or, if it did, it would forfeit excuses for its obvious enough deficiencies as one."[15] The looseness Cummings complains of would be the actual quality of an emblematic landscape, what Ronald Paulson equates with the English garden, where "one scene follows another, apparently unsubordinated but in fact related by clever juxtapositions. In this sort of structure," Paulson states pointedly, "the visitor lacks a sense of the whole."[16] The mimetic reading that works so well for georgics, pastorals, and modern realist narratives collapses with a text not needing representative description. The objects Pope identifies in his landscape are juxtaposed in the contiguous arrangement Paulson describes, rather than being subordinated systematically, for as emblems—in contrast to descriptive representations—they call up different and overlapping frames of reference.

Pope's dogs thus appear with no descriptive details that would integrate them as recognizably realistic dogs into a totalized landscape comprehended, as Cummings says Denham does, by looking "outward and downward from a height." Pope gives no such privileged perspective. The absence of privilege, and the contiguous juxtaposition of emblematic references demand a capacity for indirectness, in contrast to the direct representation modern readers expect in a literary text. Thus, if the Popean poet responds to dogs otherwise than by looking at them directly, the question becomes that of how, and if, he responds to them with care. The task before us, then, is to try to understand that indirection sufficiently to follow its consequences for the way Pope referred to his dogs.

Help with this task can be found in Earl Wasserman's thematic reading of *Windsor Forest* as the nondescriptive rehearsal of *concordia discors*, for it provides an understanding of the perceived "looseness" as an aesthetic apart from that privileging visual description. Wasserman traces this mode back to classical authors, and says that its dominance as an aesthetic guide to nature came to an end in the generation after Pope.[17] The classical notion of *concordia discors*, or concordant discord, allows for a landscape in which elements can reside in their difference—their discord—rather than sublating themselves into a unified totality. The concord is to be found in the discontinuity of a world experienced variably in both spatial and temporal terms, and the discord of variability need not be resolved in anything like the modern notion of a concord of unity through recognized sameness, or difference sublated into sameness. Criticisms like those of Cummings, in Wasserman's view, "arise from irrelevant standards"; the orientation that requires a description from a privileged viewpoint will consistently find the poem wanting. Wasserman continues: "The description is not scenic, but thematic; *we are not to see things*, but to realize the principle of *concordia discors*."[18] In the words of Cynthia Sundberg Wall, "the growing perception (and criticism) of eighteenth-century poetry and prose as visually barren, 'lacking eye,' is, in part, simply the cultural effect of the collapse of the memory storehouse."[19] Pope's emblematic references appear "loose" and "barren," because they deflect the "outward and downward" gaze of the georgic, and require a different reading from that of descriptive poetry and narrative that has dominated since. Pope's accounts of friendships take place in a nonvisual landscape of disjunction, governed not by organic unity but by *concordia discors*.

The primary effect of such discord is to preclude the privileging of the viewing subject, who would otherwise promote a single perspective of organic unity. In this discord of multiple, varying possibilities of association, readers are challenged to allow for nonorganic relations, a non-unified range of associations, and a non-totality. A relation between a man and a dog would not seek resolution into sameness through gestures of recognizing common mortality, common sensibility, or common rank—all to serve later as frames for friendships between humans and dogs—for the relation would be that of mutual difference. What a friendship of discord would entail Pope suggests in the "Discourse on Dogs," which appears in a long letter to his friend Henry Cromwell.

Pope devotes a large section of the 1709 letter to his "Discourse," beginning with this description of discordant "likeness":

> As 'tis Likeness that begets Affection, so my Favorite Dog is a Little one, a lean one, and none of the finest Shap'd. He is not much a Spaniell in his fawning; but has . . . a dumb surly sort of Kindness, that rather shows itself when he thinks me ill-us'd by others, than when we Walk quietly & peaceably by ourselves. If it be the chief point of Friendship to comply with [a] Friend's Motions & Inclinations, he possesses this in an eminent degree; he lyes down when I sitt, & walks where I walk, which Is more than many very good Friends can pretend to.[20]

Friendship as compliance works as a companionship rather than a melding of two beings through commonality or subordination. Notably Pope does not describe the dog looking back at him with any sort of loyalty or recognition. The description he does offer is as little and lean as the dog, relying mostly on the negatives of not being a spaniel (emblem of obsequious "fawning," which is derided at length in "Bounce to Fop") or of having a fine shape. The comparisons he makes between his own and the dog's appearance and demeanor, as well as with the "Motions & Inclinations" that prove their friendship, work to exclude others rather than to express fidelity or "fawning." The companionship between Pope and the nameless, ugly dog consists primarily in walking "quietly & peaceably" by themselves. This account of friendship as accompaniment leads into a series of references to famed literary dogs and humans who shared similar friendships that reflect the principle of *concordia discors*.

But first, Pope dismisses the broad tradition of describing these friendships in terms of the dogs' fidelity, saying, "Histories are more full of Examples of the Fidelity of Dogs than of Friends, but I will not insist upon many of 'em, because It is possible some may be almost as fabulous as those of Pylades & Orestes, & c." Canine fidelity is a "fabulous" cliché that Pope wants to get beyond, as he says, "for the honour of Dogs," since it subordinates dogs to the role of attendants rather than equal companions of humans. So, he says, "that the Two most ancient and esteemable Books, Sacred and prophane, extant, (viz: the Scripture and Homer) have shown a particular Regard to these Animals. That of Toby is the more remarkable, because there was no manner of reason to take notice of the dog besides the great humanity of the Author."[21] The biblical reference Pope has in mind comes from the Apocryphal Book of Tobit, when the son, Tobias, journeys with the Angel Raphael to Media, where he will meet his wife, Sarah, and bring her back to Nineveh. Twice the text refers to a dog: first, when Tobias and Raphael leave Nineveh there is the simple statement "So they went forth both, and the young man's dog with them";[22] and second, as they are returning back to Tobit and Anna's house, the angel tells Tobias they should run ahead of Sarah to prepare the house, and the text says, "So they went their way, and the dog went after them."[23] These two references are slight enough to be easily overlooked, and as Pope says, they serve no purpose to the book as a whole, or even to the section dealing with Tobias's journey. The interest Pope has in Tobias's dog would seem to lie precisely in that slightness. The references are "remarkable" only because of "the great humanity of the Author" who put them in the text, recognizing the friendship that can occur among such uncommon beings as an angel, a man, and a dog. Pope suggests that his interest is sparked by the fact that the dog does not appear as a part functioning within a systemic whole; the dog does not interact with Tobias, the angel, or Sarah in any revealing way, but simply accompanies them. "The great humanity" that Pope finds in these references would appear to be the simplicity of the statements that set a dog alongside an angel and a man as equals. In fact, this reference is "remarkable" for its lack of trope. The reference does not turn the dog into allegory or symbol of fidelity, or anything else. The humanity works in allowing for a friendship among unlike singular beings. Pope finds a "great humanity" in this unadorned, untroped reference to an un-universalized and unnamed dog, a reference that does precisely what eighteenth- and nineteenth-century natural historians and twenty-first-century post-humanists have tried to do, namely, refer to a dog without relying on humanist conceits. And yet, the references do work literarily as emblems, allowing Pope to forge "clever juxtapositions."

The "Discourse on Dogs" goes on to cite other classical references to dogs that work in much the same way, situating the human and the dog side by side so that their interactions work indirectly, precluding subordination of one to the other, but allowing for other texts to come to mind. In the one example of a face-to-face encounter—that between the homecoming Ulysses and the twenty-one-year-old Argus—Pope elides the passage to de-emphasize Homer's emphasis on Ulysses's nobility, concealed from the ignoble humans but recognizable to the noble hound. Instead, Pope turns the scene that he knew very well into a meeting of two friends who come together out of having nothing to share, both being "Unfed, unhousd, neglected," alone together.[24] For Pope, who often experienced exclusion because of his religion, politics, and disabilities, this scene works as an emblem of friendship outside of any economy of integration. Argus and Ulysses clearly feel a long lasting affection for one another, but one expressed not in the direct terms of coming together in a shared likeness, or as lord and vassal, but indirectly, in the silence of Ulysses's disguise and Argus's dying.

The conceits of humanity, good nature, and respect quietly, even tacitly, allow for a friendship among alterities, a concord of discords. The lack of elaboration in the human-canine relations contrasts with later accounts of such relations in the fact that the human subject (Pope) does not describe the way a dog looks—much less the way a dog looks *at* the human. In the modern, post-Romantic mode, the lack of description would mean that Pope does not engage directly or closely with the dogs, and would represent the archaic human-animal relations that modernity has improved upon. And the lack of description, abetted by the indirection, could be made to suggest that Pope lacked the emotional and sympathetic ties with his dogs that have become prominent in defining human-dog relations since the eighteenth century. Carole Fabricant has made this point in a different context: "What seems to me lacking in Pope is precisely . . . this capacity to 'look into the other's face' and through that act learn new and unsuspected, perhaps even disturbing things about oneself."[25] Fabricant is thinking mostly of Pope's raging sexism, shaped by "strategies of domination and containment," and her point is virtually irrefutable.[26] But her need for a poet of indirection to see a face depends on an ethical and aesthetic judgment shaped by Kant and Romanticism. Indirection foregoes the need to look steadily at another being while expecting a recognizable gaze in return. What Fabricant, like Cummings, takes as a lack might also be accepted as simply a different mode of engagement, one that does not excuse sexism but that still might offer different and "unsuspected" challenges to the modern mode of being with dogs. In writing of *Windsor Forest*, Margaret Anne Doody makes this nice observation on the hopeful world projected by Pope: "His imagined future world is one which has not forsaken differences but acknowledged them without letting them be obstacles."[27] The principle of *concordia discors* allowed Pope to enjoy the surly friendship of an ugly dog without forsaking his difference. He might have been one of the last people in the West capable of a friendship cast in the simplest terms of accompaniment.

THE AESTHETIC SUBJECT AND GOOD DOGS

The discourse of modern human-dog relations could be said to coincide precisely with the rise of modern aesthetics following what Cynthia Sundberg Wall calls the "collapse of the memory storehouse" grounding Pope's aesthetic. This modern aesthetics depends on a perspective that is strategically privileged on a number of planes at the same time. It privileges its mode of perceiving the world directly, cast as the identification of objects set into a unifying context, framed as the landscape, systematized as the environment, or spiritualized as nature. It privileges the interiority of the perceiving, judging subject as mind or spirit expressed through language, and it restricts all possibilities of subjectivity to its own version, so that a dog's subjectivity may exist only as a dumb reflection of human subjectivity. And this subject privileges its belief that it acts in the best interest of all beings that are part of its unifying context. But what has become evident is that this "all" is more exclusive than the privileged subject has let on—and, in fact, it is necessarily so. Whatever the privileged subject does not recognize within its unifying context remains illegitimate, a point that will return at notable junctures in my study.

Art historians have considered the function of the privileged aesthetic subject in the eighteenth century in detail and from different perspectives. Elizabeth Helsinger, writing about the function of landscape painting in the formation of a national identity, comments that the "conventional features of seventeenth and eighteenth-century landscape gardens and pictures (or verbal descriptions that observed pictorial conventions), all tend to enforce a separation and a hierarchy of control between the viewing subject . . . and the objects of . . . sight."[28] The control belongs primarily to the landowner who regulates the land for his own benefit—financial, aesthetic, and moral—but also to the viewer of the painting or landscape "who could learn the rules of taste."[29] The "rules of taste" often resolve into the overarching principle that dominates not only the eighteenth-century aesthetics of Shaftesbury, Reynolds, and Kant, but also the later, Romantic poetics of Coleridge that supposedly forged a direct bond between the subject and nature, and that is that the viewer should "derive a general concept from particulars, to understand the relation between the land as a local landscape . . . what can be seen by one viewer from one spot, and that elusive abstraction, the nation."[30] This principle is what Kant, at the end of the century, says governs the judgment of beauty as the combination of the manifold of particularities in the object, even so that natural beauty serves "to strengthen and entertain the mental powers that enter into play in the exercise of the faculty of judgement," the faculty that unites "particular experiences into a connected system of nature."[31] For Kant, the strength and sustenance gained from perceiving beauty instill a morality in the viewing subject. As he says in the section on "Beauty as the Symbol of Morality," "Taste makes, as it were, the transition from the charm of sense to habitual moral interest possible without too violent a leap," in that "the subjective principle of the judging of the beautiful is represented as *universal*, i.e. valid for every human being but as cognizable by means of any universal concept (the objective principle of morality is set forth as also universal . . . and, besides as cognizable by means of a universal concept)."[32] The subject possessed of taste enjoys beauty in the same way it judges an action for its morality, by comprehending the coherence of the manifold, recognizing the unification of the particulars into a coherent whole, and then asserting that it has adhered to a universal, objective standard of judgment. This last assertion enables the subject to consider its aesthetic judgment as simple and direct perception, unclouded by ideology or convention, uninterrupted by the representational function of writing. Its judgment of which dogs should be preserved and which banned has sustained itself both in depictions of good canine companionship—in paintings and narratives of the hunt, for example—and in legislative measures that outlawed many dogs in order to preserve the health of good household dogs.

It is worth noting that Kant draws this crucial analogy between moral and aesthetic judgment by pointedly referring to the rhetorical strategy of *hypotyposis*, in which distant objects are made to appear vividly present to the mind.[33] This rhetoric makes the crucial analogy possible, he says, by "transferring the reflection upon an object of intuition to quite a new concept, and one with which perhaps no intuition could ever directly correspond."[34] *Hypotyposis* works as a visual description to enact mentally the experience of directly engaging with objects in a framed setting, so that the experience—because it is mental—can correspond to a concept as if it were of the moral faculty rather than the sensuous aesthetic faculty. I want to underscore this point especially, that aesthetic judgment works analogously to moral judgment as long as the judgment of beauty relies on visual description. The effect of Kant's analogy here is to weaken any nonvisual aesthetics, such as Pope's, because it does not allow for the almost automatic blurring of aesthetic and moral experiences.

John Barrell has followed the development of aesthetic theory over the span of the eighteenth century to emphasize the ways the modern subject sustains and exercises its privilege by making the landowner represent, in his actions, in his moral, aesthetic, and even financial judgments, the national interests; for through a taste that has become commensurate with a morality founded upon universal principles, "The owner of fixed property, even when conscious . . . of consulting his own interests, would also necessarily be consulting the true, the permanent interests of the country in which his family had a permanent stake."[35] The decisions made by this privileged man affecting the landscape would thus be guided by the good taste that enables him to appreciate good art, and would morally benefit the nation as a whole. The privilege here is considered to be wisdom, or common sense, or, as Wordsworth puts it in 1800, a purity of vision that enables him "at all times to look steadily" at an object by seeing it within the unified whole.[36]

The abstraction that Barrell and Helsinger have shown to be necessary in identifying the local or regional with the nation established a clear limit to the totality that was admired as landscape or made to serve as nation. The limit setting a frame around the totality was at once nebulous and real, in that it reflected taste—which was affirmed in a circular logic by the privilege of the aesthetic subject—and set clear distinctions between who or what belonged in the landscape and who did not. Within the framing limits, variety was a vital quality expressing the bounty of nature, and differed from *concordia discors* in expressing the vibrancy of parts interacting toward resolution into the aesthetic whole of the landscape. Visual description makes a landscape appear present and real by bringing the variety of visual details together into a vibrant whole whose parts are visible in their cohesion, and morality. But at the same time each part had to be unvariable in itself, had to conform to an essential standard, an "as such" that constituted its essential being defined according to its place in the landscape, and that determined its effect on other particulars. Self-consistency precludes discontinuity. The privilege of the landowner thus lay not only in an elevated view of the totalized landscape but also in the moral capacity to delimit the landscape by determining which parts best conformed to their abstracted quiddity. For, as Barrell makes clear, the morality of the privileged subject depended on this ability to perceive a particular in terms of an abstraction, in terms that transcend temporal experience. Following this same need to extol the wealth of parts while limiting them to a comprehensible degree, Coleridge, in the early nineteenth century, defines beauty in a way that discloses the basis of the strength and sustenance gained by the subject. He writes, "the most general definition of beauty, therefore is . . . Multëity in Unity"; and notably he adds the pedantic point that he uses the "forgotten terminology of the old schoolmen, the phrase, *multëity*, because I felt I could not substitute *multitude*, without more or less connecting with it the notion of 'a *great* many.'"[37] With his qualification, Coleridge underscores the aesthetic need to bound the prospect, to limit the degree to which the manifold is present as the multiplicity of abstractable and constant particulars. As Kant asserts in regard to the sublime, there is a maximum beyond which the comprehension of parts in their unity cannot go.[38] Unless there is a limiting frame, there can be no discernible whole, aesthetically or morally, and instead of gaining a clear vision through its abstracting of particulars, the subject would lose itself in indeterminacy. Both the morality of the viewing subject and its dependence on some delimiting frame figure significantly in the subject's consideration of the landscape, for, according to Kant, "Nature proved beautiful when it wore the appearance of art; and art can only be termed beautiful, where we are conscious of its being art, while yet it has the appearance of nature."[39] For nature to wear "the appearance of art," it must be perceived in the unity of its manifold. The visual description allows the imagination to experience it as an integrated unity, which universal morality demands be preserved. In the mind's eye, therefore, natural scenes are already art, national treasures to be protected.

Viewing the landscape as if "it wore the appearance of art," in Kant's terms, means that the aesthetic subject frames the totality to delimit which parts can then be appreciated and regulated according to principles of tradition, religion, and higher nature. The "parts," of course, consist of the signifiers of contained variety, such as topographical details, climate, the indigenous people, plants, and animals, along with activities of the inhabitants, that together shape a region into a living, harmonious community with its traditions preserved as a collective memory in fables, histories, and genealogies. Such elements of contained variety are generally made to denote a regional authenticity threatened by the advances of history, on the one hand, and by exploitative intrusions of inauthenticity on the other, thus standing in need of preservation by those capable of recognizing them.

In the landscape as written artifact, the signifiers of variety must also signify interrelatedness, the capacity to affect other parts and to be affected in turn. The aesthetically and morally regulated landscape signifies the potency of nature, the originary force or spirit of creation. Thus the parts—topography, climate, human and animal inhabitants—must signify that spiritual potency through interactions that alter the active particulars leading to coevolution, or mutual improvement. The actions of the privileged landowners not only improved the land and nation, as Barrell indicates, but the landowners themselves. The morality of improvement lies in the acts of improving and in being improved by those actions. "Improvement," supplemented in different measures by such terms as "development," "evolution," or "progress," was one of the great watchwords of the day, as I shall discuss below, and continues to ground the modern self-privileging in numerous ways.

The aesthetics shaping the landscape naturalized the laws excluding bad dogs, and connected the good dogs with the aesthetic appreciation of natural beauty. The similitude that Kant forges by making nature beautiful when it wears "the appearance of art," and art beautiful only when "it has the appearance of nature" undergirds the modern relations humans look for in their good dogs. In this similitude, as Derrida says in his critique of Kantian aesthetics, art works "must resemble *effects* of natural *action* at the very moment when they, most purely, are works [opera] of artistic confection." This similitude Derrida identifies as an "analogical *mimesis*," and explains that for the Kantian judgment, mimesis "is not the representation of one thing by another, the relation of resemblance or of identification between two beings, the reproduction of a product of nature by a product of art. It is not the relation of two products but of two productions. And of two freedoms. . . . *mimesis* displays the identification of human action with divine action—of one freedom with another. The communicability of pure judgments of taste, the (universal, infinite, limitless) exchange between subjects who have free hands in the exercise of the appreciation of fine art, all that presupposes a commerce between the divine artist and the human one."[40] The similitude Kant posits between the painted and the natural landscape carries over into the performatively aesthetic subject viewing both painting as if it were nature and nature as if it were a readable artwork, open to exegesis through the principles of art criticism. The landscape appears as a work of art to be judged and improved, but it appears as though it were utterly transparent, giving the reading and judging subject direct contact with the divine author. The reading and judging—or, let's say, the natural historical comprehension—of the landscape works mimetically with the divine production: the privileged judge admiring and improving the landscape produces and sustains the "*effects* of natural *action*." The objects in the natural landscape thus attain by analogy the status of "encrypted signs, a figural writing set down in nature's production," which the aesthetic subject, well educated in taste, comprehends as the expression of an analogous subject, namely, the divine author of nature. The mimetic relation between the aesthetic subject and the landscape—and whether it be that viewed out of doors, as a painting, or a georgic description almost ceases to matter—becomes, in Derrida's words, "a language between nature and man." Even more to the point of human-dog relations, Derrida identifies this language as an "in-significant non-language," and "silence."[41] When Derrida rejects the understanding of Kantian mimesis as "a relation of resemblance" in favor of "the relation . . . of two productions," he underscores the basic claim of post-Popean aesthetics to apprehend the essential goodness and beauty signified by the written landscape as though it were voiced by God; and in terms of dogs, this means deciding which belong and which are bad, immoral, a social threat; and he shows just how much privilege the judging subject grants itself in its claim to recognize and reenact the creative freedom exercised by the divine author in the creation of unified nature. The reading that recognizes a good dog's place in the landscape, and the judging that excludes a bad dog are both valued as performative reenactments of the divinely creative act of organizing nature into a spoken grammar of presence, a free and productive answer to the divine author.

THE TECHNOLOGICAL SUBJECT AND IMPROVEMENT

The linguistic exchange supposedly uniting the human subject and nature in the written landscape also provides the basis for the technological regulation and manipulation—the "improvement"—of the landscape. Here is where the privileged comprehension of aesthetic judgment and the transformational capacity of technological knowing come together. Read as signs of divine speech, the landscape generally, and dogs particularly take on an order that pleases the subject instructed in taste. Signifying the language of nature, the landscape with its variety of dogs presents itself not only as though it were art, but as a kind of grammar or order that indicates the direction in which the text might be improved for fuller expression to bring the "two productions" into greater presence. Kant says that nature "with its variety and heterogeneity" must conform to the laws of an order, which the understanding must "find out"; and for Kant this very discovery consists in "introducing into nature the unity of principle."[42] The laws governing this order, according to Kant, are identical with those of the understanding, so that the subject is said not to impose its laws on nature but rather to "attain a concept" of the order of nature through that identity. Within the linguistic exchange between subject and divine nature, the abstractions, relations, exclusions, delimitations, and so on that the subject needs in order to comprehend a multëity in unity become the qualities of the landscape itself. The "improvement" that had far-reaching effects on the English landscape throughout much of the eighteenth century was guided by the aesthetic comprehension of the laws of nature signified by the regularity of the landscape, and was enforced by technological intervention into the parts of the totality, restricting the extent of their variability in conformity with "the bringing of unity of principle into nature." In "bringing" such conformity to the landscape, the morality and privilege of the subject justify the interventions as "improvement." Taste is no longer an appreciation of nature as it appears on its own, but becomes the active mastery over the framed and regulated landscape. But mastery is presented not as subjugation, which would seem less like "improvement" than exploitation; rather, mastery is presented as "bringing unity," through a productive engagement with the divine author, to unformed nature. A prominent improvement effected in just this way was experienced by dogs, whose discontinuity in size, shape, and demeanor posed clear challenges to the framing of the landscape as an aesthetically ordered space and morally legislated possibility of experience. Because dogs responded directly to humans, their function in the landscape constituted a forceful experience of the landscape itself offering itself to engagement; dogs' appearance and their behavior needed, therefore, to adhere to the laws that are both of nature and of the understanding. Another way of saying this is that dogs needed to be normalized in their bodies and performative abilities in accord with the aesthetic and moral health of the regulated landscape.

Nature read as the expression of a divine author calls to the judging subject for a productive engagement that will complete the expression by making it into a landscape framed as though it were art. Following this mode of thinking, F. W. J. Schelling says in the first decade of the nineteenth century, "The Word which is fulfilled in man exists in nature as a dark, prophetic (still incompletely spoken) Word. Hence the anticipations which have no exegesis in nature itself and are only explained by man."[43] As "anticipation," nature awaits fulfillment through man's complete expression.[44] "Improvement" in this regard entails all the actions committed by the privileged subject in the name of comprehending the text of nature and bringing it to its teleological—and even, as Richard Drayton says, eschatological—fulfillment.[45] And this fulfilling expression entails both the philosophical and aesthetic systems that facilitate knowledge and the actions conducted in the name of knowledge. These actions include agricultural interventions, from crop rotation and fertilizing to draining and clearing lands; they include the landscape designs by Capability Brown and others; and they include the breeding techniques that gave rise to such modern animals as the Thoroughbred and the Foxhound. "Improvement" thus lends a moral necessity to such aggressive interventions as the intensive inbreeding program that created a new hound needed by the sport of foxhunting, and the legislative interdictions that eliminated ugly, immoral dogs and other "unqualified" possibilities of human interactions with dogs. And, as I stated above, the landscape improved by the moral and aesthetic subject improves that subject in turn.

Such logic also drives the necessity of mastering the troubling discord among both dogs and humans by grouping individuals under conceptual headings that create identities through obscured differences. It was thus out of the necessity of mastering themselves and nature that Enlightenment thinkers arranged plants and animals into taxonomic categories in which individuals acquired a conceptual identity. For Kant, "the discovery that two or more empirical heterogeneous laws of nature are allied under one principle that embraces them both is the ground of a very appreciable pleasure, often even of an admiration," and in contrast, the failure of such a comprehensive organization—"a representation of nature" in which "a heterogeneity of its laws" persisted—"would be altogether displeasing to us."[46] Still driven as they are by a logic of necessity and by Kantian identification of the laws of understanding with the grammar of landscape, the categorical divisions remain inescapably vital to the modern discourse, so that virtually the only way we can speak of animals is from within the conceptual frames of breed and species, and the only way we can speak of humans is through race and gender understood within taxonomic alignments.[47]

Dogs cease to be fluidly discordant beings when breed becomes the primary way to understand what a particular dog is. Breed has effectively transformed unpredictable relations between self-determining and free productions to generic (albeit signified as mutually affective) relations between the freely performative human and the preformed canine product. In fact, the language governed by ethnicity, race, breed, and species becomes the very essence of the discourse on nature: to speak and write about animals—whether wild or domestic—means to institute and enforce these organized conceptual differences. Taxonomies no longer appear as mere technological tools; they have become the shape that technological knowledge of the regulated landscape itself takes, and as such they reveal the extent to which technology—as the organization of the mythically unframed, ungrammatical discord into a manageable linguistic system signifying the divine call for man to complete the "still incompletely spoken" word of nature—has transformed the knowledge or appreciation of nature and dogs (and humans) into an active reformation and regulation of a resource. And this is not to mention the extent to which technology has restricted and narrowed the landscape and the animals—particularly dogs—within it.

The technological view of animals as resources aligns their meaning in a relational organization with other resources, enforcing the regulatory control of that organization by expanding the taxonomies to account for virtually any possible variant in terms of its relations with other varieties. Martin Heidegger explains that the effect of technology on the Western view of nature is that "Everywhere, everything is ordered to stand by," to become a resource; and as such the landscape becomes available in the same way both to an activity as overtly and intrusively manipulative as the electrical industry and to one that promotes conservation of animal habitats the way hunt culture does, for in both cases nature consists of a field of objects valued as resources to be improved as products.[48] Heidegger describes the view toward the landscape manifested in modern technology as a "challenging," which amounts to a demand that objects fulfill the requirements of the privileged subject. As an example, Heidegger points out that "the coal that has been hauled out in some mining district has not been supplied in order that it may simply be present."[49] Rather the coal is made to provide energy, and as a resource the coal remains incomplete in itself; only when it is improved as energy does it serve a vital function. We can easily go beyond Heidegger's example and say that the landscape is no longer looked upon except as the source of such coal, or—what may seem more benign but in fact still perpetuates the discourse of modern technology—as the source of scenic attractions for tourists educated in the tasteful appreciation of nature, or where the huntsman can engage in sport. The freedom for judgment, joy, production, or performance is appropriated by the human, who transmutes the freedom or possibilities on the part of other beings into a desire to join with or serve humans as a resource. Modern techno-science "sets up nature to exhibit itself as a coherence of forces calculable in advance."[50] Taxonomies enable humans "to know" breeds in advance by recounting information that always reaffirms the taxonomic relations. Just as Kantian aesthetics makes the laws of nature identical to the laws of the understanding, so taxonomic delineations project technological knowledge onto the landscape, to make beings like dogs and other animals into functions calculable in their service to technology itself, to the landscape needing, calling for the technological drive to improve and to regulate. The knowledge afforded by breed taxonomy amounts to the calculation that an individual dog will act within a limited range of possibilities determined by the breed standard, which has been almost inextricably intertwined with a wholly modern landscape formed "as a calculable coherence of forces."[51]

The importance, even urgency, of coming to terms with what this techno-aesthetic framing means begins to come clear in Heidegger's point that the modern ordering of nature "drives out every other possibility of revealing."[52] The restrictiveness of this modern mode of technology will always impose itself upon, will challenge nature by way of excluding whatever does not contribute to the systematic, organic, unified, tasteful conceptualization of the landscape. It excludes by way of improving the resources, to make them serve more efficiently or tastefully; and it excludes by relegating something to the non-status of what does not belong, what threatens to intrude and disrupt the system—whatever violates the natural grammar, or is distastefully cacophonous, or is simply and forgettably irrelevant. Such, as I shall show in later chapters, is the cur, which, unlike the mutt, holds no relation to breed—except as contaminating excess—and consequently no relation to the landscape overseen with pleasure by the techno-aesthetic subject.[53] The cur also invokes the sense of disgust that Kant says cannot be represented "without destroying all aesthetical delight," the non-categorical object "insisting, as it were, on our enjoying it, while we violently resist it."[54] Curs appear in the regulated landscape as variability itself, which interrupts the aesthetic exchange between the two full presences of the privileged judging subject and the divine author of nature. In terms of the written landscape, a breed dog is the trace of nature, promising and deferring a mutual coming together of the judging subject and the divine author, a recovered continuity with the lost primordiality of pre-technological nature. A cur promises nothing, as its variability raises the disgust that turns the grammar promising a meaning into a confrontation with manifoldness, which voids any expectation of a future understanding or any certainty of an originary past.

The critique of technology I have just summarized becomes complicated when Heidegger expands that critique in other contexts, especially when he does so with reference to his distinction between humans and nonhumans. In one such notable passage from *An Introduction to Metaphysics*, he says, "What do we mean by world when we speak of a darkening of the world? World is always world of *spirit*. The animal has no world nor any environment. Darkening of the world means emasculation of the spirit, the disintegration, wasting away, repression, and misinterpretation of the spirit."[55] All of this comes, in Heidegger's view, from the technology enforced by America and Russia, the two cultures holding Europe in "pincers." Heidegger's anxieties and biases lead to a view of Europe losing its way, effectively reversing the process of completing the dark, "incompletely spoken" word valued by Schelling. In the work *On Spirit*, Derrida engages these biases to show that Heidegger would find an antidote to technology in revitalizing the "spirit" of a race, specifically the German, or we might say the spirit of those able to judge and improve the world from an enforced position of privilege. As Derrida states, Heidegger seeks a return to a primordial power, one that "originarily unites and engages, assigns, obliges," and thus overcomes "the instrumentalization of spirit," through a "spiritual unity."[56] In Heidegger's anxiety, nostalgia for a primordial unity provides the antidote to the danger that lies next to animal world poverty. And technology takes on the character of the fragmenting, interrupting evil that we need to resist in order to effect a more perfect union with spirit, which is to say nature, Being, thinking. What I have been referring to as the landscape, the always already technologized nature, would be the instrumental text we could lay aside in order to engage once again in the true pastoral where canine muteness was itself the voice of creative, originary nature, of the author of nature. In fact, as my examination of modern aesthetics has shown, the qualification to judge, to read the landscape promises the spiritual unity Heidegger sees as the antidote to technological "darkening"; and that same aesthetic judgment colludes with technological improvement and regulation of the landscape to make the unity even possible.

In recognizing that the landscape in which we interact with dogs has been shaped technologically (even *as* the technology vital to aesthetic judgment), most evidently in the faces and possibilities we have imposed on dogs, I do not mean that we might, or should, free ourselves from that landscape and either return to a mythic pastoral or move ahead to a more enlightened union. But I do think it is important to recognize how our relations with dogs have been written irrevocably by this landscape into conventional, generic aesthetic and moral terms. The technological landscape can only seek to expel the disgust of the undefinable cur. The repulsion permeates the landscape, and in multifarious ways. A breedless dog interrupts the regulatory economy even without attempting a canine insurrection or resistance. But the disgust, the general anxiety over currishness drives the technological regulations for order and respectability, on the one hand, and leads to calls for a nostalgic return to the spirit of originary creativity on the other. Technological disgust and anxiety, this infectious excess, might also be termed surprise, possibilities available in the landscape we have inherited.[57]

The dual aspect of modern technology as systemic knowing and systematic manipulation has played a central role in transforming and regulating modern human-canine relations, to make them almost wholly dependent on the discourse of breed. The importance of breed as an identifying qualification arose quite suddenly in Britain in the latter half of the eighteenth century alongside two other cultural events that were by no means unrelated: first of all, within the Agricultural Revolution the drive for "improved" crops and animals led men like Robert Bakewell and Hugo Meynell to develop breeding strategies that promoted desirable qualities in agricultural and sporting animals, and excluded displeasing surprises; in other words, the creation of improved breeds of several valuable animals became a determined effort throughout the rural landscape. And secondly, natural historians were mapping out the taxonomies defining the categorical abstraction against which an individual was measured, and orienting relations between categories, such as "dog" and "man." Both of these activities are manifestations of the technological discourse on animals that Derrida has characterized "the one that occurs most abundantly" in the modern era.[58] During "the last two centuries," Derrida asserts, human-animal relations have been dominated by "forms of *knowledge*, which remain inseparable from *techniques* of intervention *into* their object, from the transformation of the actual object . . . namely, the living animal." This fundamentally modern equation of the knowledge *about* animals with the ability to transform and manipulate them through breeding has the effect of reducing "the animal not only to production and overactive reproduction," but also to "all sorts of other end products, and all of that in the service of a certain being and the putative human well-being of man."[59] If nature has always been technologized as a landscape, what distinguishes this modern mode of technology is the stance taken by the privileged subject toward it. In this modern mode, the subject takes technology not as the structure of significations, but as a manageable mode of interrogation that can be made to serve the human. Technology in this sense consists of a tool apart from the written landscape, lying apart from and in wait for the subject. It is no longer simply the landscape as written supplement to the lost pastoral of "nature," but now supplements the supplement, turning the landscape into the signifier of human need. This supplementary nature of modern technology will become evident when I take up the creation of the Foxhound.

CONDITIONAL SIMILITUDE AS THE CANINE SUBJECT

When Derrida takes up the thinking about the war that has raged throughout the modern epoch of human-animal relations—the war over whether or not to feel compassion for animals—he says that this thinking begins at the abyssal limit between the human and the animal, a limit that is multiple and multifarious. It is this thinking at the abyssal limit that I attempt to invoke throughout my study; it is by keeping this limit—or these limits—in view, along with the means through which we enforce them, that thinking can begin to break up the collusion between aesthetics and technology, to allow for less violent, more responsive engagements between humans and other animals, engagements that do not close off the freedom of one participant by allowing it only to perform as an "end product." For beyond "the so-called human," Derrida says, "there is already a multiplicity of organizations of relations," and "these relations are at once intertwined and abyssal, and they can never be objectified."[60] The multiplicity in the types of, or orientation in, relation between humans and dogs has been narrowed since eighteenth-century breeders and taxonomists began to define and improve upon the dogs allowed in the landscape. In order to encounter dogs apart from the narcissistic reflection provided by regulated breeds, we have to open ourselves to dogs in their discordant alterity. And, in order to begin opening ourselves up to that alterity—even to consider what alterity entails—we must consider the mechanisms that have perpetuated the restrictive framing of possible human-canine relations; we have to understand how that difference has been aesthetically framed, or even disguised, as likeness. For through that disguise, the technological violence committed against dogs and other animals remains concealed. It is breed discourse and its attendant elements, I contend, that should be understood not simply as part of a historical progress in human-animal relations, but as one of the most effective means through which the techno-aesthetic subject has "challenged" dogs by demanding that they not "simply be present," as Heidegger says in his example of the coal, but that they serve as a resource for the privileged subject alone, perhaps even offering something like the spiritual unity Heidegger posits as the antidote to technology. The technological intervention that is perpetuated through breed discourse colludes with the aesthetics of the privileged subject by producing a canine face in such a way that it can be recognized and can be responded to within conventionalized limits that narcissistically serve human needs or desires. This aesthetic doctrine allows for compassion, sympathy, and responsiveness—the qualities that would seem to be at odds with the violence of technological intervention—but only along predetermined lines. A dog must be tasteful, or useful, or simply must belong; it must reflect the aesthetic (human) subject that finds gratification in responding with care and taste to the framed landscape and to the dogs allowed a place and role within the landscape. If, as Derrida says, the human relation with animals "is passing through a critical phase" where thinking about abyssal alterity has become a necessity "henceforth more than ever," then, I believe, we can facilitate this thinking by critically assessing how the collusion of technology and aesthetics has framed our privileged relations with dogs.[61]

The relations that humans have developed over the past two hundred years with dogs bear special consideration for several reasons. The discordant variability of dogs, as I have already stated, posed the same problem to natural historians as the variability of humans, and it was no coincidence that the early development and delineation of canine breeds occurred at the same time—and through the efforts of some of the same natural historians—as the delineation of human races. Canine variability was taken to be the natural analog of human

John Dixon, after Thomas Gainsborough, *Henry Duke of Buccleuch*, 1771. © National Portrait Gallery, London.

variability, and so to comprehend the conceptual laws governing the one would also disclose the laws governing the other. In this way dogs served as the particular analog of humans in the landscape, by way of the conceptualization of breed or racial identity. The silence of dogs became, to call on Derrida's account of economimesis, the natural language that spoke to the meaning of human variability. And this mimesis developed through the eighteenth century to make dogs into a prominent reflection of the privileged aesthetic subject whose capacity for judgment found affirmation in the recognition that dogs might possess an interiority directly analogous to human interiority.

The mimetic relation assumed that dogs possessed a human-like sensibility, a capacity to respond to external forces (climate, topography, and the other regional characteristics) that led to their variability. It was their sensibility, their capacity both to respond and to feel, that, according to the general narrative, made dogs willing companions to humans (and their willingness is always stressed, as we shall see), and, in turn, gave dogs a visibly present face to which humans might respond with compassion. This was the face of mutual regard, of loyalty, of mutual comprehension—it was the face that looked *as if* it knew what its human reflection meant, and *as if* it wanted to speak, to tell humans of its loyal feelings and that its greatest desire was to be wanted by humans. And it was this face that made dogs readable by the privileged aesthetic subject who found affirmed there in the dog's gaze the truth that techno-science had successfully delineated the natural order. No wonder, then, given the many ways the modern human-canine discourse supports the mimetic relation between man and nature, that for Kant comprehending the design of nature "is the ground of a very appreciable pleasure."[62] Such pleasure derives from the coordination of nature with the order of human understanding, "for our judgement calls on us to proceed on the principle of the conformity of nature to our faculty of cognition";[63] this is to say, we look at the landscape in the expectation of finding the order by which our judging functions. In the case of dogs, and other agricultural animals, the expected pleasure is ensured through the technological processes of improvement. The dog looked at by the modern subject has been shaped as a breed; its appearance, talents, disabilities, and behavior have all been predetermined and oriented, in Derrida's words, toward "the service of a certain being and the putative human well-being of man."[64] Shaped and regulated by breed, modern dogs face us less from an unexpectable alterity than as a prosthesis of Western narcissism that promotes a vision of the caring human as capable of recognizing and appreciating the inner life of another being, such as my beagle who looks just like the winner of Westminster. The modern dog lover looks at the breed dog *as if* it were a free individual who willingly and happily chose to engage in just this way, at this time, with this person with surprising predictability.

My study considers the discourse of human-dog relations as it has been constructed through the conditional similitude of the "as if." Derrida examines the conditional similitude in numerous contexts, generally as similes or analogies, as in the analogies between human judgment and divine authorship driving an "economimesis," but most often as the constructed relations projected onto the world that support the claims of a narrow brand of knowledge or judgment. Certainly, analogy, along with non-contradiction, serves as one of the grounding principles of the Western philosophical tradition, and is thus unavoidable as an aid to critical thinking, even as it warrants its own critical attention as a *dispositif* normalizing thinking that sustains the privileged status of a certain kind of human engagement. Post-Enlightenment aesthetics guides the caring human into one kind, one breed of bonding with dogs, a recognition of the dog's face. Breed technology shapes and regulates dogs physically to give them consistently recognizable faces, and social technology regulates them with laws and taxes, determining which ones legitimately belong with the landscape. Aesthetics generates narratives to support a legitimate dog's belonging in the landscape, enriching it beyond the moment to the history of freely productive nature. Aesthetics and technology collude, in short, to transform dogs into human products that are praised, delighted in, bonded with *as if* they freely presented themselves to human appreciation, and *as if* the landscape in which they live were the freely productive nature produced by God for human enrichment. And with this collusion, the "as if" works as unobtrusively as can be, allowing the conditionality to pass *as if* unnoticed, while the similitude takes on the force of direct, unobtruded recognition of a lesser, mute subject in its presence before the appreciative, compassionate, and observing subject. Two beings are discursively aligned into subject and object, forging a similitude through the concealment and expulsion of any nondiscursivity—the abyss of difference. The conditionality of the similitude subsists in its unobtrusiveness, that it adhere to the conventions of modern aesthetics of difference suppressed. This similitude enables the modern dog lover to recognize the modern dog as a similar but less developed subjectivity who presents itself freely and fully, framed by breed discourse that ensures a proper aesthetic engagement between caring human and eager dog. Dogs serve as mute signifiers of the human subject's own capacity to read the grammatical structure of the landscape, which is broadly structured just like the human understanding. And it is this same similitude codified through breed discourse that precludes any other possibility of canine subjectivity.

The challenge in thinking critically about breed discourse—which takes a step toward abyssal thinking—lies precisely in the entanglement of technology and aesthetics that I have been pointing out. For a big thrust of the aesthetic doctrine of the eighteenth century came from the attention paid to the feelings of the vulnerable cast in picturesque modes. Animals, children, and peasants were often seen as possessing pure feelings, pure bonds to the living landscape, because of their primitive status.[65] These bonds, untainted by culture, supposedly provided a direct link to a primordial, preindustrial past—perhaps even to the heart of romanticized "nature" itself. The capacity to recognize and engage with these vulnerable figures and their pure (primitive) feelings was a significant component of the taste denoting the aesthetic subject. Out of this capacity grew many of the modern humanitarian institutions, such as the animals rights movement of the nineteenth century, as Hilda Kean has shown in detail.[66] At a more discursive level, it is also a key component in the modern humaneness that people began to bring to their treatment of animals.

This humaneness, this caring for animals as victims has generally been seen as the counterforce to the technological violence directed at animals. To an extent this is a just view. But, and this is the challenge at hand, a good part of the humaneness, arising as it does from eighteenth-century aesthetic discourse, perpetuates the image of animals as lacking; in considering animals first as mute victims for whom we must speak, the discourse of modern humanitarianism relies on the privileged perspective of both aesthetics and technology, and considers the animals it cares for in terms of their pure (primitive) role in the system of the landscape, which remains subject to technological management. And finally, humanitarian discourse perpetuates the confinement of animal subjectivities to lesser versions of the human, allowing them to appear only *as if* they were not what they are.

This is where the deconstructive, and post-humanist, vigilance of Derrida and others provides guidance in understanding the ways a well-intentioned and caring approach to animals can perpetuate the ability of modern humanistic "man" to commit acts of violence against animals. As long as humanitarianism works within a system of similitude in which the regulative conditionality is barely noticeable, its efforts at a caring responsiveness will allow animals only to be smaller, incomplete versions of the techno-aesthetic subject, awaiting our improving interventions. The mimetic relation established in the eighteenth century between humans and dogs, for example, leads simultaneously to the recognition of mutual care, based on the anthropocentric view that if a dog has feelings they must be almost like human feelings, and to the use of dogs as the corporeal analogs of humans in laboratory experiments. Erica Fudge has pursued the rhetoric that makes rats and dogs into human analogs, stating that "in the laboratory the animal body stands in for the human body."[67] She summarizes the argument for this substitution with a touch of irony thus: "A rat cannot fully understand the painfulness of the pain it is experiencing, whereas a human can. . . . there is pain, but at the same time there is no pain at all, so the animal, by extension, suffers, and doesn't suffer at all."[68] Fudge's reductio ad absurdum of the mimetic underpinning to animal experiments makes plain that the privileged subject governing such experimentation must uphold its privilege by claiming an interventionist knowledge while insisting on its own separate humaneness. And in Fudge's astute analysis, the capacity of an experimenter to claim that animals subjected to pain are treated humanely implicates the anthropomorphic narratives of human-animal communication: "while Lassie may have a mind of her own, it is a mind that drives her back to her true 'master.'"[69] The bond portrayed in such depictions—some of which I shall examine in a later chapter—reinforces the certainty of the privileged subject that it can know what and how much a dog experiences.

The heartfelt declaration "the dog is sad," with which Fudge characterizes the anthropomorphic humanitarianism, demonstrates a human's capacity to empathize with an animal other.[70] But it also—and this is the problem with all anthropomorphism—precludes any allowance for utterly nonhuman modes of being-in-the-world, for currishness. This is no less true of humanitarianism than it is of Heidegger when he declares that animals are "world poor," that the dog running up the stairs does not comport itself toward the stairs *as* stairs; Heidegger not only gives way to a dependence on the quiddity of things in the world, such as stairs, but allows for no other comportment.[71] It is such an allowance, in contrast, that Derrida raises when he writes of "pluralizing and varying the 'as such,' and, instead of simply giving speech back to the animal, . . . marking that the human is, in a way, similarly 'deprived,' by means of a privation that is not a privation, and that there is no pure and simple 'as such.'"[72] Without an essential "as such" marking the human—the face, the soul, language, auto-affection, whatever—there would be less of a need to frame a dog in terms of an "as such," judging it in terms of its conformation to a breed standard. Essentializing standards against which variability is measured to keep it from expanding, as Coleridge would say, into a *great* variability become necessary through the discourses that order the world into regulable and knowable wholes. Without an "as such" defining the human, canine variability would not necessarily be subjected to the "as if" of conditional similitude—that makes dogs serve as stand-ins for humans, as being like but less than their world-making, mindful, soulful analogs.

In making dogs—or nonhuman animals generally—world poor, so that they are forever cast *as if* they were what they are not, as if they were non-technological, the modern subject enforces its own privilege as the only being capable of instituting a signifying relation, for the elements—such as dogs—in the landscape cohere into the textual medium for the real relation, that between the human reader and the diviner author. Later in the same work where he identifies a dog as world poor, Heidegger expands on this poverty to define "world" as "the manifestness of beings as such as a whole"; he goes on to say, "Something enigmatic emerges from such a characterization: namely this '*as such*,' beings as such, something, '*a as b.*' It is this quite elementary '*as*' which . . . is refused the animal."[73] In Heidegger's characterization, humans alone carry the capacity to consider an individual in relation to something, either something else or its own essential self. The dog would not consider stairs *as such*, or the man *as if* he were a dog *as such*. Canine poverty, then, would mean that a dog does not consider the man categorically, comparing him to what he is not; and, needless to say, the impoverished dog would not consider a rat analogically while denying that its pain is not real pain because it isn't canine pain. What Heidegger "refuses" dogs when he declares them world poor, it would seem, are the gestures arising from within an economimesis that make any other subject less than canine by only ever describing them *as if* they were canine, or *as if* they served as expressions of a doglike divine author to the canine landscape.

A number of critics in animal studies assert their capacity to respond directly to an animal (and in Donna Haraway's case, a dog) before them by separating themselves from humanist discourse to open a space that both human and animal share. This assertion, in my estimation, extends the techno-aesthetic privilege by ignoring that a response and engagement are already written within a discourse—whether one that regulates as strictly as the breed taxonomy or less overtly through efforts to ground a commonness by recognizing an "animality" in the physical existence or vulnerability of both human and animal.[74] As Leonard Lawlor has astutely pointed out, "biological continuism, in a word, biologism, is the mere reversal of Platonism," and as such actually perpetuates the sovereignty of the modern subject in the assumption that the abyssal human-animal difference is either singular or a simple boundary to be crossed or annulled.[75] "Animality" understood as some common mode of being identifies a part of the human that can also belong to a nonhuman, and opens the mimetic relation Derrida describes as the "in-significant non-language" that is dependent in large part on conditional similitude that tropes the silence of nature into a grammar and the muteness of a dog into a readable face, but only on condition that nature remains silent as predicted.[76]

The construct of the conditional similitude puts a dog on call to be like a human when conditions are right, such as when a natural foundation for racism is needed, or when a laboratory needs an object for its experiments, or—more inclusively—when the privileged subject needs affirmation that it is responding tastefully and morally to the framed landscape. And this is where the danger of both humanist gestures of projecting a human subjectivity as a canine face, and of finding animality within the human becomes most apparent. As the conditional similitude turns dogs into resources for human substitutions, it also makes the human into the spokesman for the dog. In saying that a dog looks *as if* it were sad, we make ourselves the vocal substitutes for the dog, speaking for it *as if* it had a subjective interiority framed analogously to ourselves. In making ourselves the linguistic replacement or representative of the dog based on a recognition that we share an animal likeness, we ensure that the being we speak for, the being in whom we have projected a mute and lesser version of our inner selves, will never be heard on its own terms, or any terms that exceed likeness, or that exceed our understanding of "animal." As Derrida says, the being we have recognized as being like us "loses the power to name."[77] We deny the dog the capacity to look at the human (or stairs) in any other way, through any other frame than what the privileged techno-aesthetic subject demands for itself; such a denial only affirms Heidegger's view of the animal being poor in world. Without acknowledging the effect the techno-aesthetic subject has on the dog it speaks for, we shall not escape the violence committed in the name of knowledge, or that humane violence that cannot see itself as violent, of committing another to muteness by speaking in its name. Such violence is also sustained in the various performative arenas through which humans and dogs supposedly both enter of their own accord to engage with the other; the joy with which such engagements have been described since the eighteenth century requires forgetting that the dog has been technologically shaped to have no choice but to engage willingly in such an arena. To acknowledge this effect has required, throughout this introduction, that I attempt to delineate the forces acting together to situate dogs in ways that they look "as if," and that enable the human to read that similitude as one without conditionality, as a direct and full engagement transcending or sublating difference.

Matthew Calarco opens a line of thinking in much this same regard when he suggests that a profitable orientation for animal studies would be the "genealogical analysis of the constitution of the human-animal distinction and how this distinction has functioned across a number of institutions, practices, and discourses."[78] It is precisely as such a genealogical analysis that my study of breed discourse traverses literature, sport, natural history, and the law; and in uncovering the forces contributing to that discourse, I hope to show some of the ways breed discourse delimits the range of engagements humans today think of as being possible with dogs. This represents one key step in opening a different thinking about dogs and about animals generally. For an alternative to the techno-aesthetic mimesis appears when Calarco says, in the context of his reading of Levinas's ethics, that "ethical experience occurs precisely where phenomenology is interrupted and . . . [is] not easily captured by thought. . . . This would, it seems, require us to proceed *as if* we might have missed or misinterpreted the Other's trace."[79] The procedure Calarco offers here could have the effect of turning the conditional similitude on itself, confronting the modern dog lover with the discursive qualities of his or her knowledge and appreciation of dogs. No longer proceeding as if the dog possessed a human subjectivity, or as if the human could find a canine experience within its subjective frame, we could begin apart from the presumption that the perspective of one subjective interiority pertains to any other being. The discomfiting emphasis on conditionality opens a possibility well beyond the challenge of technology that makes a being calculable in advance, and of a similitude that assigns a dog a recognizable face, a trace not of something missed or misinterpreted, but of the unmistakable appeal of an "other" directly in front of us. The implication of this possibility is one that I shall be able to explore fully only after tracing the genealogy of the techno-aesthetic subject's delineation of dogs into modern breeds. What I wish to add to Calarco's "genealogical analysis of the human-animal distinction," therefore, is an analysis of the strategies upholding that distinction while claiming to overcome it.

My own taxonomy of human-canine encounters, linking the responsive relations of pet-companionship with the exploitative relations of dog shows, vivisection, and hunting (or even linking shows and vivisection, or vivisection and hunting, or subsuming all responsive relations under pets), is intended to underscore the human subjection of dogs in the variety of possible modes of interacting available today. Sports like foxhunting that involve packs of dogs, or like shooting, agility, or fighting that involve individual dogs, develop their self-justification from real or imagined traditions that allow dogs to project recognizable characters—their function as signifiers within a conventionalized discourse. Much of that is not so difficult to recognize, but what has been difficult is how the modern expressions of compassion and concern for the care for dogs (and other animals) have perpetuated their subjugation by upholding the sovereignty of the techno-aesthetic discourse of breed.

My hope, then, lies in bringing to the fore the breed discourse that took shape in the eighteenth century and persists in many twenty-first-century accounts of human-dog relations. These accounts are instructive not only for the ways they replicate eighteenth-century and Romantic narratives of canine-human relations in novels and breed histories, but also for their insistence that the interactions they make possible—and for which the dogs participating in them have likely been specifically bred—occur through the mutual and free decisions of all partners involved. Dogs serving in these techno-discourses signify fidelity to their master—the human who has mastery over the subject assigning the signifier—as much as to the discourse in which signification becomes possible. As a canine theme, fidelity is no less dishonorable to dogs today than it was for Pope. My hope depends, therefore, on dismantling the effectiveness—the naturalness—of the discursive conventions that conceptualize dogs into a predictable catalog of character types. Pursuing such hope, the succeeding chapters culminate in the examination of breed discourse in light of Derrida's critique of numerous modern discourses.

More than any other thinker of the past generation, Derrida has given a focus to discussions of human-animal relations, opening fruitful possibilities and making newly apparent the pitfalls of relations that had seemed benevolent. But, even though I frequently turn to Derrida to orient my questioning, this is not a study of his work; nor is it a study of Comte de Buffon or Walter Scott, to both of whose texts I devote chapters. Rather, this study is always about dogs, and about the way humans have shaped dogs into regulated and recognizable faces with whom certain types of engagements are possible. Similarly, while the chapters in one sense span a historical period ranging from the early eighteenth to the early nineteenth centuries, they each attend in a more important way to one or more of the elements—institutions, practices, and art forms—contributing to the modern discourse of human-dog relations. My concern is to understand why we humans in the West have come to interact with dogs as we do today. This study, therefore, presents not so much a new theory of human-canine or human-animal relations as a genealogical analysis of the grammar shaping and governing the landscape of human-canine relations so that the conditionality of asserted similitudes can remain hidden; once the grammar loses its transparency, once the laws expelling disgusting curs can be seen to govern pervasively in our everyday gestures, once we no longer have to find a sameness, the possibility of surprise might open.

As Diana Donald shows in her magisterial study of animals in art, dogs began to attract a particular interest in the eighteenth century that grew, by the time of Landseer in the 1830s, into "an astonishing cult in nineteenth-century art and literature," celebrating "the dog's intelligence and devotion to man"; indeed, Donald says, "these two traits were treated as virtually synonymous."[80] As I have shown at length throughout this introduction, this modern relation is driven primarily by the formation of the techno-aesthetic subject and the expressions of this subject in particular cultural avenues: law, natural philosophy, sport, and popular literature. The following chapters focus on the forces shaping modern human-canine relations in the eighteenth and early nineteenth centuries, and these can all be put under the heading of breed, as the categories distinguishing and regulating canine variability, and as the cultural discourses normalizing human-canine relations.

The first chapter begins by examining the development of laws aimed specifically at restricting dog ownership and regulating the types of dogs that could be kept; these laws express in the fullest way the anxiety over the unbounded variability which, toward the end of the century, was successfully framed into a grammar through the taxonomies that ultimately led to breed divisions. Associations between types of dogs and classes or regions—associations

Edwin Landseer, *The Old Shepherd's Chief Mourner*, 1837. Victoria and Albert Museum, given by John Sheepshanks, 1857.

fed in part by painterly analogies—made sense out of the very potent analogy between canine and human variability, so that taxonomies of canine breed and human race quickly became less descriptive and more definitive. At the same time, the Agricultural Revolution was achieving considerable success in its improvements, most notably the creation of the Foxhound, through new, disciplined breeding techniques; these techniques, and the exploitation of aesthetic rhetoric to make them seem less an intervention in, than a participation with the living course of nature, are the topic of chapter 2. It is both here and in the following chapter that I examine the originary narratives that became a central element of the breed discourse, as they obscured the artificiality of the breed designation by situating the ancestors of most modern breeds in a mythic pastoral setting in which the dogs supposedly fulfilled a clear and meaningful function. The third chapter focuses on Walter Scott, who celebrated his dogs in novels and letters, and contributed significantly to the mythic connection of breed and region. Scott was one of the first to describe nonsporting dogs in terms of breed identity, and his visually descriptive narrative strategy reinforced the emphasis on the conditional similitude that made physical appearance into an expression of almost human sensibilities, so that a good dog was not only a moral dog but called up moral judgments in the humans admiring him. Scott also reinforced the analogy between breed and race by casting it in narratives of a romantically pre-Enlightenment past to make it seem older than it really was. The popularity of Scott's novels ensured that the views of dogs defined as breeds dominated the discourse of human-dog relations. I skip over much of the nineteenth and twentieth centuries, not because little happened, but because the very great deal that did happen unfolded with the necessity of a logic determined earlier on. Of course breeds proliferated and pedigrees were institutionalized, and of course Darwin detailed the physiognomy of expression; all this took place as affirmation—disguised as discovery—of the breed landscape. My concern lies with the discursive, cultural forces framing that landscape, and that enable it to seem so natural as to be unconditional. The fourth and final chapter, therefore, examines twenty-first-century accounts of dogs as pet-companions and partners in regulated practices like sport and scientific research to show the extent to which the discourse of breed persists in dependence on the techno-aesthetic subject. At the end of this chapter, by engaging with some of the most serious thinking on animals in our time, I speculate on the possibility of being with a dog abyssally, apart from the conditions imposed by the discourse of similitude.

For all the while, canine alterity does occur, and even within the enframed landscape enforced by the discourse of modern human-canine relations: the dog other is not the dog seen in terms of breed, but rather is the cur who remains illegitimate, recognizable, perennially unwanted. The cur remains beyond the recognition of both aesthetics and technology, even while it slinks through all the best efforts to condition it out of existence. In calling a dog "man's best friend," we attach the existence and possibility of the being we hardly know—and have refused to know in so many ways—to the concept "man." We—i.e., "man"—then proceed to restrict our best friend by allowing it to act only under the conditional "as if"—as if it were the one looking to us for friendship, to be best friends, to be like a human. It is not the dogs who need us for friends; on the contrary, and this is what we—"man"—most resist conceding, it is the privileged subject who needs dogs, but only some dogs, the dogs who present to us a history of our privileged role in the landscape, and who are eager to perform for us, and even to sacrifice themselves out of love for us. And these are the dogs that have been framed into breeds that perform in predetermined ways. With the modern force of technology, "we" create dogs that have no choice but to perform in predetermined fashion, and then we congratulate ourselves on "our"—man's—dogs' love for "us." All "we" have to do is forget the curs who are unwanted, nobody's friends, referents of no collective pronoun, disruptive of the discourses through which we frame our friendship and through which we even create our friends.

Much of the thrust of a post-techno-aesthetic responsiveness to dogs would begin with the question of what would happen if one were to approach another, not as a member of the "we," but as a cur? If I said, I am a cur—a statement far removed from President Obama's account of himself as a mutt—I am unwanted, disruptive, incessantly barking, incapable of serving a function; could I become a friend, say, to another cur? Would these two unwanted beings cease being curs if they became friends to one another? Would they find a likeness to recognize one in another, the likeness perhaps of being unlike, of being unrecognizable, of mutually inciting Kantian disgust? Would one be made—technologically or otherwise—into the conditional, mute reflection of the other? Or would recognition, along with the whole mimetic force of modern aesthetics, cease to dominate the approach of one being toward another? Would possibility—unrestricted, unhistoricized, open possibility of indeterminacy, of monstrous variability and of disgusting individuality—become a fluid arena of interest in others? Who, or what would be a cur's best friend?

Legal and Legible
Breed Regulation in Law and Science

ON THE TWENTIETH OF MAY 1722, ALEXANDER POPE'S BROTHER-IN-LAW, CHARLES Rackett, was arrested for poaching in Windsor Forest. Rackett, his son Michael, and two servants had with them some horses and dogs.[1] The circumstances of the arrest, its consequences for the Rackett family, and its effect on Pope's poetry all remain unclear. It has generally been understood within the context of anti-Catholicism, with its fear of insurrection against the Hanoverian reign; these political antagonisms found an immediate and effective image in the conflict over poaching, which in Rackett's case merely meant encroachment on the royal forest by a person whose rank did not qualify him to hunt, or to approach within ten miles of the forest with large dogs. As Pope's *Windsor Forest* makes plain, the notorious laws regulating who could enter the forest, and who could keep hounds, had long been part of the English countryside. These had been relaxed during Anne's reign, and then reinforced by George I. Such restrictions took different forms over the next century and reflected the broader drive to restrict the discord that had supported Pope's aesthetics. That desire for control led not only to various calls to regulate dogs, but also to the technological innovations that eventually took over as the Agricultural Revolution and the push for "improvement" in which the Foxhound was created as the first dog breed.

Of course many people in Britain kept dogs, and many—like Pope—even kept large dogs within the restricted ten-mile range of a royal forest, but the law prohibiting people from officially keeping and owning their dogs was in place and could be used whenever those of the proper rank might wish; and, in fact, throughout the eighteenth century the Game Laws were enforced often enough for their existence to be felt as a fact. These laws, extensions of the old Forest Laws written by Canute, existed well before natural historians began to divide the world into genera and species, and it would be specious to suggest that they gave rise to the technological manipulation of the countryside. But the process of modernizing them, to regulate the large number of dogs kept by all classes of people, reflected a significant shift from Pope's allowance for concordant discord in favor of a unified landscape in which populations of humans and dogs were not so much excluded as managed. That such management sustained a certain privilege can be seen in the fact that the parliamentary debates over strategies of regulation occurred alongside delineations of relatedness among humans and animals by taxonomists like Buffon. The taxonomies established concrete analogies between canine appearance and human appearance at the same time that they divided humans into races. And the taxonomists employed much of the same aesthetic rhetoric as the lawmakers.

Thus it is that this chapter will link together the laws regulating dogs, and the natural histories that began organizing the discordant and fluid varieties of dogs into stable types. Special attention was given to dogs by the natural historians because the prominent aesthetic doctrine replacing *concordia discors* bonded dogs and humans as mutual reflections, evident in literary works like Gay's *Fables* and in numerous portraits pairing humans and dogs.[2] Even after all the laws restricting dog companionship and ownership were repealed, the divisions they enforced endured through the efforts of natural historians who created their classifications as reflections of them.

The different laws framing and narrowing modern relations between humans and dogs sought to institutionalize the comprehensive vision of the privileged subject through the surveillance of threatening political forces that appeared as insurrectionists, or merely as interlopers accompanied by dogs. Later in the century these unpopular laws shifted to a call for regulation through taxation that claimed more benign motives in hygienic control of rabies and in the moral concern over the mistreatment of dogs by the lower classes. During this same time, the legalistic enforcement of class difference was transposed into a comprehensive knowledge of dogs and humans through taxonomies. These taxonomies organized dogs into breeds, and changed discordant variability into set and preservable character traits that linked different individuals into similar members of a breed. Once stabilized and enforceable, breed differences gave rise to narratives of breed origin and purpose, and served as naturalizing analogies to the human racial taxonomies intertwined with canine categories. The development of breed and racial taxonomies complemented the legal framing and regulation of the mimetic landscape and facilitated—even necessitated—enforcement of the framed totality of "dog" by raising the necessity to preserve both purity and heritage of the newly devised categories.

FROM THE GAME LAWS TO THE DOG TAX

Although the Game Laws may be said to have taken various forms throughout their existence, they served the consistent purpose of restricting the hunting of certain prey animals—deer, hare, and game birds—to the aristocracy. Toward this end, they technically prohibited access to the sixty-nine officially designated forests throughout England, and they regulated the possession of dogs. The laws allowed for the seizure or destruction of "guns, dogs, nets and engines kept by unqualified persons to destroy game."[3] In his seminal work on the Game Laws, P. B. Munsche frames the period from 1671, the year the Game Act revived the exclusionary aspects of the old laws, to 1831, the year of the Game Reform Act that effectively abolished the land qualifications for hunting rights, as the era when hunting was enforced as the exclusive privilege of the gentry.[4] This was the time when terms like "forest" and "game" were legally defined to hold restrictive meanings. A forest had clear boundaries with access limited to the aristocracy. Game indicated the specific animals that those people able to enter a forest found pleasure in hunting and that anyone not possessing the required degree of land-based wealth were restricted from hunting or interfering with. The restricted spaces, the animals classified as game, and all the elements of the hunt—particularly hounds—became metonymies of class privilege. For my purposes, what matters is that the accoutrements of hunting—guns, nets, "engines," and dogs—also sufficed to mark a person as a poacher. The metonymic relation that could exist between a gentleman and his hound was a legal, social, and grammatical solecism among the lower classes. Outside the aristocracy, dogs could not be claimed as companions, for they held the potential of signifying unqualified activity. Indeed, "by 1707, the penalty for possessing a snare or a hunting dog was the same as that for killing game," which is to say that the snare and dog outside the restricted context became equivalent signifiers of an intent that was itself equivalent with the actual performance of poaching.[5] Citing various reasons, such as the gentry's fear that money would gain ascendancy over land-based wealth, Munsche stresses that during this era "the property qualification for sportsmen was enforced with increasing vigour."[6] Dogs accompanying unqualified people could be seized and destroyed, and apparently without any provision for size, shape, or ability (such as nose or speed).

The actual effect of the law on the number of dogs in England seems to have been minimal, since dogs appear to have remained almost ubiquitous. But the fact of the laws, the sense that they were needed, even when not consistently enforced, is what matters most. In "The Force of Law: The Mystical Foundation of Authority," Derrida draws the "unstable distinction between justice and *droit*" that can help us to understand the need and effect of these severe, yet haphazard, laws. "Justice" he describes as "infinite, incalculable, rebellious to rule and foreign to symmetry, heterogeneous, and heterotropic"; it is, in effect, the "mystical" foundation named in the article's subtitle. And *droit* he describes as "the exercise of justice as law or right, legitimacy or legality, stabilizable and statutory, calculable, as system of regulated and coded prescriptions."[7] The mystical quality of justice gives it an equivalency with nature, as the creative force that makes the world of beings appear as it is, as the mystery signified by the written landscape. This justice tends to be nebulous, and it is just such nebulosity that makes it effective in regulating the landscape. Derrida explains that "to be just or unjust and to exercise justice, I must be free and responsible for my actions."[8] But at the same time, "this freedom or this decision of the just, if it is one, must follow a law or a prescription, a rule."[9] A right lies in the *exercise* of justice; the active, free decision can be performed by those capable of acting freely, and capable of engaging with the originary, creative force of justice, of nature as the embodied expression of divine will—in other words, by the privileged. In this unstable distinction, *droit* would belong to those who have both the right to hunt and the right to exclude others from doing anything approximating hunting; these rights have no real meaning or function apart from enforcing the privilege of those who possess them and excluding those who do not. The instability Derrida emphasizes brings into focus the way such an unpopular institution as the old Game Laws could remain intact so long: "It turns out," he says, that "*droit* claims to exercise itself in the name of justice and that justice is required to establish itself in the name of a law that must be 'enforced.'"[10] Any enforcement of the Game Laws, of the restrictions on dogs, would have been an appeal to the just order of nature that distinguishes qualified men from all others. For "privilege" itself denotes an individual's capacity for self-rule (indicated in the etymology: *privus*, separate, *legis* genitive of *lex*) as opposed to rule imposed from without. Privilege is thus in itself the capacity of the subject who knows the objective world sufficiently to govern it. In the words of historians Tom Williamson and Liz Bellamy, "The great landowner was mythologized as a wise and powerful figure. . . . [whose] benevolent omniscience was a result of his landed status, for as owner of the nation he was seen to be able to understand its needs."[11] Supposedly, those without privilege derived from property lacked the capacity for self-governance, and effectively lacked the capacity to judge the world and themselves as a subject, and by extension lacked autonomy sufficient for aesthetic judgment. The qualified expressed their privilege through the right to hunt, and to enforce the laws restricting other people's ability to hunt; these rights are at one with the capacity to judge the beauty and justness of the landscape, managed by the privileged through enforcement of laws keeping rights exclusively for them. The nebulous justice of the Game Laws would have been implicit in all the exclusionary gestures of the privileged; the incalculability of their justice excluded the possibility of anyone arguing rationally against them, since reason (as the mystical governance of nature) lay at their foundation. As long as this nebulous—or mystical—foundation to the laws remained unassailable, their repressive heavy-handedness could be challenged no more than could the natural order of the landscape, no matter how hated they were.

The Game Laws were no less unpopular than the archaic Forest Laws, because they overtly excluded the majority of people from the right to hunt or to have dogs, while enforcing the privilege of the aristocracy. In order to enforce the freedom and judgment of the privileged, they necessarily excluded the non-privileged. The tenor of the laws reflected the view that non-aristocratic people (and political outliers, like Pope's brother-in-law) were all potential poachers, and that the companionship of dogs was not something deemed a right outside the aristocracy, because, in lacking the qualification, the unqualified lacked the judgment to enforce, to enact, the law; they could not manage the landscape by enforcing its limits. The unqualified were simply not privileged; they lacked the autonomy—freedom and responsibility—necessary for judgment. We might also say that they had not interiorized the nebulous and mystical justice that gave the *droit* of privilege its unassailable force; the qualification to hunt, based as it was on land ownership, foregrounded the mystical value of inheritance. Being excluded not only meant being barred physically from appearing in the landscape with a dog, but being disqualified from participating in the landscape as an intentional subject capable of performing an intervention. Unqualified persons were only ever objects of judgment, and of the law. Thus, when Derrida makes the point that "we would never say, in a sense considered proper, that an animal is a wronged subject," he gets to the heart of what the bare fact of these laws meant in their distinction between the qualified and unqualified.[12] The people and dogs lacking qualification were not "wronged subjects," because only those qualified to exercise their rights by creating laws that upheld justice could be called "subject." Only the qualified subjectivity, with its judgment, its privileged position, possessed rights; and these rights, upheld by law (*droit*), served as the human form of natural or divine justice, just as the landscape represented the divinely authored nature. The unqualified lacked—along with privilege, qualification— the subjectivity capable of judgment—aesthetic, moral, or legal. And thus, "What we confusedly call 'animal,' the living thing as living and nothing else, is not a subject of the law or of law (*droit*)."[13] The long-term effect of these laws was to delineate subject from nonsubject; this delineation split the species delineation between humans and dogs, so that some humans were deemed nonsubject, and some dogs were deemed almost-subject, or at least a metonymy of subject, and as the active bond between human and divine agents. The real force of the laws qualifying the rights of privilege is indicated by the comment of the Norfolk squire Robert Buxton, who sneered at the idea of the "lower orders" having pets, for "no industrious man would wish to keep a dog."[14] This standard reflected the general assumption that the "lower orders" were void of the aesthetic capacity that enabled foxhunters to find joy in their hounds, and that enabled ladies to recognize a return of their affection from a lapdog.[15]

That dogs had become a metonymic reflection of aesthetic capacity in the modern sense, combined with the ethical justice of inherited social rank, meant that fruitful companionship

James Macardell, after Joshua Reynolds, *Lady Charles Spencer, Duchess of Marlborough*, early 1760s. © National Portrait Gallery, London.

between them and humans could only be possible for the privileged, those men possessing the ethical capacity for moral governance and aesthetic joy. In chapter 59 of the *Critique of Judgement*, Kant equates the beautiful with the morally good, since in the act of judgment "the mind becomes conscious of a certain ennoblement and elevation above mere sensibility to pleasure from impressions of the senses, and also appraises the worth of others on the score of a like maxim of their judgment."[16] Such judgment, such "elevation above mere sensibility" was demonstrated by the privileged in the exercise of their qualification both to hunt with hounds and to make laws restricting other forms of human-dog relations. The equation of aesthetic judgment with moral judgment and with social law institutionalized the aspersion of non-hunting relations between humans and dogs (or, a bit more broadly, non-privileged relations, since relations between lapdogs and ladies were somewhat acceptable, though still aspersed along gender lines[17]) as immoral and unjust, because void of feeling, sympathy, or understanding.

When E. P. Thompson, in his examination of the Black Act, argues that the strident reactions against poachers in the early decades of the eighteenth century stemmed from fears of a Jacobin uprising, he foregrounds the political forces driving such responses. The hated Forest Laws were transformed in the Black Act as an urgent need to protect the kingdom against a persistent threat akin to today's War on Terror. Then, as now, the threat remained indeterminate and ever-present, and provided the locus where the right to exercise justice through the force of law was enacted. The act passed in 1723, Thompson says, "was so loosely drafted that it became a spawning-ground for ever-extending legal judgements," and it "signalled the onset of the flood-tide of retributive justice."[18] Poaching had been common enough prior to the Black Act that London restaurants had relied on it for their meat and poultry.[19] But with the Hanoverian accession, deer were given renewed protection to preserve the supply for the royal hunt. This privilege, along with the political need to stifle any Jacobin threat, encouraged gamekeepers to enforce the right to kill dogs, which only heightened tensions among the residents of the countryside. As Thompson states, "No power provoked fiercer resentment than" that of gamekeepers "to seize and kill hunting dogs. . . . Again and again the killing of dogs sparked off some act of protest or revenge."[20] Confrontations between gamekeepers and dog owners continued throughout a good part of the century, even after any Jacobin insurrection had vaporized, with legal judgment tending in favor of the keepers.[21] The unpopularity of these laws, and of any law associated with the Game Laws, shifted attention from overt restrictiveness to management through taxation.

Threats of poaching—basically incursions into privileged spaces by the unqualified—like proclaimed threats of disease or underground conspiracies, express the anxiety over the lack of containment, over the excess threatening the divine order of nature represented in the justly regulated landscape. This is the force behind law that leads Derrida, looking for "the superstructures of law," to point out that "the founding and justifying moment that institutes law implies a performative force, which is always an interpretative force," one functioning through the same terms as the aesthetic judgment I have outlined in the Introduction.[22] The parliamentarians revising old Game Laws, or creating new laws of taxation, are thus performatively engaged with the vital organization of the landscape where the laws will have their force. From the perspective of privilege, these laws are not imposed from without, but carry the force of the judging subject interacting productively with the life and justice of the landscape. "To be just, the decision of a judge," Derrida observes, "must not only follow a rule of law or a general law but must also assume it, approve it, confirm its value, by a reinstituting act of interpretation, as if nothing previously existed of the law, as if the judge invented the law in every case."[23] As an intervention, the lawmaking and law-enforcing by the privileged subject takes on the quality of poetic engagement with the divine author of nature through the landscape. Derrida's account of a judge's decision following and inventing a law reflects the pleasure Kant describes in the discovery by the faculty of understanding that the laws governing its judgment of nature also govern nature itself; and it reflects the "commerce between the divine artist and the human one" functioning in the aesthetic judgment of nature.[24] The poetically performative engagement with nature can thus occur in scientific observation and in juridical decisions that shape the landscape into the one setting in which meaningful relations can occur.

The performative engagement of legal judgment is already predetermined, since it takes place between the privileged techno-aesthetic subject and the author of nature represented in the framed landscape that must be protected against any excess threatening its unity. Excess is most recognizable in the variability of dogs and in their ability to engage in various relations with humans, and with different kinds of humans. Such excess, such fluidity and indeterminacy pervading dogs themselves and the possible relations they have with humans attracted the charge of immorality, and was referred to as the threat of disease, because of the threat to the static social order of the landscape and the barely unnameable threat of miscegenation. And as a threat, it extended from moral issues to health issues, while the driving anxiety was the discomfort over variability that weakens any assertion about what a dog is, any assertion that a dog can be known as a singular kind of animal engaging in only a limited number of possible relations with humans.

Such is the impulse that drove the efforts to institute a dog tax throughout the eighteenth century, efforts that finally paid off at century's end. A tax seemed less onerous than the overtly exclusionary laws, even though it was intended to serve the same ends of limiting, and normalizing, the kinds of relations between humans and dogs, and limiting—naming—the kinds of dogs that appeared in the landscape. Calls for a tax on dogs throughout the eighteenth century consistently followed a conventional form of pointing to the threats posed by unrestricted dogs—attacks on horsemen, poaching, disease, and the limitless proliferation of dogs serving no utilitarian purpose. The guiding aim, usually brought up last in the proposal, was to reduce the number of dogs kept only as companions by people incapable of aesthetic judgment and moral self-governance. Though the tax was only passed in 1796, calls for it began long before, reflecting the enduring desire within the privileged discourse to restrict the meaning of dogs, to allow human-canine relations to arise only within determinate parameters.

Proposals often introduced the canine threat in terms of mismanaged resources, emphasizing the consumption of food by poor people's dogs, as when William King claims in 1740 that

> Even the Labourer, who gets his Bread by the Sweat of his Brows, and the Stroller, who begs his from Door to Door, will waste and consume a great Part of it upon their Dogs; one or more of which they will each of them constantly keep in this great Scarcity of Corn. This is one of the Inconveniencies, which arise from suffering all Men to have full and free Liberty to keep as many of these useless Animals as they please; even tho' they want Bread for the Support of their Families.[25]

King takes pains to emphasize that he is no lover of dogs. But when poor people keep them just for their companionship, dogs are not only useless in his view, they exacerbate the nagging problem of poverty. As Munsche notes, Pitt's government "wanted a tax on 'luxury', not a new game law, and that is what it got."[26] George Clark's proposal of 1791 likewise condemns the immorality of allowing people to keep dogs as luxuries, which are "generally in some degree pernicious."[27] So, for fifty years proponents of the tax focused on the lower classes who did not *need* dogs and kept them only as pernicious luxuries, unlike the aristocracy who *needed* their packs as performative metonymies of their aesthetic and moral functions in the landscape. "Useless" and "inconvenient" dogs—which became a sweeping reference to dogs of the lower classes—provided a focus for the general and persistent anxiety felt by the gentry over the uncertain relations among beings—humans of different classes, and animals of dizzying variety—threatening, in their excess, the very justice and aesthetic order of the landscape. "Useless" dogs had no function as signifiers of anything beyond excess interrupting the exchange between privileged subject and divine author; thus, as "inconveniences," the non-aristocratic dogs posed a real threat that went beyond—at least in the aristocratic view—chances of malnutrition.

It is the excess found in lack of restriction and containment that makes the numerous and unidentifiable dogs a persistent threat not only of morality but also of public health. King charges that dogs would certainly facilitate an epidemic of plague, if there were one, and with only slightly less hysteria, he raises "the frequent danger of Madness."[28] The MP introducing the bill, John Dent, asserts that "thirty three persons in Manchester within a twelve month had been admitted into the infirmary" with rabies.[29] This is where we can see privilege maintaining a restrictive boundary even while seeming to loosen the severity of the Game Laws. Unregulated dogs are a disease, a plague, infecting the landscape.[30] The madness of rabies, Clark says, degrades humans "from the image of God, to the condition of a brute animal."[31] As Harriet Ritvo has stated, rabies was looked on "as yet another manifestation of unsettling social forces."[32] The threat is not just disease, but degradation, with hints of miscegenation, allowing unfettered lower-class people and their dogs to mix with privileged and aesthetically just people and dogs.

These sensationalist appeals helped the framers of the bill to present the tax as a regulatory exigency to curb the disease and degradation threatening the landscape, rather than a restrictive barrier as in the Game Laws that overtly excluded most people and dogs. But the reality of regulation becomes clear when King says, "All Men who can be thought to have any proper Business for a Dog, shall be at their full and free Liberty to keep one without being Tax'd for the same; but that, if they keep more, they shall pay a certain Tax for all of them excepting one."[33] His hope is that when dogs become expensive appurtenances, the people who cannot afford them will kill them, resulting in the reduction of the dog population by half.[34] The remaining dogs will, he assumes, "be less liable to become a Nuisance [*sic*] and Detriment to the Public, inasmuch when People pay for their Dogs, they will take better care of them, and keep them within due Bounds."[35] King's combination of "Detriment to the Public" with concern for the welfare of dogs follows the convention of blaming the poor for their lack of morality and sympathy that excludes them from active and free participation in the landscape. The effect is to justify the treatment of them as objects rather than as subjects of law, a gesture we shall see more of further on. When King takes up the consideration of "who shall be thought proper Persons to keep a Dog," he distinguishes two categories: those "who hath anything of Value to lose," determined by having land "to the Value of Ten Pounds a Year," and those "who have any Trade which may require the use of a dog; such as Tanners, Curriers, Fellmongers, Butchers, and the like."[36] These two groups of legitimate dog owners King distinguishes from sportsmen, and—more sharply—from the "Set of Strollers, who go by the

Name of Gypsies and Tinkers, who always keep a Number of those mischievous Animals, and undoubtedly with no other View but to kill Sheep, Lambs, and Fowls, and to rob Gentlemens [*sic*] Coney Warrens, &c."[37] Three types of dogs thus hold legitimacy, determined by the person associating with them; another broad range of dogs continues to threaten the landscape, if not literally with disease, then with the similar incursion of poaching.

The question that arises from reading King's distinctions between legitimate dog owners and illegitimate ones is whether it is the people or the dogs he wishes to control. And the answer is both: the same problems arise from the presence of the unregulated dogs as from that of itinerants who have "no Place of Abode." The working men—butchers, tanners—along with property owners, serve clear signifying functions in the social structure, and their dogs would replicate that utility. But the "strollers" represent the fluid, unregulated movement within the social body that has often been made akin to disease so that anxious moralists like King feel strongly the need to purge it. A person or dog whose relation to the landscape is not immediately evident poses a threat to the systemic order—to morality, health, and law.

Dogs are ubiquitous, with "scarce a villager who has not his Dog,"[38] and a tax, with attendant requirements for registry and collars, would control the movements of immoral, inconvenient dogs and people. This conventional polarization runs throughout the treatises supporting a tax: the qualified alone have the privilege to engage with dogs, and their stability—the natural justice of the landscape—is threatened by drifting itinerants, whose dogs "are kept in an unrestrained state."[39] Since the unprivileged lack the legal right to hunt, along with the aesthetico-legal capacity to define the landscape, their "unrestrained" relations with dogs are incomprehensible to a parliamentarian as anything but a violation or disruption of the moral, legal, aesthetic landscape. Unregulated movement by "strollers," Gypsies, and tinkers, and undefined relations between these people and useless dogs pose the threat that always demands enforcement of the law in which right (*droit*) exercises itself. This "set" of people and their "mischievous" animals provide the threat that must be removed—sacrificed, as Derrida puts it—as an essential step in "the founding of the intentional subject, and the founding, if not of the law, at least of law (*droit*), justice and law (*droit*)."[40] The justice of the landscape is thus concurrent with the intentional, the judging subject, who improves the elements, judges the beauty, and interprets the law. Writing the laws that prohibit dangerous people and dogs carries much the same force as landscaping the great estates or hunting foxes: all these activities bring the aesthetico-legal subject into "commerce" with the divine author.[41] Landscaping and legislating both write the landscape into its meaningful form, the discourse in which the subject can read its own significance in judging which "set" of humans and dogs are legal and which not. Just as in the Game Laws, Clark must exercise his right, asserting his own legality as a subject, by casting indeterminate human-dog relations beyond the law:

> In too many instances, I am persuaded, those Dogs are kept for some better, or at least for some more profitable purpose, than to gratify the eyes and ears of their masters. The practice of poaching is too prevalent to make these Dogs useless pieces of furniture. And the ill effects poaching has upon the manners of those who follow it, is, I conceive, a sufficient justification for restraining their ability to practice it.[42]

Clark cannot allow that the poor might be capable of either aesthetic pleasure or friendship, and so dogs that only "gratify the eyes and ears of their masters" are dismissed as being an impossibility among the unprivileged. A good-looking dog—a hound, say—cannot be appreciated for itself by a poor person who lacks the agency necessary for such an aesthetic judgment. Conversely, possession of a dog by a person without the legal qualification to hunt could only follow the traditional equation of poaching. Non-aristocrats lack aesthetic sensibility to the same degree they lack the legal right to hunt: any agency attributed to the unqualified could only be that of criminality.

Similarly, Edward Barry, on the eve of the passage of the Dog Tax, warned that the poor lacked the sensibility to treat their dogs well. The poor, Barry complains, "are of all people the most rigid to *exact* their demands, while they are the very foremost to vociferate against others, for appearing to act in the same manner," and thus they reveal themselves to be incapable of sympathy by refusing to entertain any political view other than that benefiting them.[43] By direct extension of this inflexibility, Barry traces the brutish character of the lower classes that makes the dog tax a humane necessity:

> They further evince a peculiar tyranny of temper, in their savage correction of such animals as are entrusted to their care, particularly of horses; they delight in barbarous sports, and their very children take pleasure in torturing dumb creatures![44]

A poor person could only use an animal badly, and for illegitimate ends. The effect of this distinction is not only to limit the number of legal dogs, but the kinds of relations possible between humans and dogs, and between people of different lifestyles and different dogs. By determining that only a certain range of people may enjoy dogs and only within a limited range, these legal interventions—already determined by conventions of justice—reshape infinite and variable possibility into a legible grammar. The conventionalized exercise of parliamentary right calls for legal enforcement to limit meaningful relations with dogs to those who already possess the capacity and the right to judge particular beings aesthetically and legally.

As Ingrid H. Tague stresses throughout her history of the dog-tax debates, many arguments for and against the tax relied on the rhetoric of sensibility, the popular aesthetic movement based on feeling and sympathy.[45] Thus, even while denying subjectivity to lower-class people, the debates ironically helped to affirm the acceptance of an inner life among some dogs—though not all. So, in mid-century, when "Brindle" published his appeal against the tax, he not only took the dog's perspective but began with an assertion of dogs' capacity for inner experience: "Consider, gentlemen, we are animals and not such senseless machines as you men are pleased sometimes to make us: we have a feeling of pain, a sense of pleasure, tread the same earth, are warmed by the same sun as our masters."[46] Brindle's appeal represents another significant step away from the *concordia discors* of Pope's landscape, one that precludes the possibilities of dogs having inner lives utterly and incomprehensibly different from humans'. This appeal thus reflects an important development in human-canine relations, one that had measurably positive consequences in the higher expectations for treating dogs; but this development occurred within, and as part of, the broad discursive development of breed. Brindle's plea is against the wholesale slaughter of feeling, sensible beings that some parliamentarians in the 1770s asserted as the primary aim of the Dog Tax. Brindle's reference to a "senseless machine" creates a simplistic opposition between the reactive being and the human subject, with no other possibilities. Anything like a canine landscape with its own order of judging or of intervening, for example, became all the more inconceivable as the legal landscape of privilege and justice attained universality, became technology always already naturalized. Sympathy for a canine subjectivity—as important as it was for the animal rights movement—was only possible in terms of normalized sameness. This sameness cast dogs as having a diminished ability: they possessed sensibility, inner lives, but not sufficiently to qualify as subjects of the law able to judge and to intervene in the landscape as intentional agents, or in a capacity beyond that written, legislated for them.

The appeal held out by a dog tax of leading many dogs—good and bad—to their death raises the question that became increasingly prominent as the century progressed, of how to distinguish good from bad, given the huge variability among dogs. So Brindle gets right to the heart of the pro-tax argument: "To varnish over their inhuman scheme," he proclaims,

> the projectors of it only pretend to design the destruction of the *mad dogs, saucy dogs* and *worthless puppies*. But, because some animals are a disgrace to the dog-kind, must the whole species suffer? Because there are *odd dogs* and *queer bitches* and now and then *a dog in a doublet*, must the generous hound, the loving spaniel, the useful turnspit, and the honest mastiff suffer?[47]

The witty allusion to oddness, queerness, dandification—disgraces to the kind—implies that to separate such beings from those recognizably (and the use of the clichéd epithets only makes the implication more pointed) "generous," "loving," "useful," and "honest" can only proceed from an ulterior motive—as indeed it does.

But separating the "odd dogs" from the hound, spaniel, turnspit, or mastiff was quite the point, and increasingly so toward the end of the century. Dogs kept for determinate functions, especially involving labor, sport, or protection of property, were not the ones that made the gentry and upper classes anxious. Rather it was the dogs that seemed odd or queer because of their apparent superfluity, because unregulated people would keep them for unregulated, unconventional, surprising companionship—all collapsed under the legal and moral headings of poaching and abuse. In the end, as Lynn Festa recounts, the "Act for granting to His Majesty certain Duties on Dogs" (36 Geo. 3, c. 124) passed in 1796 because it distinguished between different types of dogs, assessing them, she says, "based on kind, usage and quantity." Festa summarizes the tax bill thus: "All individuals keeping either a hunting dog ('a Greyhound, Hound, Pointer, Setting Dog, Spaniel, Lurcher, or Tarrier') or 'two or more Dogs of whatever Description or Denomination' were to pay the sum of five shillings per dog, while those who paid assessed taxes were assessed three shillings for any dog they owned not embraced under the former category (such as lapdogs). The poor—those who did not pay assessed taxes—were only subject to the dog tax if they kept a hunting dog."[48] While allowing for the possibility of human-canine relations based on companionship (exempting "the poor" who kept dogs other than "hunting dogs"), the bill institutionalized the general distinction between dogs based largely on class. This distinction represents an important step toward the modern regulation of canine variability by chaining the signified of "dog" into different framed types, at this point still determined through class association. Festa argues persuasively that the shift in the debates away from overt prohibitions of people and dogs associating and toward regulation through taxation had the effect of making dogs into things that could be owned, and basing human-canine relations almost entirely on the human capacity to own a dog. The choice of the relationship, and the form it took, belonged primarily to the human who could select a dog for a function, like hunting or herding, or for companionship. But, as a taxable piece of property, an owned dog reflected not just the class privilege that had been enforced through the Game Laws, but even more a commodity chosen ethically and aesthetically by a human subject as a piece of property, in Festa's words, "so intrinsic to the person as to be in a sense constitutive."[49] The purchase of a dog enabled the non-gentry to acquire, if not the full privilege of owning land, then at least a legal connection to the landscape. When the debates began openly addressing the consequence of people killing large numbers of dogs, the question became, Festa notes, "not so much whether it is acceptable to kill dogs as which dogs it is acceptable to kill"; the answer, of course, depended on the value of the dog, which might now be determined not so much by who owned the dog as by whatever a potential owner sought in the possession.[50] Dogs thus acquired a determinable value apart from companionship. In owning a dog, a person was not just a privileged landowner or a potential poacher, but the possessor of something that acquired the force of a sign.

The exemption in the bill of the households owning only one dog enabled the "poor," as Tague observes, "to keep dogs without penalty whilst taxing the hunting dogs of the landed elite at a higher rate than other breeds. . . . Ironically, in the eyes of the law the dogs of the wealthy were luxuries, whilst for poor people, dogs—even 'useless' pets—were necessities that they could not live without."[51] Thus the more lenient views of the poor and their nonsporting dogs seemingly won the day. But it is important to recognize that, within the discourse of human-dog relations that was taking the form that still prevails, the leniency of the parliamentary bill was prefigured by the aesthetic law of the landscape enforcing exclusionary privilege and limiting variability. The poor could keep dogs only *as though* they were qualified to have sporting hounds, and *as though* the pet dog were a hound that only the most privileged humans could keep because of their traditional claim to the land and to political and legal power. Even small dogs could be made to signify their owners' capacity for judgment, if

James Gilray, *John Bull Baited by the Dogs of Excise*. Prints and Photographs Division, Library of Congress, LC-DIG-ppmsca-07654.

the dogs could be more than "just" dogs. As commodities, dogs began to signify an owner's capacity to choose and purchase a recognizable part of the landscape—maybe not the land itself, but possibly the history of the land embodied in the dog's ancestral participation in the rhythms of the landscape. And, as I shall show in the next chapter, the breed designations facilitated the acquisition of an artifact of the mystical force undergirding privilege through inheritance. Once dogs became identified as breeds, they could serve as a purchasable signifier of taste and heritage. The poor could legally become dog owners, and could select their dog on the basis of historical and cultural associations, and these associations very often preceded the relationship between the human and the purchased dog. In being legalized as taxable goods, dogs now represented clearly conventionalized relations with the landscape. Even though the unqualified might still be said to lack the sensibility sufficient for performative engagement with the landscape or with the beautiful hounds within it, they were allowed their commodified dog that could signify a broadening of sensibility on the part of legislators. The sacrifice of the unprivileged and their dogs necessary to the judging subject did not cease; the legalization of dog ownership codified human-dog relations into legible components of the just landscape. Codified through taxation, the relations between humans of all ranks and their dogs were better regulated, incorporated into the legal structure of ownership, than left as indeterminate threats to the landscape of privilege. Ownership facilitated a more subtle and durable regulation of human-dog relations by shaping them through the discourse of breed identities. As I shall show next, breeds acquired some of their meaning through analogy with human races and through narratives that claimed to trace breed origins.

TAXONOMIES AND READABLE DOGS

Legislative management of dog ownership, and even companionship, reflected the Enlightenment faith that the landscape could be managed as a whole. The creative intervention legalizing dog ownership also performed an act of shaping the landscape into a legible text in which particularities were aligned in clear and meaningful relations voiding any unpredictable interactions. The legal measures aimed at managing dogs functioned within the Enlightenment discourse of totalized knowledge that also, and at the same time, led natural historians to organize canine variability into breeds. It is worth invoking again Derrida's claim that "the founding and justifying moment that institutes law implies a performative force, which is always an interpretative force."[52] Just as the generation of laws regulating the populations of the landscape entailed an active shaping and framing of the landscape, so the delineation of taxonomies entailed the mapping of the same landscape to organize the jumble of canine variability into a legible text, or catalog of signifiers. The organization of the landscape into taxonomic divisions expelled the discord of Popean aesthetics as an incapacity to look directly and sympathetically at other living beings, just as it expelled non-codified human-canine relations. Concordant discord and contiguity were replaced with categorical relatedness and systemic continuity. Taxonomies provided the grammar in which canine variability could be read as analogies of likeness. These analogies grew into mutually sustaining discourses of human races and canine breeds, each validating the other as natural evidence of the accuracy of taxonomic perception. The taxonomies produced in this era have continued to govern Western thought about natural beings, evidenced in the reification of race as the explanation and regulation of human variability, and breed as the explanation and regulation of canine variability—reflective structures that each have served as the naturalizing basis of the other.

Theorists in animal studies have considered analogies between animals and human races from various perspectives. In these discussions, animality is generally aligned with the racialized other, while the human stands for the white, unracialized subject; to be dehumanized, then, is to be animalized through the alignment of race with animal otherness—to be disqualified as a "subject before the law." In one of these discussions, Christopher Peterson asserts that "The potency of the animal trope lies precisely in its fungibility, its potential as a placeholder for virtually any excluded other."[53] Peterson goes on to criticize Carrie Rohman for attempting to overturn the logic of racism by simply privileging animality over the human.[54] In these accounts, the human-animal dichotomy replicates the Cartesian division of body and mind, albeit with certain provisos. Thus, Rohman says, following Derrida's discussion of carnophallogocentrism and Judith Butler's account of abjection, that "In short, becoming human requires passing through a field of discourse that defines the human as not-animal."[55] Vanessa Lemm, working primarily with Nietzsche's texts, traces a distinction in modern discourse between civilization and culture, the first of which "distinguishes itself as the forgetting of the animal," and the latter of which "recovers [the] fullness of life in the dreams, illusions, and passions of the animal."[56] In remembering or recovering "animality," these studies maintain the basic dichotomy of *the* human and *the* animal that depends on the singularity of the two opposing terms. This is the singularity Derrida criticizes in his accounts of *l'animot*—the discourse that collapses the countless singular beings into essentialist categories whose one relation is that of simple opposition.

I would like to argue that accounts of opposition do not get at the problem of race in any way that avoids perpetuating race itself as a dominant mode of configuring human variability. While simple opposition has its history of institutionalized slavery and oppression, race itself gains its potency from taxonomic delineations of variable characteristics. Human variability was set in analogous relations with nonhuman variability, to make racial difference seem real and meaningful as categorical distinctions generated by the discovery that nature adhered to a grammar. The delineations of racial and breed categories worked as performative readings of the legible landscape in which physiognomic details signified a continuity with regional origin. The interplay between the creation of race and the creation of dog breeds played a significant role in the reification of breed and race, since dogs were aligned, by the early taxonomists, in a particularly potent analogy with humans. The natural historians delineating the analogous taxonomies—particularly Buffon—performed a creative intervention in the landscape of the same sort as the parliamentarians writing the Dog Tax law, infusing meaning into variability by emphasizing similarities that made for predictable and regulative alliances: dogs could begin to be recognized as types with shared origins who reflected the types of people with similar origins, and all types demanded the exclusion of any individual deemed untypical because discontinuous, interruptive. The recognition that variability could be organized categorically as races and breeds performed a foundational interpretation of the justice grounding the privileged subject as judge of the laws governing individuals in the landscape. Laws against miscegenation, for example, could be said to have become necessary through this interpretation that sacrifices illegible variability (in the same way it sacrifices *concordia discors*) in order to ground the judging subject's privilege in the landscape.

The legalization of dog ownership came about in part from the recognition that dogs are virtually ubiquitous, but also through distinguishing dogs into a hierarchy of types directly aligned with social classes. Dogs do not always signify an animalized otherness, or at least not to the same degree. Nor do dogs stand in the same relation to the humans making the laws and grammatizing nature as do other nonhumans, such as game animals, or even domestic animals, or even the other domestic animals that hold equivalent status in the legalistic and aesthetic landscape, such as horses, and particularly the Thoroughbred. The parliamentarians debating the Dog Tax began with the simple distinction between the dogs they wanted close to them and the dogs they wanted to keep away; they ended by granting dogs an inner life that officially recognized in them new, codified possibilities for companionship. The process through which dogs were made legible within the economy of the landscape entailed casting them as analogies of humans. To an extent, we could say that dogs were thus humanized, but only to an extent, and that limit remains clear and a key aspect in the shaping of human-dog relations, as later chapters will show. For now, what matters is the construction of the analogy between humans and dogs that makes dogs seem less than other.

Two elements will stand out in my discussion: first is that the analogy aligns not just the two species, but human and canine variability. It is in this alignment that racial categories are relevant, since the categories dividing dogs into proto-breeds served to reify human races, and to make breeds and races into signifiers of a lost primordiality, one that has only ever appeared "in its own disappearance," as Derrida says about the inscription of self-presence in the system of writing.[57] Second, and linked to the first, is the alignment of categorization—the naming that goes into delineating and dividing groups among conditionally similar species—with aesthetic and moral judgment, so that the signification of the loss generates the force of written law naming individuals otherwise than as variable, idiomatic, or unrepeatable beings. The taxonomies of the natural histories establish the grammar through which racialized humans and breed dogs have been read.

Given that the creation of law occurs as a performative engagement with the life of the landscape, it was no accident that "improvement" of animals into breeds, and the organization of human variability into racial categories should occur as analogies. Kelly Oliver has considered the function of this perceived human-animal analogy at length. In observing the differences among animals, Oliver argues, humans learned how to construct the taxonomic system that allowed for the category or species "man." Following Lévi-Strauss, Oliver says that "man can distinguish himself from other animals only because he first learns to distinguish animals from one another." She extends this insight further when she asserts that the metaphoricity on which taxonomies are built "also is a response to the animals. The logic of metaphor that makes men human is a response to the animals in their midst."[58] Such logic works as the necessity of mastering the discordant diversity of animal forms by creating identities that obscure differences. It was thus out of the necessity of mastering themselves and nature that Enlightenment thinkers arranged plants and animals into taxonomic categories in which individuals acquired a conceptual identity.

For Kant, a concept is the uniting "in one representation the manifold that has been gradually intuited, and afterwards reproduced."[59] Such uniting distills the particular beings of the manifold, with all its monstrous variability, into their essential qualities so that they can be "combined in a certain manner," which Kant calls synthesis; "knowledge is first produced by the synthesis of a manifold," and "synthesis is what really gathers the elements for knowledge and unifies them into a certain content," he says.[60] A century later, when Nietzsche critiques the nineteenth-century science that had grown out of the Kantian drive to categorize, he says a concept "is formed by arbitrarily discarding these individual differences and by forgetting the distinguishing aspects."[61] Kant's unifying synthesis requires forgetting differences and "distinguishing aspects," which is to say, singularity, the unexpected. The "one representation," which for Kant reproduces the manifold, has to forget "the distinguishing aspects" of the singular beings in order to reproduce the category shaped through isolating sameness. And with this one organizational principle, diverse species of plants and animals are valued according to their reflection of, and proximity to "man." The categorical divisions remain inescapably vital to the "zoological, ethological . . . forms of *knowledge*" that, according to Derrida, orient the modern response to animals, so that virtually the only way we can speak of animals is through the conceptual organizations of breed and species, and the only way we can speak of humans is through the conceptual distinctions of race and gender.[62]

As Harriet Ritvo has shown, most modern dog breeds appeared after the Napoleonic Wars, but efforts to fit canine varieties into types were being made decades before that as part of the discourse of regulation reflected in the debates over the Dog Tax and reflected in the agricultural interventions into the landscape under the name of improvement.[63] For the prevailing view of monogenesis—that each species originated from a single set of parents and then "degenerated" from the original form through climatic influences—asserted that variability among animals and humans alike masked essential and unchanging qualities that might be developed, "improved," through regulation of form and habit. Michael Banton points out, for example, that Adam Smith describes "the savage" as having interest insofar as "he possessed the unrealised accomplishments of the child."[64] In seeing "the savage" as the child, taxonomists were recovering the "proper name" of the particular being, or the species, or the community. Standing above and apart from cultural differences, taxonomists broke through those differences in order to recognize a genealogical sameness uniting people—and by analogy, dogs—into a common developmental history. Such sameness made the designation of a "savage"—human or dog—meaningful as the prototype of the privileged, beautiful, and qualified human or dog. Taxonomists were literally writing into natural law the traces that concealed the writing of the landscape, concealed the writing of social law as enacted by the parliamentarians.

Other efforts to connect body types and demeanors to essential qualities focused on observably useful traits, such as the violence and affection of the pit bull, that overshadowed those considered less useful, or that were not apparent; in Nietzsche's terms, "the distinguishing aspects" of individualities were forgotten. Once physical appearance could be semiotically connected to "interior" or ethical qualities such as temperament, intelligence, or responsiveness, those details that acquired such semiotic status were privileged to become the empirical determinants of breed and race, and degree of evolutionary development. As Phillip R. Sloan notes in his study of Buffon's contributions to racism, "From the 1770's onward . . . the central issues in the race question are empirical issues, questions in which anatomical data, physiology, zoogeographical analysis, and tests on the interbreeding criterion are presumed to be decisive, taking precedence over all philosophical, ethical, and theological tenets."[65] As the privileged traits were isolated and distilled, they incurred demands that their purity be preserved. The preservation of purity became one of the means of regulating possible relations by ensuring inheritable continuity. Just as miscegenation raised racist anxiety, so poor people could keep ugly dogs and privileged people could keep beautiful dogs, and neither the dogs nor humans of different classes could intermingle. But even more to the point, once purity among dogs could be authorized through recorded pedigrees, it not only became an exclusionary standard but also demanded a narrative connecting individuals to an idealized primordiality necessitating the pedigree's preservation and continuation. These narratives became the breed histories that define dogs and delimit the possibility of relationships between canines and humans.

The discursive emphasis on purity and preservation running through narratives of the breeds, their putative origin and history, also inflects the racial thinking that grew up at the same time. Writing about the philosophical justifications of racial divisions that appeared as part of the larger discourse arranging animals into taxonomies, Robert Bernasconi justly asserts that "it is not so much the reality of race as racial purity that has been at the center of discussions of race over the last two hundred years."[66] As the lines dividing a fluid variability hardened into differentiated categories of breed and race, the standard of purity occluded the individuality of any dog in a human-canine relation, in the same way Peter Fenves observes to have happened in Enlightenment racial theory: "Race can assume the function previously assigned the individual: it . . . represents the lowest *self-sustaining* species of animalia . . . that maintains itself intact, in contrast to ever 'lower' ones that appear and disappear more or less at random."[67] Individuality came to be occluded by the category that now defined it; the less a dog varied from the breed ideal, the more evident the dog's characteristics were said to be, and the more evident the dog's "character" with which a human might engage directly. Reification of taxonomic categories necessitated both authoritative records of genealogy, and narratives that connected a canine type to some vital function in the landscape and that indicated the dog's direct integration into regional qualities, like climate and topography. Thus Kant, explaining the "great dissimilarities in form" that can appear within the unified genus of humans, points out that "the condition of the earth (dampness or dryness), along with the food that a people commonly eat, eventually produces one hereditary distinction or stock among animals of a single line of descent and race."[68] Race, like breed, signifies the generic origin in a primordial physicality, a specific region anterior to the modern landscape constituting the individual's "proper name" that can only be recovered by the racial or breed name.

Given an originary *telos*, the breed acquires the meaning of having once been integrated in the naturally organized (i.e., preindustrial) proto-landscape, so that its meaning becomes that of the resource that still remains as a capacity to function within the modern landscape. Positing a capacity among humans and animals to respond to environmental forces, Kant also insists on a seminal constancy: "Any possible change with the potential for replicating itself must," he says, "have already been present in the reproductive power so that chance development appropriate to the circumstances might take place according to a previously determined plan. . . . For nothing can become a part of an animal's reproductive power that is foreign to it, since this would make it possible for the creature to distance itself gradually from its original and essential determination."[69] This potential for replication endures through all the variations of a species, race, or breed, and provides Kant with the meaning a category of beings holds to the landscape, the trace of primordiality. Such meaning provides the teleological reference that enables a breed to occlude individuality and difference. As Susan Shell points out, for Kant the "key to the conception of organic form is the principle of germinal constancy . . . : nothing can affect the germ which constitutes an organism's original inheritance from the first propagator of its species."[70] Breed provides the organic form governing the "germinal constancy" among individuals so that each individual foregrounds the undiscarded, unforgotten traits that become the signifiers of its conceptualized breed, and the breed narratives purport to establish "the first propagator," not so much by naming an individual dog as by identifying dogs with categorical functions that can be reinterpreted in the modern landscape according to set conventions. In Kant's view, according to Shell, "we understand living beings teleologically . . . because we cannot think the possibility of such a living system [as this particular organism] without supposing a concept of what the organism is 'to be' in the mind of some hypothetical author."[71] The modern landscape has been authored both by the nebulous force of justice and by the creative interventions of lawmakers, landscape architects, and agricultural improvers working in the name of justice. Kant's English contemporary, the huntsman William Blane, writes in almost the same terms, answering the question of whether dogs were originally divided into various sorts, asserting

> that every virtue and faculty, size or shape, which we find or improve in every Dog upon earth, were originally comprehended in the first parents of the species; and that all this variety we behold in them, is either the natural product of the climate, or the accidental effect of the soil, food, or situation, or very frequently the issue of human care, curiosity, or caprice.[72]

The "hypothetical author" Kant needs to orient individual organisms teleologically into racial categories appears in Blane's account as nature, the transcendent intentionality that shapes dogs physically through climate and soil, and as man, who shapes dogs for his purposes. Notably, to emphasize the role of authorship, Blane creates an analogy between the variability of dogs and that of humans:

> That we are all, of every nation and language, the sons of Adam, we have the testimony of God, which to honest Hunters (who are generally of the orthodox party) is of sufficient authority. . . . and yet what an incredible and monstrous variety is risen among us, in humour and constitution, as well as shape and colour.[73]

The "honest hunter" is not only recognizably Kantian in his dependence on a divine author—replicated in nature and man—but also adheres to the eighteenth-century effort to account for difference by recovering an originary selfsameness. Teleology in the form of adaptability to climate, human demands, or divine intention shapes a breed through generations to ensure that specific traits will be germinally constant sufficiently to categorize them as a breed apart from other breeds. What matters for Enlightenment philosophers like Buffon, Kant, or Blane, however, is differentiation itself, which necessitates the principled observation leading toward taxonomic arrangement into classes, races, species, and breeds that will turn the "incredible and monstrous variety" into a comprehensible organization of difference through historical and romantic narratives. These narratives ground the organization by delimiting the possibility within which differences can bear recognizable meaning. Recognizable and meaningful differences can occur only at the level of categories into which individuals are synthesized. Variable individuality, at the level of the manifold, is forgotten, for, as Kant says, "knowledge is produced by the synthesis of a manifold." The individual remains unknowable within the economy of the written landscape, except as it can be named as belonging to an originary category—breed or race.

Under the logic of metaphor described by Oliver that conceptualized the "monstrous variety" of dogs into the taxonomy of breed differences, breed as a "principle of germinal constancy" became the natural referent that proved the accuracy of racial divisions. Once it was teleologically differentiated, breed provided the metaphorical model for human variability. Any account of "man" necessarily had to adhere to the taxonomic divisions of races in order to seem in accord with the natural economy designed by the "hypothetical author"; and once established as a natural fact, racial distinctions demanded preservation. Although breed delineation appeared to preserve natural variety, it was in truth the regulation of the purity of artificially defined breeds, which then, through "the logic of metaphor," was made to serve as a natural ground for the regulation of human races. One implication of Oliver's study is that the language governed by race, breed, and species becomes the very essence of the discourse on nature: to speak and write about animals—whether wild or domestic—means to institute and enforce these organized differences, and to speak and write about nature meaningfully as knowledge can only be done taxonomically from within the landscape. As the very shape modern knowledge of animals and man takes, taxonomies reveal the extent to which such knowledge has framed possible human-canine interactions through a discourse of regulated intersubjective recognition reliant on conceptualization. The possibility of discovery or surprise between individuals is reduced to predetermined reflection by the dog of the human.

The technological view of either dogs or humans as "resources in reserve," to use Heidegger's phrase, establishes their meaning by aligning them in a relational organization with other resources. The taxonomic organization of the variable manifold facilitates the technological mode of knowledge that regulates beings by grouping them, so that their behavior, performance, appearance may be, as Heidegger says, "calculable in advance."[74] Taxonomies enable humans to "know" dogs as conceptualized breeds by recounting information that always reaffirms the calculable taxonomic relations. The knowledge afforded by breed taxonomy amounts to the calculation that an individual dog will act within a limited range of possibilities determined by the "principle of germinal constancy." Breed histories provide the germinal information that explains seemingly every aspect of a dog, from its color, shape, size, to its behavior and lifespan, just as racial histories purport to recount the innate qualities of persons.[75]

The breed histories that began to be told at the start of the nineteenth century tie a dog to a specific region, and thus reflect the prevailing view of race, epitomized in Buffon's (and Kant's) monogenetic theory, which considers a single source for each species (rather than for each variety within the species) and attributes racial and breed differences to external forces such as latitude and climate.[76] In his account of the ways domestic animals differ from their savage ancestors, Buffon adheres to the accepted view that physical differences among canine breeds, like those among human races, "are produced by climate alone."[77] In his article on the dog, Buffon elaborates on the reason that this one species should display so many varieties: "Of all animals the dog is . . . most susceptible of impressions, most easily modified by moral causes, and most subject to alterations occasioned by physical influence."[78] What makes dogs and humans like one another is their difference within their species, which Buffon attributes—for both dogs and humans—to susceptibility to impression, or, in a word, to sentiment. And so Buffon, in a gesture of grandiosity, draws out the crucial analogy:

> In man we prefer genius to figure, courage to strength, and sentiment to beauty; and therefore we are induced to think that the chief excellence of an animal consists also of internal qualities. By these he differs from an automaton, rises above the vegetable tribes, and approaches the human species. It is sentiment which ennobles, governs, and gives activity to all his organs and propensities. Hence the perfection of an animal depends on sentiment alone . . . When his sentiment is delicate and improved by education, he is then fit to associate with man, to concur with his designs, to aid, to defend, and to caress him.[79]

Because man defines himself as a possessor of "internal qualities," and in particular sentiment, he values the appearance of these qualities in other beings, delimiting the difference between himself and the other with this apparent sameness. As Kant says, the mind "appraises the worth of others on the score of a like maxim of their judgment."[80] Later taxonomists, such as Oliver Goldsmith and Sydenham Edwards, repeat the attribution of a recognizable interiority to dogs that makes them closer to humans than any other animals; these attributions quickly assume the force of generic law, so that for Goldsmith the dog is "the most intelligent of all known quadrupeds, and the acknowledged friend of mankind," and for Edwards the dog is "not only the intelligent, courageous, and humble companion of man, he is often a true type of his mind and disposition."[81]

In short, dogs are friends and companions to humans and because of the analogous interiorities, a relation identical to that characterized by William McNeill as "an otherness that is manifest within the element of the Same."[82] Dogs and humans, in this view, are the same, in that they share common conventionalized interior sentiment, evident in the differences they each manifest within their own species. The "element of the Same" McNeill refers to can be seen in the grammatical organization of the landscape that puts individuals into a systemic continuity. It is this continuity that is continually being re-presented through discursive strategies, such as analogy, that reinforce the conventional mimesis extended through similitudes that support judgment so long as their conditionality remains unapparent. Thus for Buffon, "of all domestic animals, as the dog is most closely attached to man . . . it is not surprising that he should likewise exhibit the greatest variety in figure, size, colour and other qualities."[83] The two gestures in Buffon's account that reflect the modern mode of human-canine relations are, first, the references to a common interiority that brings dogs and humans together, and second, the argument, from the "logic of metaphor," that the commonality of sensibility explains how both species can vary so much within themselves. In this taxonomic view, humans situate canine otherness "within the element of the Same," turning dogs into a resource of knowledge about "man."

Thus Buffon describes the developments of canine breeds and human races as parallel histories. If regions of excessive cold "produce only dwarfish and ugly men," then the same regions will produce dogs that "are very ugly and so small that they do not exceed a foot in length," while in regions that produce the most beautiful humans, "we find the most beautiful and largest dogs."[84] Following this same analogous relation between humans and dogs, Blane turns directly from his amazement over the "monstrous variety" among humans to ask, "But is there not a more substantial distinction between Curs and Greyhounds, Turnspits and Beagles? I can hardly grant it; or if there be, it will be easily accounted for by . . . giving just allowance for food and climate."[85] The perceived analogies between dogs and humans serve to ground in nature the divisions of humans into races, and—more to the point—by making the canine breeds into divisions that have always already occurred within the language of nature.

Prior to the domination of breed discourse, canine taxonomies generally focused on "types." One of the earliest English writers on dogs, Dame Juliana Berners lists thirteen canine types prevalent in the fifteenth century: "Grehoun, a Bastard, a Mengrell, a Lemer, a Spaniel, Raches, Kenettys, Teroures, Butchers Houndes, Dunghyll dogges, Tryndeltayles, and Prykeryd currys, and smalle ladyes poppees that bere away the fleas."[86] Of this list no more than five types are recognizable as meaningful categories today: the "Grehoun," the spaniel, the Rache—a scent hound—and "Teroures." "Butchers Houndes, Dunghyll dogges . . . and smalle ladyes poppees" describe dogs a person might encounter in various places around the community, while

"Tryndeltayles" (referring to the curled tail—a trundle is a wheel or circle) and "Prykeryd currys" actually describe appearance. John Caius, who published a list in the sixteenth century, bases his distinctions on use, a standard that remains in a vestigial form in the originary breed narratives of the nineteenth century and after. He thus derives three primary categories: "gentle, or hunting" (the "gentle" designation is important, since this includes the lapdogs kept by ladies); "homely," or those serving mostly agricultural roles; and the "currishe kind."[87] Among these three broad categories, Caius identifies eight types of hunting dogs according to their reliance on scent or sight, and their speed; three types of spaniel based on the game they are turned to; small "comfort" dogs, also of the spaniel type; dogs of the "coarse" type that can be called by ten different names but seem to belong to the same large, violent type; and the "mungrell" that includes Turnspits and dancing dogs, as well as those cross-bred from wolves, foxes, or bears. The different types identified by both Dame Juliana and Caius are broad and loosely defined, relying on the various uses dogs might provide—from "comfort" to turning a spit—and to some extent reflecting class alignment. This looseness continued all the way through the eighteenth century, when written pedigrees—along with the regulative breed discourse—attained their authority.

In 1800–1805, Sydenham Edwards published the first English book on dogs since Caius that did not consider them primarily from the perspective of field sports, and is among the earliest catalogs both to depict and to identify dogs in forms and names recognizable as modern breeds.[88] *Cynographia Britannica* is not only rare but incomplete, ending in mid-sentence. Nonetheless, Edwards's comments on the dogs included in *Cynographia Britannica*—together with those of William Taplin—provide a good sense of the varieties of dogs that had been delineated between the establishment of the foxhound and the explosion of breeds in the 1820s and '30s. Both Edwards and Taplin organize dogs nationalistically, privileging those that are native to Britain, and claiming a superiority over the dogs of other nations: "England has long been eminent for the superiority of her Dogs and Horses, now preferred in almost every part of the world," Edwards says in his introduction. These two roughly contemporaneous taxonomies follow the conventional analogy of earlier taxonomists in deriving canine types through alignments with climate and activity. And, not surprisingly, Edwards's and Taplin's divisions reflect the alignment of canine varieties with social classes and with primordial bonds that had become necessarily enforceable with the passage of the Dog Tax. These emphases, which I shall evaluate successively, all had the effect of naturalizing the restrictively interventionist framing of variability into a legible system. After these taxonomies, "dog" no longer referred to a variable being but became a set field of categorically distinct beings historicized with a mythic pastoralism, and recognizable by their predictable appearance and predetermined character. It is not surprising, even this early, that the delineation into manageable "breeds" should be accompanied with warnings against miscegenation.

In his opening sentence, Edwards proposes "to give a more satisfactory account of the Dogs found in England, with their uses, habits, and appearance than has hitherto been offered to the public."[89] Edwards thus follows the general mode of integrating behavior and appearance of dogs into a canine ethos oriented teleologically toward serving humans. He goes on to comment on the many kinds of dog that have disappeared, such as the Turnspit, the use of which "the mechanical arts have superseded," and the Mastiff, lost with the introduction of "new modes of protecting property."[90] Once a need disappears from the landscape, the assumption goes, so does the dog that had served it; this is a point worth noting, for it situates dogs in the role of signifiers expressing the intent of the divine author of nature that is comprehensible to the aesthetic (and cataloging) subject.

Referring, then, to the sixteen varieties of dog listed by Caius, Edwards says it is not his purpose "to give every possible mixture and variety of Dogs, which by repeated crossing in various breeds, become almost infinite, but to adhere to what are termed the permanent, as the mixtures or crosses may be referred to the original races."[91] By limiting himself to "permanent" and "original races," Edwards confines his task to describing real and distinct differences, as though he were identifying elemental distinctions in the landscape that already bore their semiotic weight. In establishing this empirical basis to his catalog, he winnows out the impermanent and non-native types of dogs, with the implication that he identifies genuine and indigenous breeds. This catalog—like Taplin's—extends and focuses Buffon's racial analogy as the social and moral perception of the proper name that Derrida says conceals writing.[92] These catalogs present the framed landscape as though it were nature, legal and legible as the trace of primordiality. Edwards thus asserts an accuracy in his delineations, and it is this that not only gives his classifications their appearance of naturalism, but makes them into enforceable standards to which individuals should conform.

Taplin shows himself to be very much a man of the eighteenth century when he begins his catalog by expressing near despair over the variability and fluidity of his subject:

> It is universally known how exceedingly dogs differ, not only in their habits, faculties, and the propensities, but in the various figures and formations of the bodies. . . . From these causes, as well as the remote, infinite, and incredible mixture of races, and ramification of crosses, the total impossibility of enumerating each distinct breed, or species, is admitted by every naturalist who has hitherto promulgated an opinion on the subject. . . . Surprize, and hope of perfectly infallible investigation, must totally cease in respect to the fruitless minutiæ of various sizes, form of the heads, length of the muzzles, directions of the ears, formation or structure of tails, variation and variegation of colours, quality of the coats, and quantity of hair.[93]

Taplin overcomes his Enlightenment anxiety over the variability of dogs by relying heavily—albeit with serious qualification—on Buffon's categorizations. He cites the French naturalist's comment that of the thirty-seven varieties "(or races)" of dogs, only seventeen "ought to be ascribed to the influence of climate," which is to say, in effect, that only these can be thought of as being originary in that they were not produced through crosses. All other dogs, "including the King Charles's dog, are nothing but mongrels produced by the commixture of the above seventeen races."[94] Taplin includes articles on all but five of the Frenchman's varieties, and adds another twelve of his own, mostly by dividing the hound into Staghound, Foxhound, Harrier, and Beagle, and adding a few recently imported breeds, like the Newfoundland.[95]

As followers of the authoritative Buffon, both Edwards and Taplin adhere to the monogenic theory of variability, which facilitates the conceptual organization of their taxonomic categories by explaining the defining traits as effects of climate, topography, and activity on the essential, primordial shape and character of dogs. As with the contemporary racial theories, such emphasis depends on the notions of aesthetic responsiveness to the environment shaping both the physiognomy and the interior sensibility, that is, a continuity between external environment and interiority. When Edwards attests to the world-renowned superiority of England's dogs, he says, "Whether this superiority arises from the climate, or from the pains taken in their breeding, education, and maintenance, I do not undertake to determine; the Fox-hound and the Bull-dog out of this island are said to lose their properties in a few years; if so, then there must be some local cause of their perfection in this country, and their degeneration in others."[96] As genuine and original elements of the landscape, these dogs provide evidence, in their appearance, of belonging to the landscape; their responsiveness to their environment becomes a sign of the organic interrelatedness of all the genuine members of the landscape. Following the shift from the exclusionary prohibitions on human-dog relations in the Game Laws to the definition of human-canine companionship as ownership fostered by the Dog Tax, these catalogs helped to create the "natural" basis for such companionship by establishing an organic continuity between primordiality and the purchasable dog. In distinguishing native and permanent breeds from mongrels and immigrants, the catalogs allow dog fanciers to begin thinking in advance of the meaning their companionship with a dog will hold for their performance in the landscape, reenacting what Kant terms an "original and essential determination."[97]

By the time Edwards and Taplin wrote their catalogs, Buffon's identification of the Shepherd's Dog as the primordial ancestor of modern varieties had become the standard view. Following his usual method of setting dogs and humans in an analogy that explains both, Buffon says, "In every country inhabited by savage or by half civilized men, the native dogs resemble this race more than any other." So "savage" men can be seen with "savage" dogs, working in primordial fashion, as the child to the adult. In order to set this "half-civilized" dog at the source of modern canine categories, Buffon has to isolate the essential quality that will enable others to be forgotten. He thus continues by saying, "This dog, notwithstanding his ugliness, and his wild and melancholy aspect, is superior in instinct to all others."[98] The Shepherd's Dog's "instinct" aligns him with the "half-civilized" savages—i.e., instinctual men—because of his desire to work in a certain way: "He alone is born fully trained . . . guided solely by natural powers, he applies himself spontaneously to the keeping of flocks, which he executes with amazing fidelity, vigilance, and assiduity."[99] The Shepherd's Dog's primitiveness—like that of the men with him—is synonymous with his ugliness. His ugliness makes him the dog of uncultivated, unimproved, savage nature. His "natural powers" are close to the potency of nature itself, so that he needs no training, but performs "spontaneously." This nature is not the framed and improved landscape for which modern men write laws and natural histories; rather it is the mythic primordiality from which the modern landscape was made through legal and agricultural interventions. The Shepherd's Dog's "instinct" to work for men is the secret "proper" name that, in Derrida's account, is occluded by the arche-writing, then revealed as the third level of writing strips away what had been "*perceived* by the *social* and *moral consciousness* as the proper," namely, the non-native and impermanent identities and classifications.[100] And so, Buffon concludes, "we shall be confirmed in the opinion, that the shepherd's dog is the true dog of Nature; that he has been preferably bestowed on us for the extent of his utility . . . and, lastly, that he ought to be considered as the origin and model of the whole species."[101] As part of this same mythicization of the human-canine-nature relation, Buffon says, "The machines and instruments we have invented to improve or to extend our other senses, are not nearly so useful as those presented to us ready made by nature, which, by supplying the defects of our smelling, have furnished us with great and permanent resources for conquest and dominion."[102] Dogs, in Buffon's account, have made the technologizing of nature possible, as primitive man first used them to fill in for his lacks, and in that way began to learn how to create machines and instruments. Following the process of analogy,

Buffon explains that primitive man recognized that dogs possessed abilities he did not, and began to make use of them in order to appropriate those abilities. In Buffon's words, "The training of the dog seems to have been the first art invented by man; and the result of this art was the conquest and peaceable possession of the earth."[103]

Setting the Shepherd's Dog at such an origin makes all descendants of this dog—which would be every domestic canine, along with any intervention toward conquest and possession—signifiers at once of the primordial bond between man and the pastoral pre-technological nature and of man's development of technology. The subsequent delineation of dog breeds that Edwards and Taplin conduct would be the historical consequence of that originary human-canine bond. The breeds Edwards and Taplin find in the landscape signify the originary foundation of the landscape itself along with human-canine relations in the mythic nature. Canine variety grammatized into socially recognizable meaning affirms the expressiveness of the landscape *as though* it were nature and the judgment of the privileged subject reading the landscape in commerce with the divine author. As David Bindman points out in his discussion of Kant's thinking on race, the value of race as a concept lies in its capacity to "reconcile the greatest diversity . . . with the greatest unity in origin," and raises the need for "a guiding principle" by which an observer will "look for features in nature that explain their origin."[104] The Shepherd's Dog would signify that guiding principle as the origin in nature of the human-canine bond along with the human domination over nature, the technologizing (or writing) of nature into the landscape. Technological regulation of a totalized

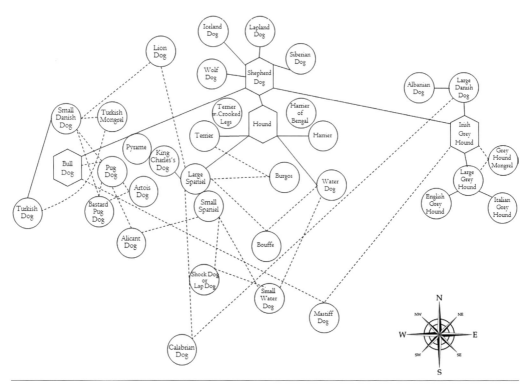

Genealogy of Dogs from Comte de Buffon. *Natural History, General and Particular*, trans. William Smellie, 2nd ed., 9 vols. (London, 1785).

landscape thus appears in a Hegelian sense as the *telos* of the originary human–Shepherd's Dog interaction. Taxonomies, then, conceptualize disparate beings into a regulable organization as the completion of knowledge, of natural history, the narrative synthesizing the manifold into reproducible representations, and all founded on such a myth as a Shepherd's Dog driven by the mystical force of nature (what else is "instinct"?) to fulfill his potential by herding "man" toward the just technological development that will improve the landscape for the benefit of all beings, but mostly himself.

In contrast to the "civilized" Foxhound—the dog most advanced from the Shepherd's Dog, and whose gentleness is proof "of the wonderful perfection he has acquired"—are a small group of dogs both Edwards and Taplin find distasteful.[105] The bulldog, which some fanciers had identified as the national English dog, Taplin finds too closely associated with "that class of people who delight in a sport formerly in great estimation (with the lower orders)."[106] In the Lurcher, Taplin sees a primordial originality that ultimately excludes it from the aesthetic landscape. He recognizes a direct lineal descent in this dog from the Shepherd's Dog crossed with the greyhound, and refined through "breeding *in and in* with the latter," so that little of the Shepherd's Dog remains recognizable.[107] "In and in" was the strategy of breeding offspring back with their parents and with one another, used to develop Taplin's beloved Foxhound, making the Lurcher into a negative parallel of the canine primate. Taplin qualifies any suggestion of refinement in this dog by saying it is "neither more nor less, than a bastard-greyhound, with some additional qualifications, but without their beauty." And lacking any "beauty," it is "little calculated for the sports of the great," and is "doomed to obscurity by the rusticity and unattracting singularity of his appearance." What is worse, the Lurcher, like the bulldog, has unhappy class connections: "We find him almost invariably in the possession of, and in constant association with poachers of the most unprincipled and abandoned description; for whose services of nocturnal depredation of various kinds, they seem every way inherently qualified."[108] As with the brutish violence of pit-fighting, poaching must be continually condemned and expelled through legalistic prohibitions like the Game Laws and Dog Tax, and through the taxonomic registration of the dogs involved as emblems of ugliness and criminality.

All these low-class dogs are epitomized in the category Edwards describes as the non-categorizable—the cur. Edwards describes this variety in terms that reflect many of the qualities Taplin associates indirectly with bulldogs and Lurchers: "The Drover's Dog, or Cur," Edwards says, has been produced by "chance" and carries the qualities of the lowest classes and weakest character: "restless manner, shuffling gait, incessant barking, vagabond appearance . . . incapable of any great design, or regular chain of action."[109] Writing at the very dawn of the great age of modern breeds, Edwards and Taplin both perpetuate the class bias that shaped much of the debate leading up to the Dog Tax, and this bias has also perpetuated racist discourses that objectify beings by imputing to them a diminished subjectivity incapable of the aesthetic judgment of the privileged techno-aesthetic subject. Curs, bulldogs, and Lurchers epitomize beings that are unrecognizable to the privileged subject, except as objects of disgust. Curs have "little value," Edwards implies, because they have not been intentionally bred—or improved—for any particular task, and because they lack any genealogical connection to a region; they are simply an accident. And so curs embody in their demeanor a lack of direction, orientation, or even locale; they have no character because they belong nowhere. In terms of the techno-aesthetic structuring of the landscape, this can only mean that, unlike the beautiful dogs serving as an analogy to human responsiveness, a cur possesses no interior sensibility, no proper name apart from chance, excess, disorder; it cannot be a good, moral, or healthy canine companion to any person capable of aesthetic judgment, who esteems dogs according to their analogous capacity for sensible intervention in the landscape. Unworthy to be a companion, a cur would not even be owned, or ownable.

These are the dogs on whose expulsion the taxonomic system depends as part of the regulation of the landscape. Bulldogs and Lurchers can be identified in terms of a putative (though unauthorized) genealogy, and so can even be identified as a type; their crime is to participate in the illegitimate activities of the lower classes. But the cur is the dog of no type; it remains singular, simply as the dog apart from design, order, relatedness. As Derrida says of disgust in Kantian aesthetics, "It is unrepresentable. . . . it is unnameable in its singularity. . . . The disgusting X cannot even announce itself as a *sensible* object without immediately being caught up in a teleological hierarchy. It is therefore in-sensible and un-intelligible, irrepresentable and unnameable, the absolute other of the system."[110] As the embodiment of chance, according to Edwards, curs threaten the grammatical unity of the landscape. They are always individuals that are not calculable in advance. They remain unknowable because they cannot be read categorically through any conventional narrative tying them to a clear origin. They threaten the taxonomic regulation of the landscape through their individuality; they pose the danger of miscegenation, erasing the sharp regulatory boundaries between breeds, and they threaten the privileged subject's ability to

Sydenham Edwards, *Cur, or Drover's Dog*. © The Right Hon. Earl of Derby/Bridgeman Images.

know what a dog is, what conventionalized face it presents. The disgustingly individual cur can never be looked at directly, and so challenges the heteronormative mode of friendship through which modern human-dog relations have come to be described. The cur is expelled over and over again in order to perpetuate and expand breed discourse, which depends on regulation and conceptualization of type. This expulsion not only enables the founding of the regulative aesthetic-legal system of the landscape as written by natural history, it also, and at the same time, founds the judging subject. The disgust expressed by Taplin and Edwards is necessary to establish their authority as natural historians delineating the canine taxonomy, and as judges of canine beauty, morality, value as potential objects to be owned.

This is the discourse that drove Parliament to enact the Dog Tax as an official delineation of legitimate and illegitimate dogs and human-dog relations, and it made taxonomic divisions appear to be empirical descriptions of canine characters as it discarded and forgot individual differences among dogs—that is, as it sacrificed the currishness possible in any particular dog. That Edwards relegates curs to the same status of brutishness and chance to which Barry relegates poor people affirms the fact that the analogical structure aligning legible and legal human-canine relations through shared sensibilities works conjointly with the foundation of the judging subject. The human subject has to comprehend the canine population apart from the accidence of particulars, and through the technological (or written) landscape of categorical organization. Comprehending dogs as breeds, historically and necessarily intertwined into the landscape, enables the judging subject to apprehend a reflection of its own capacity for aesthetic, moral, and legal judgment. Thus it is that Kant draws a direct correspondence between the judging subject and the landscape: "The universal laws of the understanding, which are at the same time laws of nature, are just as necessary . . . as the material laws of motion."[111] Dogs in the landscape capable of legible sentiment reflect the aesthetic subject's interiority, and respond to the immediate and proper environment, just as humans judge the landscape comprehensively in their interventions. Taxonomic alignments like Edwards's organize canine variability systematically—and semiotically—into reflections of the different class and racially inflected human capacities for aesthetic judgment; and all these in turn sustain the landscape as the legible and transparent work that brings the privileged subject into direct dialogue with the divine author.

The nascent taxonomy of breed division and relations—which is to say, the delineations that arranged canine variety into a semiotic system—asserted its legitimacy through expanding the divisions and refining the categories. In this sense the proliferation of dog breeds participates in the carnophallogocentrism that David Wood defines as "a mutually reinforcing network of powers, schemata of domination, and investments that has to reproduce itself to stay in existence."[112] Not only must sexual activity be regulated and authorized by official pedigree records to extend the purity of lineal descent, but breeds themselves must be proliferated to reinforce the networks and schemata of taxonomies mapping out the semiotics by which dogs can be recognized as reflections of the aesthetic subject's responsiveness.

Such legitimation already occurs within *Cynographia Britannica* in the category of terriers. Edwards distinguishes terriers, on the authority of previous taxonomists, as a type unto itself, and as "an original native of this island." And he allows the Terrier type enough variability within it to be capable of the subsequent division into distinct breeds. During the two centuries since Edwards published his taxonomy, "terrier" has expanded so much that it has become the largest of modern "groups." Rawdon Lee, at the end of the nineteenth century, devotes a full volume to the numerous breeds of terriers in his three-volume work *History and*

Description of the Modern Dogs of Britain and Ireland; he refers to a terrier show in 1893 with "162 classes provided for terriers."[113] In 1805 Edwards lays the groundwork for this expansion of terriers into multiple breeds when he differentiates one terrier from another: "The most distinct varieties are the crooked-legged and the straight-legged. The white kind have been in request of late years. Much of the variety in the Terrier arises from his being a small dog, and often bred for mere fancy."[114] This statement clearly shows that terriers had already begun to be bred for pets, as particular types. Terriers expanded into the largest group of breeds, and very often on distinctions as arbitrary as leg shape and color. The Norwich and Norfolk terriers of today are differentiated primarily by ear shape, and Cairns, Westies, and Scotties were once distinguished only by color. Along the way, as individual differences were discarded, forgotten, and regulated out of existence, these arbitrary distinctions acquired semiotic values that made them anything but arbitrary, so that a Scottie is not just a black (or gray or brindle) Westie, but an altogether different terrier with its own breed narrative.

While the Dog Tax of 1796 did indeed open the possibility of canine companionship to all classes of humans, it also necessitated the dictionaries defining dog varieties and what sorts of "new" relations they make possible ("new" relations must always reenact the originary significance, or they would not be recognizable as relations, new or outmoded). As a commodity, dogs became something that could be collected. With this shift, canine variability lost much of its monstrosity, its accidence, and took on the appeal of a fancy that actually sought out differences and, through both the breeding practices developed with the Foxhound and the associations formed between race and region, began to distinguish breeds semiotically and through the authority of sanctioned pedigree records. Canine variability acquired a double signification, as the analog providing the natural base to accounts of racial categories among humans, and as an object of fashion. The associations developed by natural historians of a dog's putative origins became intertwined with fashions granting and withdrawing value according to relations with popular figures, regions, or events. So it is that "breed" began to supplant the more broadly delineated "type" as the distinguishing quality of a dog. And fashion began to make different breeds more and less popular as their associations with people, political parties, regions, or events were foregrounded.

An example would be the spaniels kept by "Our unfortunate Monarch, Charles the First," whom Edwards has confused with Charles II, the monarch known for the affection he showed his toy spaniels. Carson I. A. Ritchie says that "Charles II was the first male dog-owner to make a real fetish of lap-dogs," which were the black and white spaniels brought to court by Henrietta of Orange.[115] Ritvo argues that it was such associations between dogs kept solely as pets and the aristocracy that gave rise to the fancy that took over the nineteenth century: "The elaborate structure of pedigree registration and show judging metaphorically equated owner with elite pet," and "the institutions that defined the dog fancy projected an obsessively detailed vision of a stratified order which sorted animals and, by implication, people into snug and appropriate niches."[116] Small dogs like the Cavalier and Blenheim spaniels that had once been kept only as lapdogs retained the associations with the Stuarts and nobility generally, and, once the tax turned dogs officially into a commodity, the associations could be bought and kept as a plain emblem of that association.

The parliamentary debates that instituted the Dog Tax and the taxonomies of natural history together legalized and naturalized the range of possible human-dog relations. Law and science authorized which readings humans could conduct of the dogs in their midst. Derrida observes that establishing laws, or systems of law, produces "proper interpretative models to read in return, to give sense, necessity and above all legitimacy to the violence that has produced . . . the interpretative model in question."[117] In a real way that cannot be overlooked, the law creating the Dog Tax defined which dogs could exist in the future, which ones had a legitimate function in the landscape. And scientific authority delineated and grammatized the relations humans and dogs might have with one another. These relations constitute the interpretations that humans assign to dogs through historic associations with regions and activities (herding, hunting, guarding, etc.) within a mythically primordial landscape. Expansion of the canine taxonomy not only meant that the sheer number of dog breeds grew, but that breed as the authorized, and socially recognized, character of dogs was naturalized into the easiest—and necessary—way to describe an individual dog. As the class analogies between dogs and humans were cast into parliamentary law, the racial analogies were cast into natural law. And just as these analogies affirmed and reified class and racial differences among humans, they legalized and naturalized breed distinctions with the same authority of law and nature. Breed differences were created and maintained through a technological violence of inbreeding and culling; they were given meaning by an aesthetics of mimesis that subjected the canine being to a programmatic reading in service to human sovereignty.

Once canine variability could be arranged into breeds, it lost its monstrous quality by acquiring the historical significance regulable within technology. Breeds enabled post-Enlightenment natural historians to comprehend dogs in themselves and as representatives of animality more broadly, and to apprehend individual dogs as animals possessing an inner life comparable to that of humans related through analogies of class and race. The creation and expansion of dog breeds, beginning with the Foxhound, made Enlightenment taxonomies seem more than strategies to enforce the regularity of the landscape; they worked as codices of mute nature, the grammar revealing that nature had all along constituted a linguistic coherence. Even more, they brought originary nature and its divine author into direct, comprehensive presence. Kant makes this claim thus: "Natural history would presumably lead us back from the great number of seemingly different species to races of the same genus and transform the presently overly detailed artificial system for the description of nature *into a physical system for the understanding*."[118] The interpretive model legitimated itself in its claim to be nature, not merely the legal calculus framing the discordant variability of dogs into a readable landscape. If dogs exist as breeds—especially if they have always existed as breeds that humans have only just begun to recognize the organization of—then the variability of animal nature could be seen as a unified totality, rather than an open field of contiguous events that might or might not hold relevance to human reason, language, and history. Once nature was thought of as a totalized system, its fundamental elements—from oxygen and electricity to forests and animals—could be interpreted for their contribution to the ecosystem. These interpretations not only make human institutions such as racism seem reflections of nature, but make the technological governance of animals—dogs particularly—into the primordial relations to be discovered by objective science.

The taxonomies of breed thus perpetuated the regulations of the Dog Tax and the Game Laws. When the Dog Tax was repealed in 1828, it was not as a result of the liberalization of human-canine relations toward other possibilities of interaction, but because the surveillance and regulation sought by laws and taxes were attained by the division of dogs into breeds and the assignment of narratives of origin and character to those breeds. The taxonomic organization of breeds claims for itself a determinate and direct knowledge of "the dog," as the being that has willingly shaped itself into different varieties through a responsiveness to nature and to the needs of man as the improver, completer of nature. The sensibility that enables dogs to respond to nature compels them instinctively to reflect human judgment. This knowledge of "the dog" is confined within the framing enforced by the taxonomy and discourse of breed as the trace of the instinct driving primordial dogs into the service of man.

A breed gives us something we can, and must, describe, with empirical rigor, as the differences of an individual dog, and then—this is the most important step—situate those differences within a taxonomy that forges the particularities into a historical concept. The descriptive taxonomy of breeds, along with the tax law defining dogs as property, established conventionalized identities that dogs might hold within the regulated landscape and by which they might be known. To know a dog through its breed identity is to recognize it through the *as such* of its authorized category, and to recognize it conceptually—not individually—within the mimetic economy of the landscape. The taxonomy of canine breeds enframes the totality of "the dog" into a field of particularities that can be apprehended within the comprehensive whole. Every encounter with a breed dog reinforces the taxonomy through the act of judgment that situates the particular within the totality. Every encounter with a particular dog within the enframed totality makes "the dog" knowable in its presence, which is predetermined by the breed. At the end of his discussion of Derrida's reformulation of the conditional similitude into a questioning of the *as such*, Joris van Gorkom emphasizes the conditionality of similitude by pointing that "To know or recognize the other *as such* means that the other has lost its alterity. It is precisely this impossibility of the 'as' or 'as such' that is underscored by the 'if' or 'as if.'"[119] The force of breed discourse is that of the law that requires dogs to be present apart from any alterity, and apart from any currish individuality open to an indeterminate and variable future. Without legal alterity, breed dogs are assigned a presence that will always occlude and deny any undetermined, contingent possibility. Relations between humans and dogs are happily calculable through a mimetic economy that compels a dog to reflect a human in predictable ways, again and again. The breed descriptions generating knowledge of a dog in its presence silences possibilities for relations between humans and dogs that do not necessarily or wholly participate in this mode of writing, this landscape. The indirection that had oriented the engagements between Pope and his canine friends, for example, appear now as uncaring, lacking in the "capacity to 'look into the other's face.'"[120] Not only does indirection allow for contingency to abound, but it allows too much for nondescriptive, non-knowing silence, as when a poet and dog walk "quietly & peaceably" by themselves.

Once the law made dogs into property, and the taxonomies made them present as breeds, dogs held value only insofar as they were pure—otherwise their *as such*, their breed, would only be indeterminate and mediated by conditionality. Their "proper name"—the instinct that drives *them* to work *for* humans—would remain unwritten, as much as the mythic foundation to the landscape. Breed purity ensured the aesthetic pleasure of the human subject able to own the right kind of dog. And so protecting the purity of breeds, their *as such*, went beyond the keeping of paper records for pedigrees and the legal restrictions on which persons might possess them. Purity demanded expelling variability from bloodlines through the technological strategies that had successfully created a modern Foxhound, which will be the focus of the next chapter.

The Modern Landscape of Sport
Representations of the Foxhound

MANY OF THE BROAD CONCERNS RAISED IN ANIMAL STUDIES OVER THE PAST DECADE have been formulated in ethical terms of how humans treat animals, how humans respond to the animal gaze and recognize animal others for their capacity for responsiveness. Through laws and through taxonomies, a different—though not unrelated—element in human-canine relations gained real footing in the eighteenth century, and that is the overarching distinction between desirable and undesirable dogs, attractive and unattractive ones, for this distinction separates the dogs one might wish to respond from all others. This is an aesthetic concern that I would say predetermines any of the ethical questions about responsiveness or recognition. During the time that the English Parliament was turning to taxation as a method for reducing the numbers of undesirable dogs, many of the men holding a real stake in the debates were also involved in a long-term project that would transform existing hounds into a singular hound that would respond to their need to hunt foxes for sport. The result of this successful project—itself, perhaps, an offshoot of the Agricultural Revolution, when plants, animals, and the terrain of England were subjected to intense interventions for their improvement in desirability—was the first modern canine breed, the Foxhound. Although the techniques used to create this breed could not be called aesthetic in any sense, they were described as a performative intervention demonstrating sound aesthetic judgment. Similarly, foxhunting has been described since the eighteenth century as an aesthetic performance uniting and completing the landscape. The unimproved space in which sport and agriculture had previously been conducted called out in some way for a human intervention that would improve the space; the most significant intervention was that provided by the conceptually framed Foxhound.

Derrida begins the close scrutiny he gives Kant's aesthetic system by recalling that Kant himself refers to "the lacunary character [*Mangelhaftigkeit*] of his work."[1] Derrida then poses the question that will orient much of his reading: "and what if it [the lack, the lacuna] were the frame?"[2] In relating the lack to the frame that Kant emphasizes as being key to beauty (as opposed to the sublime) and to an aesthetic theory, Derrida can begin thinking of the frame as that which is not within an artwork, nor without it;[3] thus he turns to the *parergon*—to which Kant refers in "The Analytic of the Beautiful" as being "only an adjunct, and not an intrinsic constituent in the complete representation of the object. . . . Thus it is with the frames of pictures or the drapery on statues, or the colonnades of palaces."[4] Of Kant's examples Derrida says, "What constitutes them as *parerga* is not simply their exteriority as surplus, it is the internal structural link which rivets them to the lack in the interior of the *ergon*."[5]

Consequently, "No 'theory,' no 'practice,' no 'theoretical practice' can intervene effectively in this field if it does not weigh up and bear on the frame, which is the decisive structure of what is at stake."[6] With this statement, Derrida is orienting his own reading of Kantian aesthetics, and at the same time pointing out that for that very aesthetics a sound judgment must work at this same degree of intervention. In other words, a performative judgment in the landscape must engage with "the decisive structure," with the frame that is apparent in the lack, in the need at the heart of the landscape. In answer to the questions "Where does the frame take place?" and what is the *parergon*, Derrida responds, "The whole analytic of aesthetic judgment forever assumes that one can distinguish rigorously between the intrinsic and the extrinsic. . . . Hence one must know . . . how to determine the intrinsic—what is framed—and know what one is excluding as frame *and* outside the frame."[7] Within the Kantian system, and, by extension, within the regulated landscape of modern human-canine relations, the capacity to make this determination is what distinguishes a sound aesthetic (and, for that matter, legal) judgment. Not only does the lack begin the judgment as intervention, it also orients the sustained performance, to become the *Zweckmäßigkeit ohne Zweck*, the aim lacking an actual goal that counts for disinterested beauty. Thus, from its putative beginning to its fulfillment (in what Taplin calls the most perfected hound, for example), the aesthetic intervention is focused on, engaged in, and determined by a lack, the interaction with a need. What is more, this need, Derrida says, is effaced as frame—since an obvious framing would only signify an artificiality that would make the intervention academic—by naturalizing it.[8] The interventions that shaped the legible landscape in England and elsewhere were thus framed as natural engagements, even as they created and enforced the frame to include some readings while expelling others. What this means in terms of the Foxhound is that the manipulation of particular dogs to create a reliably consistent breed has been narrated as a conscientious response to a natural need, as part of the broad drive for improvement characterizing the Agricultural Revolution.

The prominent accounts detailing the creation of the Foxhound adhere to a distinct set of narrative strategies to synthesize characteristics into a breed. If the histories of the Foxhound fail to identify a singular origin, they do succeed in turning the lack of origin into a conceptual frame that singularizes *the* Foxhound as an aesthetically necessary dog, as *the* necessary dog in the completed framed landscape. In addition, by setting the creation of the Foxhound alongside the Agricultural Revolution, the histories make the Foxhound an aesthetic emblem for the broader transformation of animals, plants, and the earth into resources to be improved by eliminating undesirable qualities. In reading these histories, I hope to continue the examination, begun in the previous chapter, of the discursive strategies employed to make regulation and restriction appear to be performative interventions with nature, to read the silence of nature as if it were a plea to be brought closer to man. Along with those histories of the breed, the accounts of modern foxhunting reiterate the aesthetic function of the hound created specifically for the sport. Foxhunting, in these descriptions, repeats the unifying function in the landscape accomplished by the creation of the Foxhound. Hunting with hounds is described as bringing together humans, animals, and scenery into an active affirmation of the judging subject's ability to comprehend natural beauty directly. These accounts, along with the new catalogs of breed dogs that began appearing at the start of the nineteenth century, played a large role in conventionalizing descriptions of other dogs into conceptual breeds that still dominate the way we speak and write about our relations with dogs. The numerous calls for an improved hound guide the histories to present this intervention as a response to a natural need, while conventions presenting foxhunting as a performative unification frame the landscape as an arena in which a predetermined meaning can be repeatedly discovered for human-canine interactions. I shall show first of all what it meant for an eighteenth-century man of privilege to turn dogs into a resource to be developed and improved, and what it meant that this intervention was cloaked in the terms of an aesthetic responsiveness, a sensitive reading of the needs of the landscape.

As the conceptual framing of a plurality of dogs into a conceptual singularity, "breed" consists, on the one hand, of the regulation of dogs' sexual reproduction, and on the other as the historical narratives of origin that are meant to explain such matters as temperament and physiognomy by way of assigning a readable character to a category of dogs. To a great extent, these narratives are spurious, fabricated through general conventions that make the narratives themselves into a genre, a *Geschlecht*, a literary breed. And in this sense, "breed" directs our relations with dogs prosthetically, as affirming reflections of the interventionist subject that I have been referring to as techno-aesthetic. The manipulation of dogs toward the putative *telos* of attaining the performative ideal of a single function—not individually, but as a genealogical grouping—shows the technological drive at work to re-form a being into a mimetic representation guaranteed to facilitate an aesthetic bonding, to reenact the originary presence between the aesthetic subject and the divine author through the landscape as though it were nature. And the narratives that relate that technological intervention and then describe the improved hound as a central integrating force in the landscape show the aesthetic discourse at work in presenting technological intervention as a performative engagement with vibrant nature. It should be remembered that this "nature" stands at a distant remove from the "savage" (to invoke Buffon's term) nature; it is the landscape in which the modern Foxhound brings sportsmen into a communion with a vibrant wholeness, a prosthetic representation of a wholly mythic pastoral.

In the mid-eighteenth century, three events occurred that changed the way humans looked at and interacted with dogs (and that could be outlined in terms of the biopolitics directing the power of the discursive landscape): sporting men turned their attention to foxes; farmers began employing new strategies for improving their crops and animals; writers and painters began to portray foxhunting as an aesthetic engagement with the landscape. These three developments all facilitated each other in fundamental ways to give the Foxhound a native, naturalistic value that did not pertain to the Dutch Pug, the King Charles or Blenheim Spaniels, or even—at least until later—the bulldog. The men who put their stamp on foxhunting at that time—such as Lord Yarborough of the Brocklesby Hunt, Lord Rutland of the Belvoir, and Hugo Meynell of the Quorn—were country men with sizable land holdings; and many others who rode to hounds and owned large estates also patronized the arts (and held seats in Parliament). Sporting interests, agricultural interests, politics, and aesthetics thus overlapped with one another in constituting the collective outlook of the landed gentry—or at least those members of the gentry involved in creating the Foxhound itself and the discourse of what this hound meant to the English countryside. And because the countryside was attaining a renewed importance in the British national identity, the rise of foxhunting as the foremost sport in the countryside—and, consequently, of the Foxhound as the foremost dog—acquired a high value as a signifier of an indigenous means of engaging in the landscape. The Foxhound developed a cultural significance greater than that of other canine types that had fashionable followings in the eighteenth century, such as the nonindigenous Pug and toy spaniels. As a countryside pursuit, foxhunting changed with the landscape that was being subjected to sustained developments as agriculture was modernized through enclosure, drainage, and the building of fences—all of which contributed to the speed and distance of individual hunts. The "institutional framework" that Mark Overton outlines as the complex of forces (*dispositifs*) that increased productivity in eighteenth-century agriculture entailed not only the physical changes to the landscape—which had already been taking place for almost two hundred years—but also broad social changes, such as land ownership, relations between owner and worker, and the growing population, which was pointed to as the necessity for increasing efficiency and productivity.[9] That interventions with the landscape should be governed by a sense of needed improvement was in fact due to the technological perspective that had already cast the landscape into a field of resources to be managed, to produce more food, more timber, and better sport—or, put another way, to serve a growing population, to serve the navy, to serve the aesthetic tastes and sporting interests of the privileged. This necessity provided the frame that gave the countryside a landscaped cohesiveness, with select humans filling the need with their drive for improvement. These "improvements" might have had an appearance of a definite aim—a faster-growing cow, or a quicker hound with a better nose—but the more enduring aim appeared to lie beyond the simple outcome of a changed animal product. The larger and more nebulous aim seemed, in fact, to lie in aesthetically engaging with the intrinsic dynamics of the landscape, in identifying the necessary potencies and making them more necessary.

Consistently, accounts of the Foxhound praise the "science" of the breeding programs, situating the developmental phases of particular hounds or packs as progressively responsive steps toward the ultimate solution of a riddle: how to create the best hound for hunting foxes through open country. Narratives on the development of the Foxhound conventionally begin with the primordial state of the English countryside when there was no Foxhound. This was a time when hunting in England varied widely among the different regions. The general understanding held that the differences among hounds reflected the differences of regions—the kinds of quarry, the terrain, and the climate—in all the ways developed by taxonomists. So William Blane observes "that a couple of right Southern Hounds, removed to the North, and suffered to propagate, without art or mixture, in a hilly mountainous country, where the air is light and thin will by sensible degrees decline and degenerate into lighter bodies, and shriller voices, if not rougher coats."[10] Like Buffon, Blane identifies climatic and regional influences as the key forces shaping dogs and humans physically and temperamentally. Such a view accorded closely with the belief that hunting with hounds was integral to the landscape, and that the different kinds of hunting were appropriate modes of engaging in the specific climates—thus hare hunting to the north, stag or foxhunting to the south. And what is more, as dogs were set into an analogy with humans for their capacity to engage with the vital forces of the landscape, their integration into the character of a region signified their proximity both to humans and to the living landscape. This medial position made them a pivotal element in the new aesthetic discourse promoting foxhunting as the primary sport of all regions.

Well into the nineteenth century (1840), Delabere Blaine, following Taplin, still pointed to climate as the primary agent in shaping canine varieties, and even emphasized its role in forming national characteristics: "It is said the shepherd's dog transported into temperate climates and among people entirely civilized, such as England, France, or Germany, will be divested of its savage air, its pricked ears, its rough, long, and thick hair; and from the influence of climate and food alone, will become either a French Matin, an English Mastiff, or a hound."[11] Blaine extends his bias in favor of northern Europe as the seat of civilization when he cites a historical authority—"Mr Griffith quoting the sentiments of French naturalists"—to give "to the ancient Britons the old English hound or talbot, as the parent of the celebrated sagacious hound of our island; and it is found by experience," he continues, "that this dog degenerates in every other part of the world—a strong presumptive proof of his being indigenous to Britain."[12] Following the principle of sensibility that makes dogs and humans physiologically responsive to regional conditions, historians like Blane and Blaine establish that the Northern and Southern hounds must have been either indigenous to Britain or very, very ancient, because they could not naturally appear in their form anywhere else. Though this notion waned in the nineteenth century, it continued to provide the link to the indeterminacy of an ancient past. So the origin of the Foxhound has been traditionally attributed to a cross between the two indigenous hounds of Britain, the Northern hound and the Southern hound that had each embodied the characteristics of their native regions. As to when and how the cross took place, no one knows, but everyone, it seems, cares.

Already in 1686, Richard Blome had complained about the hounds of both the North and South in terms that were soon locked into formula, describing the Northern hounds as "fleet of foot [but] thin-skinned and therefore not proper for coverts and bushy enclosure as the Southern Hounds which are thick-skinned and slow-footed, and not fit for the long chases that open countries afford."[13] Blome's complaint that neither of the older hounds fits the demands of modern sport specifies mutual lacks that made the Foxhound necessary. For the negative statement that neither hound had all the right qualities opened the possibility for the positive statement that a cross might combine their good traits and eliminate the undesirable ones. This positive view of a cross marked a notable shift in attitude, as most people still believed that crossing different types would only combine the negative traits.[14] But that positive view generated the ideal of the perfect hound that might be attained by human intervention.

At any rate, within a hundred years after Blome's complaint, the idea of a homogenized hound displaying the best of the two ancient regional hounds became widespread, as when William Blane advised his fellow huntsmen "to begin to breed on the middle-sized dogs, betwixt the Southern Hound and the Northern Beagle."[15] The theme of this cross enabled historians simultaneously to describe the aesthetic responsiveness of the early breeders and to protect the indigeneity of modern hounds. Working on early eighteenth-century descriptions of the Badminton hounds (the Duke of Beaufort's pack), early twentieth-century historian T. F. Dale makes a typical gesture when he claims they "show plainly their descent from the older races," carrying the qualities of the old deerhound, to which Taplin refers as "primeval stock."[16]

Dale makes a bold move, however, when he asserts that the Badminton pack provided the link between the two old hounds of the North and South, as Beaufort switched to foxhunting in the 1760s and began breeding out to Hugo Meynell's hounds as well as to the Belvoir.[17] The overt aim of Dale's assertion is to dispel the myth that Meynell single-handedly developed the Foxhound; but the less overt—and more important—aim is to identify an essential link between the modern Foxhound and the older hounds. This link turns the modern Foxhound into the preserve of the two foremost indigenous hounds of Britain, and, by extension, turns foxhunting into the modern preserve of the two earlier modes of hunting in Britain—coursing and stag-hunting. Although coursing had attained a wide popularity, and the hounds used to chase hare were supposedly derived from ancient packs of wolfhounds, the Northern hound's contribution to the creation of the Foxhound is often slighted in favor of the Southern hound. Certainly the Northern hound had as many admirers as the Southern hound, and

John Frederick Lewis, *John Crocker Bulteel, Depicted in His Hunting Attire with Two of His Favourite Foxhounds.*
Exhibited at the Royal Academy in 1829 (Private Collection), Wikimedia Commons.

even held its own against the Foxhound through the eighteenth century; but as foxhunting grew in fashion, and as more land opened up to allow for mounted chases, it was the Southern hound, with its association to stag hunts, that acquired the greater attention, as though the Southern provided the basic stock and the Northern simply made contributions to improve it.

An important characteristic of foxhunting is that the hunt field follows the hounds on horses. Unlike other game, which only legally qualified people could hunt, foxes were never protected, so that anyone could kill them. As the countryside was cleared of old forests, the muddy ground drained, and fences laid, the land was opened to new agriculture, and to this new form of hunting. Not only was foxhunting exciting for the extended fast chases that had never before been possible, but its use of horses gave it an important connection with the old royal stag hunt.[18] In short, foxhunting became enormously popular, and a prominent image of the modern landscape maintaining its tie to a mythic past.

Two elements in this part of the conventional history of the Foxhound stand out. First, the sense that foxhunting replicated the old restricted stag hunt, alongside the narrative of the cross sustaining ancient and indigenous strains, makes the Foxhound into an active bonding agent between modern hunting and archaic hunting in a mythically pre-technologized landscape. Technologization framing the landscape through laws, agricultural changes, and sport was evident enough that the mythologizing narrative—like the rhetoric surrounding the Dog Tax—made the creation of the Foxhound into a performative engagement with primordial nature to preserve and "improve" the vital elements of England. Thus Dale asserts, contrary to earlier historians, that the Foxhound "certainly was not developed out of the old harrier or beagle, neither was he modified from the bloodhound. . . . His direct descent I believe to be from the hounds kept by the great territorial families for hunting the stag."[19]

The second theme in this narrative I want to foreground is the claim that the Foxhound was a necessity. The need for the Foxhound generates the *parergon* Derrida analyzes both as providing an "internal structural link" to the organized (or landscaped) work and as being exterior frame to the work.[20] In this sense the *parergon* works not as a thing—it is, after all, a need, and thus a kind of lack—but as an impetus to act in a particular way, to pursue some end. Again, as with the presentation of legal restrictions on dogs, this narrative presenting the regulation of dogs' sexual reproduction as a response to a need makes the breeders into morally and aesthetically conscientious interventionists whose capacity for judgment enables and compels them to comprehend how a landscape seemingly calls out for improvement that only they can accomplish. The killing off of unsatisfactory dogs, the inbreeding of desirable dogs are, in this myth, benevolent acts of engagement in the living essence of the landscaped tableau they oversee and enjoy. These two elements making the Foxhound into the bonding agent with the primordial past and with the living landscape of the present impel the histories even through the lack of historical material.

Historians retrospectively and repeatedly describe the all-important cross as one that had been awaited, and that foxhunting could not do without; thus Sydenham Edwards, writing at the start of the nineteenth century, asserts that "a cross between these two is deemed preferable to either."[21] Once the importance of the cross is recognized by the historians, the narrative problem arises of how to move it beyond surmise to a documented certainty, since, as Dale states quite simply, "for such a history no sufficient materials exist."[22] The paucity of concrete, verifiable sources opens an originary gap that the narratives fill with accounts of how, in one way or another, the Foxhound fulfills the aim of the landscape; the lack of documentation itself becomes evidence within the narratives that the Foxhound provided the denouement to the plot of foxhunting's growth into an irresistible necessity, providing complete aesthetic satisfaction. Sir John Buchanan-Jardine opines that the vital cross had already taken place in the seventeenth century and in the North, so the Northern hound would itself be the embodiment of the combination that was subsequently made use of "all over the country to speed up local types of hounds."[23] Buchanan-Jardine points to the old Norman hound as the source of British hounds, most evidently the Talbot, from whom descended the slow, Southern scent hounds. But, in adding the slight variant of the climatic argument that "various offshoots of the breed gradually evolved in different parts of the country in accordance with the needs and tastes of their breeders,"[24] he makes the case that the regional variability among the older hounds belied their common source. Perhaps most fascinating of all is Buchanan-Jardine's account of the Northern hound, which is generally overlooked by the other historians. Here Buchanan-Jardine explains that until "around 1640" the hounds in the North were also probably closely connected to the Talbot, and then "almost suddenly the tide seemed to turn . . . when one finds a very fast, galloping kind of hound being bred in Yorkshire and the North generally."[25] This "sudden" development he attributes to the pack of staghounds given to King James I by Henry IV of France.[26] These noble staghounds, the surmise is, were bred with the regional descendants of the Talbot to give rise to the Northern hound. But once Buchanan-Jardine has established this much genealogy, he turns to the motif of uncertainty due to lack of documentation—"there is no ascertaining for sure"—and relies repeatedly on the "suddenness" with which the Northern hound appeared.

If both progenitors of the modern Foxhound can be shown to belong to a primordial English pastoralism, then all the hunting associated with and developed alongside this hound would also be indigenous to Britain. This genealogical foundation—undocumented and speculative as it may be—is the primary aim of virtually all the narratives on the Foxhound because it obviates the hound's artificiality: even as an engineered animal, the Foxhound as heir to the ancient Talbot and the seemingly autochthonous Northern hound embodies the heritage of the landscape as representation of a mythic British heritage. Even as a modern animal, the Foxhound has been made into a fertile emblem of the relations privileged humans hold to the land—relations that extend beyond social rights granted by law (*droit*), for these relations are cast as inherent qualities, defining characteristics of England, just like the weather, that provide the trace for the mystical justice, for the creative author of nature. Thus, the histories of the Foxhound might fail to identify the actual origin, or the moment of the all-important cross, but they do succeed in preserving (or creating) a genealogy that is both aristocratic and uniquely English. Without a concrete document verifying that a dog was born on a given date in a particular kennel, the Foxhound can only be said to have arisen from the hounds that belonged to the native, primordial landscape, *before* foxhunting. The tacit suggestion is that the Foxhound itself represents the changes in the landscape and quarry that made improvements on old hounds necessary; that is, in this discourse, despite its artificiality (as a hound whose responses to climate, topography, and quarry occurred specifically through human intervention), the Foxhound belongs to England as much as, or even more than, its more regionally distinctive ancestors did. The lack of sources pinpointing the cross becomes the essence, the proper name, of the modern Foxhound, framing the histories into descriptive accounts of this hound filling the lack in the received landscape. The necessity of the hound works just as the "instinct" Buffon ascribes to the originary Shepherd's Dog. The force of this mythic cross—as proper name—lies not simply in the fact that it happened, but that it did so in a determinate—albeit historically undeterminable—fashion, with someone at some time actively and conscientiously engaging with dogs to fill the need of the landscape, and with the dogs willingly and instinctively seeking out human aid in their own improvement.

As foxhunting spread across the different regions, it became more or less standardized (with notable exceptions, of course), and the Foxhound also took on some general standards, even while hunts sought to distinguish their packs through "accidental" features like coat color (e.g., the "Belvoir tan"). Just as the regulated crossing and inbreeding set the strategy for creating later breeds, the lack of sources for a history of the Foxhound became the template for subsequent breed historians. Consistently, these histories bypass evidence of the modernity of breed designation to establish a naturalness to the engineered, technologically created breeds by making them appear to have once held an indigenous role in a preindustrial pastoral. But, of course, the key step in creating certifiable breeds was when huntsmen began keeping pedigrees for their hounds, and for the first time ensured a factual and legal record of their lines.

Pedigrees were started for the first Earl of Yarborough's Brocklesby hounds in 1746, and these hounds were subsequently used by many other kennels as the "science" of modern breeding spread to other hunts seeking to improve their packs. Nineteenth-century historian Robert Vyner singles out Lord Yarborough's pack from all other strains of hound in the first half of the eighteenth century as being among those "from whence the most fashionable sorts are descended."[27] Dale gives the title of primacy to the Duke of Rutland (of the Belvoir), however, pointing to epistolary evidence that "the Duke had had a pack of foxhounds for some time previous to 1730."[28] But whether or not the Belvoir pack was devoted exclusively to fox, and especially whether the hounds would have been recognizable in 1730 specifically as "Foxhound" in conformation, character, and ability, are questions Dale leaves unbroached. The important detail is that by mid-century, breeders began keeping stud lists, and the uncertainty facing historians trying to unravel the relations between apparently different types of hounds, such as the Northern and Southern, ends at 1753. From that point on, the archive of recorded pedigree was as much a part of a well-bred hound as its ability in the field. With certain and detailed records, breeders knew the genealogies of hounds that performed well individually and that had descended from equally good performers and so were very likely to pass on their abilities. Individuals were continually assessed for performance in the field and for the likelihood of passing their good qualities on to their progeny. That is to say, individuals were appraised for their lack of individuality, or any deviation from the normative ideal determined by the new possibilities of hunting foxes in a particular fashion; the best individual was the one truest to type, who bore the history of its predecessors most plainly, and ensured that future individuals would extend that history without deviation.

This way of judging was taken to be inherent to the landed gentleman of the eighteenth century in his aesthetic and moral capacity to perceive the general in the particular, the ideal represented by an individual freed of its accidental qualities. The obvious archetype of such a man of judgment is Joshua Reynolds, artist, president of the Royal Academy, and author of the series of programmatic aesthetic essays *Discourses on Art*; an equally suitable example would be a gentleman like Hugo Meynell—wealthy landowner and friend of Dr. Johnson and Horace Walpole[29]—since the capacity for judgment may easily be extended beyond a gentleman's appreciation of a landscape painting that looks as though it were nature to his evaluation of the hounds in a landscape structured as though it were a painting. According to John Barrell, the aesthetic ability to appreciate panoramic landscape painting was considered by Reynolds and other aesthetic theorists of the eighteenth century as a crucial element in a landed gentleman's ability to judge all things dispassionately and disinterestedly for the good of the nation.[30] For men like Meynell, Yarborough, Rutland, and Beaufort, it was the ability to see how an individual served the ideal *telos* of hunting a particular prey, and it was the ability to see how foxhunting progressed toward an ideal—however nebulous—engagement with the landscape. That these men individually exemplified the privileged techno-aesthetic subject gives historical ground to the fact that collectively they demonstrated both the institutional normatization of that subject and the technological violence that serves as the writing of the landscape. Their claim to privilege was asserted through legal interventions—such as determining who might own a taxable dog, and who might hunt certain animals with dogs—and through the physical interventions shaping hounds for strategic purposes. These interlocking efforts can certainly be understood as a coordination of power relations to extract a surplus from living beings, as in the questioning of biopolitics.[31]

Because the shires of central England in mid-century already had a number of closely situated hunts, cross-breeding between different lines was facilitated by the number of available packs possessing either Northern or Southern blood. Hounds were then inbred within the packs to preserve or to enforce desirable qualities. Vyner points to the underlying principle of the new approach:

Hound breeding at that time was as scientifically pursued as sheep breeding, and the successful perseverance of Mr Meynell and Lord Yarborough will ever be deserving of the warmest gratitude from true sportsmen, for lighting up what might be justly termed *the dawn of science in the hunt.*[32]

This is not a haphazard comparison. Meynell and Lord Yarborough certainly belong to the broader Agricultural Revolution as the men who brought hunting into the modern age by systematically breeding a better hound. These men "persevered" through their methodical, "scientific" programs of line-breeding—that is, breeding to preserve not just the qualities of an individual but of its ancestors—and inbreeding, which duly increases the likelihood of passing characteristics to offspring since the parents are closely related. The reference to sport entering "the dawn of science"—already a tag phrase fifty years before Vyner's book—gets right to the point that such breeding programs, if not hunting itself—were governed by the teleological necessity of actively employing the capacity for judgment by improving available resources toward the ideal of complete integration—and toward complete legibility. It is in the nebulous aim of completeness that improvement identifies the lack as the essential need; and in making the lack into the guiding necessity, these interventionists made it into the frame that could integrate the landscape, perhaps even more effectively than the law or natural history.

Meynell adopted his "scientific" method from livestock breeding—particularly sheep and cattle—and considered the hounds from an overtly teleological perspective. But, as with the theme of the desired and necessary cross, here the question of precedence, and of who developed the breeding strategies taken up by others, cannot be pinned down with any certainty. At least one agricultural historian allows the possibility that sheep breeders developed their techniques of breeding for particular characteristics from hound and Thoroughbred breeders.[33] Margaret E. Derry, in her account of the innovations in livestock breeding, observes that "In the late eighteenth century, a number of British breeders attempted to 'improve' horses, sheep, and cattle. . . . The most famous of these was Robert Bakewell, and he commonly received the credit for all their work."[34] Derry's suggestion that such enormous innovations cannot be attributed to a single breeder is repeated in various forms, and repeats in its turn the factual gap of the all-important cross between Northern and Southern hounds. In this way, the judging subject is confined to no particular man, but works instead as the categorical singularity setting the judging subject against the evaluated hounds or admired landscape. Cecil Pawson, in his short biography of Bakewell, states with unabashed bias, "It is said that Hugo Meynell . . . was breeding foxhounds in the 1760s on the same principles as Bakewell. Quorn Hall is only a few miles from Dishley Grange. Meynell may have learnt from Bakewell."[35] Similarly, Dale, who takes every opportunity to assert that several notable personages exerted more influence on the Foxhound—Rutland, Arundel, Beaufort are only a few of the names—sets Meynell's reputation within the "institutional framework" of mid-century sport:

To Hugo Meynell belongs the honour of having first demonstrated to the squires and nobles of the Midlands the possibilities of the fox properly hunted. . . . Meynell it was who set the fashion of paying more attention to the breeding of hounds for the hunting of the fox, and in 1750 he began the formation of that pack which, hunting the country we now know as the Quorn, has transmitted its excellencies chiefly through the Belvoir kennels to the foxhounds of England. That pack was partly formed from hounds descended from the old Wardour Castle hounds, said to be the earliest ever kept for hunting the fox only, though of this the evidence is necessarily scanty, but it is clear the Arundel hounds were in existence as a pack in the last decade of the seventeenth century.

Whether, however, they were the only ones seems doubtful, for by the year 1750 there were several established packs, and . . . at the time the Wardour pack was hunting there were other packs in existence of which history tells us nothing.[36]

Dale is not alone in refusing to allow that Meynell single-handedly transformed foxhunting into its modern form; and he only grudgingly accepts Buchanan-Jardine's claim that Meynell's one real contribution lay in making systematic and repeated inbreeding the acceptable norm. But Dale does put a significant cast on Meynell's place in the context not just of foxhunting, but of the changing view that sporting and agricultural men alike took toward animals and the landscape, thus: "Mr. Meynell has the credit of being the first to start a quicker, more decisive method of hunting; but in fact several people had this idea at the same time. Indeed, the necessity of killing foxes must have suggested to any observant man who hunted hounds that unless he took some advantages, he could hope to bring but few foxes to hand."[37]

Dale's effort to divest Meynell of the mantle of sole innovator of the modern Foxhound holds more meaning than that of merely shifting credit to Arundel, Rutland, Beaufort, or others, for, like Derry's comment on Bakewell in regard to livestock breeding, the effort underscores the importance of considering the dichotomous structure of the landscape economy: *the* singular subject intervenes in *the* singular landscape by correcting *the* (nebulous) lack in order to move everything toward an (equally nebulous) ideal. In this structure, no particular man stands out any more than a particular hound, so long as they all share the aim of improving toward the ideal. It is in this economy that foxhunting rose to eminence in the countryside, and that a very particular sort of hound became necessary to the evolving sport whose popularity made it among the most distinctive activities in the English landscape. Just as Bakewell and others saw a need to improve sheep and cattle, so many sportsmen saw the need to develop an entirely new hound in order to provide the "advantages" Dale refers to. A singular innovator creating a new breed would allow the new hound to appear as a simple quirk or fancy, rather than a prominent episode in the overwhelming intervention of improving the natural landscape, filling in its gaps to make it more representative of primordial nature. These men collectively represent the aesthetic judgment that belongs to the class capable of creating laws that respond to social needs, in the same way that they create a hound that responds to sporting needs. And it was for understanding that such improvements were to be got most surely through a system, a science, that Meynell has been given most credit, whether or not he personally devised the strategies of inbreeding and line-breeding (almost certainly not) or simply put them to use in a disciplined and sustained program that coincided with the developing fashions in hunting and with the changes in the landscape (without doubt).

Meynell's huntsman, John Hawkes, explains that the ideal qualities Meynell sought were "fine noses, and stout runners," and that, as part of his system, "in the spring of the year, he broke in his Hounds at Hare, to find out their propensies, which, when at all flagrant, they early discovered; and he drafted them according to their defects. . . . Mr. Meynell's Hounds were criticised by himself and his friends in the most minute manner."[38] This description of the "scientific system" could apply to any breeder, emphasizing a gentleman's capacity for judging and his dispassionate assessment of type fitted to necessity (to "draft" a dog means to kill it). Such an account assumes that the gentleman (and Meynell's name henceforth might refer to the breed of sportsmen who applied the scientific strategies of improvement to dogs) had a clear idea of what he wanted and what the sport needed for the direction it was taking, and that he worked toward a specific kind of Foxhound. In determining whether or not

John Hoppner, *Hugo Meynell*. Private Collection, Leeds Museums and Art Galleries (Temple Newsam House), UK/Bridgeman Images.

to draft a prospective pack member, Meynell evaluated the hound along the measure of his conceptual ideal, the *telos* of "Foxhound," understood immediately as the canine element vital to the success of the modern hunt with hounds. Judging his hounds minutely, Meynell shows himself capable of the kind of aesthetic valuation that—to twist Barrell's words a bit—worked for the good of the landscape. Thus Taplin can say in 1804 that the Foxhound "seems after a long succession of experiments . . . to have attained the criterion of perfection."[39] By regulating generations through strategic inbreeding and line-breeding, men like Meynell and Lord Yarborough created an actual recognizable breed that would reliably and consistently pass on its qualities to future generations. This is the point made by Roger Longrigg when he says, "By 1800 if a man wanted foxhounds he bred from foxhounds."[40]

Thus, with its teleological nature, the Foxhound acquired a clear value as the one possible dog wholly necessary to foxhunting. Descriptions of the Foxhound in its development, and, once developed, in its performative engagement with the landscape situate this dog as a coagent in the human aesthetic enjoyment of the landscape. This will become an increasingly central theme in accounts of human-canine relations. Foxhounds and foxhunting serve the mimetic function of the landscape actively reflecting human understanding of the natural organization; this necessity makes the artificial hound into a sign of the privileged subject's capacity for judgment. As Derrida says, "the concept of art is also constructed. . . . to raise man up," and the "ruse and naiveté" of this self-promoting gesture by man "lie in the necessity . . . of grounding it in the absolute naturalism."[41] And, of course, this coagency retains the primordial instinct of the originary dog willingly seeking to engage with humans. Such instinct, such willingness on the part of dogs affirms the justice of the landscape, and conceals the managed and regulated aspects of the representation. The logic of such concealment works alongside the conditional similitude: Foxhounds perform co-constitutively, as coagents, with humans to bring the landscape into a harmonizing whole, but only under concealment of the fact that humans shaped the hounds to serve that single function. The insistence on the naturalism of the technologized landscape becomes evident in the numerous writings praising foxhunting as an aesthetic engagement.

In one of the best-known eighteenth-century works on hunting, Peter Beckford—epitomizing the privileged perspective—emphasizes repeatedly that Foxhounds serve a distinct aim, as he states toward the end of his treatise, comparing the Foxhound to the harrier: "When a foxhound is mentioned I should expect only a particular kind of hound as to make, size, and strength, by which the foxhound is easy to be distinguished; but I should also expect by foxhunting a lively, animated, and eager pursuit as the very essence of it."[42] The Foxhound serves the particular sport of foxhunting and nothing else—no other agricultural service, no other sport, and no other possible mode of activity or being. *The* Foxhound as a delineated concept remains singular, distinct, and unique in its necessary teleological service to the landscape. And in this way, even beyond its recorded pedigree, the Foxhound became a breed—the first of many created along these same lines.

As teleological ideal, the Foxhound is never recognized as a singular being, but always in a collective group—the pack, or as the even more broadly framed performative function of the hunting cycle consisting of fox, hounds, horses, and humans in their coordinated roles. In the eighteenth century, as now, there were certainly hounds known singularly, such as the famed Blue Cap, who in 1763 outran the hound presented by Meynell (and spurred the breeder to focus on developing more speed in his pack),[43] and Lord Yarborough's Brocklesby Ringwood, painted by George Stubbs in 1791; but such examples have been individualized only as ideals, as representing the standard for the Foxhound generally. Thus Robert Fountain and Alfred Gates, in their commentary on the Stubbs portrait, say of Ringwood, "This hound had at least forty lines back to Charlton Ringwood 1771 and would look at home in the Peterborough Hound Show of today."[44] Their recognition of Ringwood as Foxhound par excellence—typical of the responses to this painting—demonstrates the way a Foxhound is situated genealogically, in the forty separate breedings of related dogs that connect Brocklesby Ringwood to his ancestor Charlton Ringwood, and as the physical archetype of subsequent hounds.[45] The emphasis away from the singular individual is identified as one of the three breeding principles of Meynell's scientific program, and it is just this emphasis—along with the success of Meynellian science in producing successive generations of consistently improved hounds—that drove the identification of commonly desired (or "necessary") qualities among diverse individuals, to segregate the individuals according to determined commonalities conceptualized teleologically, and then to preserve the collective breed over individuals. If the proper name of breed dogs is the "instinct" to serve humans, as enunciated by Buffon, the second degree Derrida refers to in the moral and social concealment of the writing of the landscape can be recognized in this identification of hounds as a pack; for it is the group, bred to perform as a pack, that facilitates the moral

George Stubbs, *Brocklesby Ringwood*, 1792. Private Collection/Bridgeman Images.

and aesthetic engagement with the landscape, written to appear as though it were nature that needed foxhunting with just such hounds.

Accounts of Foxhounds and foxhunting providing a vital service to the countryside abound, cast as pest control or as holding together the social or economic fabric of the community. Hunt historian Raymond Carr states that among eighteenth-century aristocrats, "to hunt a country became a duty to one's fellow countrymen," since it not only served as a supposed training for military actions, but "helped to keep 'the peace of the country.'"[46] Such accounts that make the community fundamentally dependent on foxhunting not only conceal the technological framing of the countryside into a landscape serving human interests, but also reinforce the status of the Foxhound as the necessary means to a strategically nebulous end, generally preserved as the urgent claim of "absolute naturalism." Just as the early histories make Foxhounds a necessity for the creation and development of foxhunting, so now Foxhounds are necessary, in these accounts, to maintain the sport that keeps the fox population in check and upholds the local community that depends on the hunt. Indeed, the Burns report that led to the ban on foxhunting in 2000 was compelled to orient its study in the direction of a cost-benefit analysis by detailing the economic centrality of foxhunting in the countryside; the opening sentence of the report announces that the committee was appointed "to inquire into the practical aspects of different types of hunting with dogs and its impact on the rural economy, agriculture and pest control, the social and cultural life of the countryside, the management and conservation of wildlife, and animal welfare in particular areas of England and Wales."[47] Such accounts rehearse the established view of "nature" landscaped into a totalized ecosystem in which wild and domestic animals, human agricultural practices, the capitalist economy, and sport are all integrated for the benefit of the totality. What these accounts conceal is the technologized (written) quality of the totalized economic landscape, and that it could ever be written differently. The Foxhound was created to fill a need in the landscape of modernity, and that need is now recognizable in the intertwining by the Burns report of the economy, cultural life, and "wildlife" as elements that need equal protection. My claim is that a requirement such as that orienting the Burns report is merely an extension of the technological governance of the landscape reflected in the creation of the Foxhound and restrictions against unnecessary dogs. Even the twenty-first-century making of a law to ban the killing of foxes for sport functions as an interventionist regulation of the framed representation of a mythically harmonious and dynamic nature. "Man," the privileged subject, congratulates himself for recognizing and fulfilling the need of a landscape that has been written in such a way to appeal over and over for his protection.[48]

The narratives of foxhunting consistently begin with the view of the countryside as a field of potentialities in which hunting—and consequently the Foxhound—performs the vital role, to unify all particulars into a harmonious whole. For the hunting community, the countryside is shaped by hunting, and the relations between inhabitants—human and nonhuman—are determined by the hunt to reflect a panoramic view in which every element performs its conceptualized function. This view allows for meaningful relations to develop between all the categorical members of the hunt, human and animal (domestic and wild), generating, according to anthropologist Garry Marvin, "a deep connectivity . . . with the natural world."[49] Such "connectivity" is performed through predetermined relations among taxonomized categories to give the hunt its ritualistic appearance of repeatability while preserving the aesthetic function of bringing the judging subject into commerce with the creative agency of the landscape. In admiring the hounds at work—their cooperation as individuals, or coagents, with the rest of the pack, and with their human handlers—hunt supporters who cast the hunt as an aesthetic event of "connectivity" perceive the hounds as animals, and as *other*; but this animal otherness has already been enframed within the organization of the landscape into a resource for a guaranteed aesthetic event, in particular the reading of the landscape as prosopopoeia. The otherness with which humans might feel a "connectivity" has been exempted from any surprising singularity, and safely generates the mimetic recognition in which the aesthetic subject can comprehend the beauty of the landscape so long as it reflects his capacity for reading within the grammar shaped by law, by agriculture, by taxonomy, and by myth. The theme of such reading is always continuity—of the integrated landscape, of the performative coagents, and of the prelapsarian pastoral forever promised as the perfect union to come. The infinitely repeatable foxhunt provides the performative trace of the mystical union between privileged subject and divine author.

The discourse of connectivity preserves and repeats the discourse of aesthetic performativity from the eighteenth century. Just as men like Meynell "discovered" the need for the Foxhound, so modern hunt supporters proclaim the need to preserve foxhunting as the performatively aesthetic discovery of "connectivity"; these performances preserve the genre, established by eighteenth-century huntsmen, of hunt narratives that describe the visual beauty of hunting with Foxhounds. So, Beckford already situates his dramatic narrative of the proper working of a pack in just such aesthetic terms of connectivity:

> How musical their tongues! And as they get nearer to him, how the chorus fills! Hark, he is found! now, where are all your sorrows, and your cares, ye gloomy souls! or where your pains and aches, ye complaining ones! one halloo has dispelled them all. What a crash they make! and echo seemingly takes pleasure to repeat the sound. The astonished traveller forsakes his road, lured by its melody: the listening ploughman now stops his plough; and every distant shepherd neglects his flock, and runs to see him break—what joy, what eagerness in every face![50]

The music of the hounds instills the entire scene with joy, making everyone eager to participate, just as the originary Shepherd's Dog had sought to join up with humans. The one about to "break" here is the fox, so that what the observers rush to see is the drama between hounds and fox, the final run that should end in the death of the fox. The list of people getting in on the eventful scene consists mostly of non-gentry, people whom a mounted rider would see as figures tastefully placed in the landscape. Their eagerness, their joy incorporates other classes into the hunt, so that the choral unity of the working pack becomes the emblem of the countryside united by the hunt into a collective joyful "connectivity." Indeed, just as the people are united, the living nature "takes pleasure" in participating with its echo.[51]

The "connective" tableau of Beckford's account adheres to the aesthetic judgment that Barrell identifies as a characteristic trait of such privileged men; for the pleasure understood to belong to landscape painting derives, Barrell says, "from the contrast between the perception of those who are merely in the landscape, and those who are outside it, and observe it."[52] The privileged huntsman observes and approves of the connectivity aroused among the "astonished traveller," "the listening ploughman," "and every distant shepherd," and he understands that all the human figures and the hounds—and the doomed fox—come together through his aesthetic appreciation of the scene. The aesthetic pleasure of a privileged landowner like Beckford establishes a mandate that the Foxhound perform in a prescribed fashion to ensure the endless perpetuation of such joyful connectivity.

This detached aesthetic of privilege might be said to achieve its apogee when William Taplin recounts, at the end of his article on the Foxhound, the events recorded in Sawry Gilpin's painting *Death of the Fox* (1793), done at the request of Colonel Thomas Thornton, avid sportsman, travel writer, and patron of sporting art in the late eighteenth and early nineteenth centuries. The painting commemorates a twenty-three-mile run, and is described by Taplin as evidence of the perfect state achieved by the Foxhound. "The composition" of the painting, he says,

> is admitted by connoisseurs to be masterly, and the *tout en semble* sublime. So great was the attention paid to minutiæ, in the delineation of nature, that some of the dogs were actually killed and pinioned down in the very position in which they appear, in order that the artist might perfect his work; as it was impossible to place dogs alive in those difficult positions, for a length of time sufficient for the purpose.[53]

Taplin, whose admiration of Colonel Thornton is plain, performs a critique of the painting that follows the correct reading of a hunt performed in the painterly landscape. The particular details fit into the whole, and the hounds themselves were made to fit into the composition by being made into *nature morte* models—abstracted from life. For Taplin the painting is "masterly" because it is virtually interchangeable with the landscape—that "delineation of nature." For the landscape, as I have argued, has been shaped into as painterly a form as possible. Kant's relation of art and nature holds particular relevance here: even though art must be distinguishable from nature, "the purposiveness of its form must appear just as free from the constraint of arbitrary rules as if it were a product of mere nature. . . . Nature proved beautiful when it wore the appearance of art; and art can only be termed beautiful, where we are conscious of its being art, while yet it has the appearance of nature."[54] Gilpin's painting, in Taplin's judgment, has the appearance of an actual hunt performed in the actual landscape. And the landscape itself, with the legal and legible actions that keep it vibrant and performatively connective, has the appearance of a painting. Kant's conditional similitude, which plays a key role in Derrida's account of the mimetic economy that shapes the world into a recognizable representation of the judging subject in contact with the divine author, gets to the heart of the aesthetico-economic organization of modern human-canine relations. Dogs become legal and legible as breeds that perform the actions predetermined by a landscape improved into a tableau ready to please the qualified judge. Thus Kant collapses the beauty of art and of nature together in order to establish "the universal statement: *that is beautiful which pleases in the mere judging of it.*"[55] The joy expressed by Beckford, the "connectivity" described by Marvin, and the admiration Taplin has for Gilpin's painting all perform identical judgments of beauty. This is the beauty of being *able* to judge. The qualification for judgment can be acquired through the several mechanisms enumerated in this and the previous chapters—laws, historical categorizations, aesthetic education, etc.—that enable one to read an artificial, regulated, grammatized landscape *as though* the events taking place were freely spontaneous and original, and unrepeatable, no matter how often they are repeated. It is this conditional similitude that frames the landscape into a legible totality; every account of the landscaped nature works as an ekphrastic description of a painting that "has the appearance of nature."

Some of the hounds in the painting Taplin admires were killed "in order that the artist might perfect his work." These hounds, killed and posed to look *as though* they were alive, become the purest aesthetic representative of the Foxhound as a being in service to the

Sawry Gilpin, *Death of the Fox*, 1793. Courtesy of the Yale Center for British Art.

ekphrastic landscape: they have the least individuality, and can be "killed and pinioned down" into the perfect breed pose. They have been abstracted utterly into *nature morte*, a term more honest than the English, "still life." These hounds' breeding, their lives and deaths, and commemoration were all regulated as part of the sportsman's landscape through the technological oversight that serves the aesthetic pleasure of privileged men. The represented, and representational, dead hounds, who have never been individuals in life or death, perhaps can now, as we look back at the aesthetics, landscape, and animal relations that form our heritage, stand out in their lack of individuality as images of the transformation Derrida says has been taking place since the eighteenth century. This transformation involves not only industrialization—the large-scale production of animals for service as meat, or we might add for sport—but also the fact that "men do all they can in order to dissimulate this cruelty or to hide it from themselves."[56] This statement comes from Derrida's seminal animal essay, but echoes the statements from the two aesthetic essays I have been trying to keep in mind throughout this chapter. Thus, Kant's analogy linking art and nature, as though each were the other, reveals the *necessity* of grounding art in "absolute naturalism"; and "what has produced and manipulated the frame puts everything to work in order to efface the frame effect, most often by naturalizing it."[57] The cruelty lurking behind Gilpin's painting is not confined to Colonel Thornton's willingness to kill his hounds for a painting, but extends throughout the breeding programs that produce animals capable of doing only one thing, but doing it as though they were willing coagents. The commemoration of the great twenty-three-mile run, along with the mastery of the painting (and the appreciation for Gilpin's skill) conceal the fact that these hounds could have done nothing other than what they did, that the great accomplishment occurred well before the event this painting immortalizes, namely, the creation of a hound and a landscape that inevitably provide aesthetic sporting pleasure for qualified men like Colonel Thornton. The painting thus becomes for Taplin the depiction of nature at its most naturalized—that is, when it can be kept pure for a guaranteed performance, *as though* it were art that looked natural. The aesthetic naturalization guarantees a bonding with the otherness of nature by purifying the landscape of any disruptive possibility of alterity.[58]

The *nature morte* hounds might therefore stand out for us in the twenty-first century as the third level of violence Derrida detects in the belief that arche-writing represents some originary anteriority. He says that this violence "consists of revealing by effraction the so-called proper name," and at the same time "denudes" the "substitute of the deferred proper, *perceived* by the *social* and *moral consciousness* as the proper."[59] The originary canine instinct to befriend humans by serving them is here, in the painting and in Taplin's reading, revealed by the "effraction" of compelling the hounds to serve by dying, just as the socially and morally accepted name of aesthetic connectivity is "denuded" as the simple killing of hounds to commemorate the killing of a fox for sport. The written landscape may be—must be—celebrated in joy for its connectivity, but only at the expense of forgetting the exploitation and violence on which such joy depends.[60]

Donna Landry has shown how, from the seventeenth century onward, hunting discourse mythologized the huntsman's activities into a religio-aesthetic engagement with the landscape in ways that shaped pastoral writing generally. Such an elevated engagement depends, she argues, on an "identification with dogs rather than with birds, hares, or foxes," and raises "the relation between human and animal to an art-form."[61] As art, the working of the hounds demonstrated in Beckford's dramatic account and Gilpin's painting conceals the technological domination of the landscape in which, as Landry puts it, "Individuals may be killed, but hunted species are managed . . . so as to sustain them as a resource for future hunting."[62] The foundation to this standard aestheticization of hunting remains the technological view that humans can, and should, "manage" the landscape as a field of "resources" in which individuals exist only in service to the managed ideal abstractions, such as pack or species. Wild animals, such as foxes, thus earn a use-value, "sometimes merely by being allowed to feed and reproduce themselves unmolested"—and mostly by being killed. The domestic Foxhound is "allowed to feed and reproduce" itself only so long as it conforms to the abstract ideal. *Allowing* them to live turns both these animals into the objects of human choice, into the personal property of the privileged subject, or, in Landry's terms, resources, raw materials, to be developed now (into quarry) or saved for later, to be judged for conformation or "drafted," or even to be "actually killed" to serve as a model of a living Foxhound.

More to the point, within the discourse that conceals the technological management behind terms of connectivity, the hounds cease to be the product of human intention and become the free, "natural" agency of humans' aesthetic engagement with the landscape: "Cruelty to foxes is the anti-hunting battle cry," says Landry, "but the satisfaction of hounds' natural, though encouraged and disciplined, desire to hunt is rarely addressed."[63] In order to address that satisfaction as "natural," especially with the rigor that Landry brings to her historical account, it is necessary to dissimulate or hide the technological management of the hounds behind the aesthetic rediscovery of the rhythms of nature. Participation in the life of the representative landscape is given its emblem in the pack whose members must work together. Hunt narratives and paintings admiring the hounds' coordinated work as a cohesive pack present the hunt as an aesthetic event bonding humans and nature; the hounds' coordination performs the discovery that hounds find joy in chasing down their quarry. The ritualistic revelation of canine joy assures the aesthetically attuned humans that their sport fills a need in the landscape, *as though* they were riding through a pastoral, pre-technological, unmanaged scene of nature. The conditional similitude functions as the limiting, framing *parergon* that Derrida suggests appears in the act of distinguishing between the intrinsic and the extrinsic: "One must know . . . how to determine the intrinsic—what is framed—and know what one is excluding as frame *and* outside the frame."[64] Internally, the *parergon* functioned as the need for the Foxhound; then, with the instinctual arrival of that hound to fill the lack, the *parergon* framed the aesthetic affirmation that the landscape appears *as though* it were a primordial pastoral in which all beings happily and willingly participate in the hunt. The frame excludes acknowledgment of the violence—Landry's "anti-hunting battle cry," the manipulation of the hound to guarantee their "satisfaction"—along with the wholly managed aspect of hunting to guarantee, over and over, the discovery of bondedness among humans, animals, and the land. The conditionality limits what can be included, and the similitude generates categorical analogies, such as that between breed and race, that naturalize the predetermined signification of otherness.

Admiration for the Foxhound's abilities within this restricted activity depends entirely on the hounds keeping to type, performing the single function they were bred to fulfill. The use of the term "cur" to refer to any dog appearing in the hunt field that is not a Foxhound makes plain just how vital participation is. Participation—the putative resolution of difference into a coagency that enables the humans to admire their animal others rather than despising them as curs or denouncing them as Charlie fox[65]—draws a sharp line between the admirable animal and the one that distracts from purposeful activity (and the purpose is similarly recognizable only within the shared activity). In foxhunting jargon, as the Duke of Beaufort colorfully points out, a cur is "any dog other than a hound. Even the champion at Crufts would be so-called if it made an appearance in the hunting field."[66] In this restrictive discourse, all non-hound canines (with the exception of terriers, so long as they are brought in at the proper moment) exist outside the hunt, and are the dogs that would, in a serious way, constitute an Other, in that they are stripped of value or even recognizability. The cur as excluded Other in fact serves as the *pharmakon* that facilitates the reification of all breeds, or simply "breed," as the means of recognizing and understanding dogs. The unknowability of the uncategorizable cur, which I showed in the previous chapter figuring as the excess enabling the taxonomic categories to take shape, continues to manifest itself as the threat that must be eradicated from the discursive and performative landscape emblematized in foxhunting. In contrast, the Foxhound epitomizes the grammatically legible dog, the one with whom a human can sublate otherness into a performative synthesis.

The performative filling of the lack—in creating the hound that fills a need, in writing histories that naturalize the hound, in painting and describing the hunt itself as a natural event—creates and re-creates a landscape standing apart from the judging subject, which then invites the subject to reunite with it in an act of mimetic recognition. That this recognition should so consistently lead to the same expression of joy indicates that the judging subject is as much a categorical construct as the breeds and species and formed landscape. Individual hunt-lovers matter no more than the individual hounds who constitute the packs, and no more than the individual foxes whose repeated death is sustained through highly touted conservation efforts, then absurdly justified as pest control. The performance of aesthetic joy in connectivity sustains itself through repetition, and in being repeated becomes ever more natural, and even necessary. What this performative structure conceals in its naturalness and necessity is a question implied throughout animal studies and post-humanism, and it is a question that leads temptingly into speculations about animal worldliness and animal subjectivity. But at the very least, it is possible to say with some certainty that this naturalized structure excludes other possibilities, ones that might indeed bypass the dichotomies of human and animal, subject and object, legal and illegal, legible and illegible, framed and unframed—all the oppositions that come into play in the naturalized institution of breed and race.

Signifying Dogs

Popularized Breeds in the
Romances of Walter Scott

EARLY IN WALTER SCOTT'S MEDIEVAL ROMANCE *IVANHOE* (1820), THE SWINEHERD, Gurth, curses "the ranger of the forest, that cuts the foreclaws off our dogs and makes them unfit for their trade."[1] Gurth's dog, Fangs, who is large enough to kill deer, is legal under the Norman Forest Laws only because he has been "lawed." Scott appends a historical note on the process of "lawing" dogs, which entails cutting off three toes from their front feet (or only from the right front foot, as Scott has it); and he exclaims of the Forest Laws, "These oppressive enactments were the produce of the Norman Conquest, for the Saxon laws of the chase were mild and humane; while those of William, enthusiastically attached to the exercise and its rights, were to the last degree tyrannical."[2] Similarly, in Scott's first novel, *Waverley* (1814), the eponymous hero rides through "the straggling village, or rather hamlet, of Tully-Veolan," and encounters "the incessant yelping of a score of idle useless curs, which followed, snarling, barking, howling, and snapping at the horse's heels." A note says this "nuisance" was common at the time the novel was set (1745) and still exists, "but this is remote from our present purpose, and is only thrown out for consideration of the collectors under Mr Dent's dog-bill."[3] These two references show that Scott—a lawyer, as well as novelist and folklorist—was familiar with the long-term problematic legal status of dogs in Britain, and they suggest that he considered the restrictions either oppressive or ineffective. As both a dog lover and popularizer of regional and national history, Scott also understood that dogs could convey regional, class, and historical characters through a claimed originary connectivity to a place. Two dogs who appear as fully fledged characters in a pair of his late novels, *The Talisman* (1824) and *Woodstock* (1825), show that Scott also understood the discursive elements that made dogs legible—as ethical metonymies of a certain legal class of human. His letters and journals show that his affection for dogs entailed a desire to give them regional and historically based identities analogously affirming the corresponding identities among humans. These analogies work in the same direction as those of Buffon, to verify the naturalness and truth of human ethnic and racial categories. And they work within the aesthetic frame created by the necessary Foxhound, so that human-canine relationships appear as aesthetic events of bondedness occurring through the grammatical legibility of a dog. A dog becomes legible and is entered into a kinship relation with humans through a shared quality—a connectivity, or coagency—that transcends the categories of species and race, and in so doing affirms those same categories *as though* they were divisions of nature. Such affirmation reinforces the justice and aesthetic unity of the landscape in which legibility confers place, function, legality.

During the early decades of the nineteenth century when Scott lived and wrote, modern dog breeds were only just beginning to be created along the pattern established by the Foxhound. Scott's construction of canine characters in his novels contributed to the modern reading of a canine ethos—and in one instance contributed directly to the creation of a modern breed. By presenting dogs that could be read as recognizable characters, Scott's novels extended the modern discourse of human-canine relations, dependent on mutual recognition gained through codified legibility. Such recognition mostly depended not simply on imputing an inner life to dogs analogous to that of humans, but on pinpointing a particular—and necessarily nebulous—element bonding dogs and humans into a kinship based on their regional origins. This double bond of interiority and regional indigeneity created a lasting value for commodified dogs capable of being identified with breeds, as they then embodied the supposed authenticity, or essence, or power of a region or ethnicity. This value was also reflected in the function of the bond in overcoming the abyssal difference between species, so that the same gestures that establish and enforce difference then turn into accounts of connectivity; just as foxhunting works as a ritualistic reenactment of aesthetic unification, Scott's narratives lay down the conventions allowing for recognition of sameness within difference. The associations between authenticity, purity, and regional identity also reenacted the discovery of the need for the Foxhound, and thus reinforced breed as a necessity in the preservation of the landscape *as if* it were nature.

In parallel scenes from each of Scott's two late dog novels, the canine character faces one of the human characters in a direct exchange. In the first case, the exchange is legible and determinate, as the human and canine characters recognize one another fully on the basis of shared regional and class identities; the second case complicates the exchange, and even the possibility of the exchange, as it fails in the reading that should affirm a shared origin. Further, the characterization of the dog in the first novel is intertwined with animal epithets distinguishing the humans into racial categories that make the dog's characterization all the more pointed in its depiction of a good, i.e., legal and legible, dog. The collapse of the exchange in the second case is so complete that it seems almost to end any possibility of relatedness between humans and dogs based on aesthetic claims of legibility, aesthetic or originary; in this collapse, the invisible framing function of the *parergon* becomes evident enough to suggest a possibility for reassessing our relations with dogs. I shall myself frame the novelistic dogs with the mythologizing Scott performs on the dogs in his household, whom he says the fictional dogs represent; his mythopoiesis helped to reify a modern breed based on the confusion of an early novel with historical reference. This mythologizing arises from the need—evident in many of Scott's activities—to create a representation of Scotland as a primordial, pre-Norman culture available for modern consumption.

The way Scott wrote of dogs—real and fictional—disseminated the discourse enabling good dogs and humans capable of judgment to form relations grounded in regional, class, and family histories that made them complementary members of the same category. Where Pope's dogs make no descriptively direct appearance, Scott's dogs appear in a richly descriptive landscape actively engaged in "natural" relations with humans. While Pope's friendships with dogs seem almost unrecognizable today as friendships because of their dependence on archaic aesthetics, Scott's canine relations fit easily into the modern mode of connectivity between individuals seen through the categorical identities of ethnicity, race, or breed—all of which would be determined by regional origin. In shaping the genre of the novel out of romantic histories, Scott effectively creates the myth of a cultural primordiality from which the modern world of Britain originated, and which makes dog breeds—as replications of the necessary Foxhound—vital components in a heritage to be preserved. Putting dogs as characters in this vividly described primordial setting enables the modern relations depicted between them and humans to appear to be the natural mode of such interactions that have always occurred just as in the modern world: the human-canine relations in the vividly descriptive novels appear *as if* they were universal, natural relations, recognizable across the ages and cultures. The descriptive quality of these narratives thus enforces the visual engagement of facial recognition and reproducible representation, both of which support the modern dependence on breed identity that enables an individual dog to be read as representative of a type.

Scott framed the narrative in each of his novels by situating them explicitly among historical events and figures, or within a romantically primordial landscape. This figural, quasi-historical, nostalgic setting is what Judith Wilt describes as an "abandoned but still 'live' mine" from which a "historico-mythic treasure can be dug out of a materially empty hiding place."[4] The sense is that the meaning lost through modernization will appear in the romantic narrative that expands from the historical backdrop. The allure of the "treasure" of meaning is one reason for Scott's popularity throughout the nineteenth century, as the depictions of the Scottish border country made Scotland into a destination for tourists seeking the revivifying contact with their indigenous heritage. Through references to this broad, extra-narrative setting, what Ina Ferris calls the "enabling assumption," Scott delineates a setting in which characters can be vividly described and plots followed as bodies moving through a visualized frame.[5] His novels, a century apart from Pope's *concordia discors*, embrace the ekphrastic strategy, developed through the rhetoric of hypotyposis, in order to make characters recognizable as modern Europeans, even though they might be situated in a distant time or place. The vision relied upon for these descriptions is, of course, that defined as an aesthetic principle of judgment by Kant, and exemplified in Peter Beckford's accounts of the hunt, and, in the most literally ekphrastic case, by William Taplin's description of Sawry Gilpin's painting, all of which I considered in the previous chapter. These descriptions, made possible by the extra-narrative frame, transformed, in Cynthia Sundberg Wall's assessment, "emblem and detail into symbol and description in the eighteenth century."[6] Similarly, the detailed descriptions of the characters generate a recognizability through singularity: these characters appear distinct from one another, and yet not alien in that they adhere to a convention of types already established through the tradition of romance. In a word, Scott gives his characters faces through which they respond to one another, and through which readers can respond to them as active agents in a visually vibrant landscape, as though it were our own. The vibrancy makes the artificial, romantic setting appear as though it were present, as though it were nature, and the characters within appear as though adhering to the modern law of legibility.

The dogs, especially Roswal and Bevis, become characters in this very same fashion. With faces, the canine characters interact with their human counterparts in mutual responsiveness and understanding derived from similitude of origin. The canine characters adhere to romantic types as well, identifiable through regional and genealogical origins that correspond with their human friends, or allies, or kin. The bondedness of coagency that modern humans have developed with their dogs depends on the constructions of similitude found throughout Scott's texts. What makes these particular representations of the modern human-canine bond notable is that they show the recognizable and shared similitude under construction. The faces given to the dogs make them canine complements to the human characters, acting as though they are mute representations of the universal category of humanity; the similitude between human and dog remains evident on the condition that the dog submit to the grammar of legibility, concealing any alterity.

Two important qualities of Scott's depictions of dogs make them stand out sufficiently to warrant the attention of a full chapter. First of all, Scott enjoyed enormous popularity, so that his novels played a prominent role in disseminating narrative strategies in describing character and setting. Second, the fusion of romance, regional legend, and realistic description naturalized the modern form of human-canine relations, so that other possibilities appear to lack intimacy, affection, communication. Combined, these two qualities put Scott's novelistic depictions of dogs—and the depictions of relations between dogs and humans—in a central role shaping the modern view of dogs, and particularly of the relations humans expect to have with dogs. In addition, the two novels to which I shall give primary attention complicate this modern view as no other literary works of this era do, opening a way—even in its early formulation—to question this modern mode.

Laura Brown is correct when she identifies the eighteenth-century image of the lady and the lapdog as "the inaugural event for the literary representation of pet-keeping"; in the new depiction of pet keeping, Brown goes on to say, "ideas of alterity are instantly transformed into experiences of intimacy."[7] The intimacy Brown refers to in this instance serves the misogynistic effect of making both dog and woman ambiguous; enforced is "a dynamic that places the animal simultaneously within and outside the realm of the human, or—from another perspective—places the woman both within and outside the realm of the animal."[8] Thus, defined through misogynistic discourse, the newly allowable relations between women and dogs denigrates both members of the relationship, while still allowing for the possibility of a positive relation. Intimacy within these bounds can only be imagined in sexual terms, for the masculine conception of intimacy with women was similarly confined to sex. In contrast, as Brown notes in passing, depictions of "relationships between men and dogs explore notions of canine loyalty and devotion."[9] Although I disagree with Brown (and with the accepted history of pet-keeping first advanced by Keith Thomas) that the eighteenth-century shift in human-canine relations consists of creating the first possibility of intimacy or friendship between humans and dogs, I would say that the shift reoriented that possibility from Pope's indirection to the modern recognition of shared sentiments and analogous interiorities that demands a legible face.[10] And such a face is dependent on the categorization of a dog as good, as having a known history, in effect being identifiable—readable—as a breed. The loyalty Brown reads in male-canine relations supports breed legibility through its etymological tie to law (Latin, *legalis*), so that the loyal dog is good in being legal, and as a legal dog is legible. I would also say that Brown's analysis typifies the modern need to enforce abyssal differences (animal-human, female-human, male-female) in order to overcome them, in this case through intimacy; in order for such an analysis to succeed, other possibilities must remain illegible.

Two of Scott's own dogs in particular, Maida and Nimrod, draw numerous descriptive references in the letters and, according to comments by Scott himself, served as the models for the large dogs in his novels. Scott refers to them variously, even when describing a single dog, as when he boasts of his favorite, Maida:

I have got a deer-hound or blood-hound, or wolf-hound that is the most magnificent creature ever seen for height and strength. All Edinburgh is agape at him. I got him from Glengarry. He is descended of the Blue Spanish wolf-dog and the real deer grey-hound, and might have followed Johnnie Armstrong for size and dignity.[11]

Not only does this description exploit the slippage among different types of hound still possible in the early nineteenth century, but its overlapping genealogical and folkloric references facilitate the rhetorical inclusiveness of the large dog's heritage spanning back to the Highland chieftains: the connection with the Scottish chieftain Glengarry makes Maida into a metonymy of Scottish heritage, and his descent from the spurious "Blue Spanish wolf-dog" ties him to an even older time bolstered by the reference to Scottish folk hero Johnnie Armstrong. Thus Scott's large dogs—of indeterminate breed—are given a shaped canine and ethnic ethos through the rhetorical references to old Highland clans and to "real," or legible, origins, however mythical they be.

Scott's references to the dogs in terms of archaic sporting types also carry strategic class and national associations. Though Scott certainly enjoyed coursing for both foxes and hares, the hunt for stags or wolves had long ceased by his time due to scarcity of either stags or wolves: "We have only one wolf which I know of kept in a friend's menagerie near me and no wild deer," he wrote to Maria Edgeworth in 1830.[12] Nonetheless, he insists that Maida "would make no bones of a wolf and pulls down a red-deer without fear or difficulty," while being "perfectly gentle affectionate and good natured and the darling of all the children," and "sits beside me at dinner—his head as high as the back of my chair."[13] Scott values the heritage of the dog as a hunter with all the class associations. Though it is extremely doubtful that Maida ever pulled down a deer, Scott imagines him as both deer-slayer and "darling" because he then appears as a kind of retainer: Scott himself becomes the image of clan chieftain enjoying the loyalty of a great warrior dog that attracts "the admiration of the populace of Edinburgh who crowd round him whenever he trots out along with me or with the carriage."[14] Thus Scott creates a romanticized ethos for himself—Laird of Abbotsford—buttressed by the hound whose

Edwin Landseer, *Walter Scott's Maida (A Scene at Abbotsford)*, 1827. Tate Images, Tate Britain, London.

size alone holds the historical resonance of class privilege. Caroline McCracken-Flesher argues that Scott helped define "a Scotland that could be posited against England and as past against present."[15] Scottish value, in this view, can only be nostalgic, and depends on the re-creation of the past through romances that, according to McCracken-Flesher, are not certain but rather strategic, as "shifting, shaping signs."[16] In his enterprise of defining a national identity, Scott also defined the range of canine identities that belonged to Scotland—i.e., that attained identity by Scott's nostalgic placement of them in the mythic past.

Just as the size of his hounds enables Scott to create associations with Scottish primordiality and class privilege, so with his small dogs he insists—along with the common theme of their being gifts from prominent Scottish personages—that they are among the last of their kind, rare specimens of a specifically Scottish dog. Rarity, with its connections to the primordial past soon to be altogether lost, becomes directly associated with purity of breed and class, as Scott indicates in a letter of 1827 to Mrs. Hughes, to whom he had promised a puppy from Spice—one of his favored terriers: "It is difficult to get the real breed & Spice who is the best I have seen has had no puppies this year. It is singular that the race is very difficult to perpetuate or preserve."[17] Purity of race and breed would seem to be marked singularly by its fragility, in that it cannot be preserved (and pure-blooded dogs are under greater threat than impure dogs, as evidenced by Scott's fear and frustration over "The Distemper which is particularly fatal to dogs of high blood"[18]), as well as by the difficulty in perpetuating it.[19] The "high blood" and rarity that keep Spice infertile and delicately susceptible to disease signify both that she is "the real breed," and that the breed itself carries its own threatened loss of ethnic and cultural authenticity, which would be the loss of the trace of primordiality on which the legibility of the landscape depends. Threat of loss functions just as potently as the lack necessitating a Foxhound: to preserve a breed (which Scott recognizes only in its loss) necessitates the mythologizing narratives, recognition of value, and projection of modern value to a mythically authentic past. Scott's gestures of perpetuating or preserving that authenticity in fact popularize modern dog breeds whose value lies in their generic re-creation of a romanticized past. Dogs like Maida and Spice (the two he refers to most throughout his letters and journal) create the direct, living connection to what Richard Maxwell describes as "a partly constructed and perhaps partly genuine tradition" of Scottish cultural character.[20]

Spice was one of the terriers given to Scott by local breeders who developed the breed of Dandie Dinmont terriers following the popularity of the novel published thirteen years earlier, *Guy Mannering* (1814). That novel contains, as a minor character, a Scottish farmer named Dandie who raises terriers to hunt foxes, all named either Mustard or Pepper. The dogs themselves get little descriptive attention, but because of the enormous popular attention sparked by farmer Dandie, vividly cast as representative of the romantic Scottish past, the terriers acquired considerable appeal as living artifacts of the landscape depicted in the fictional narrative. The breed of Dandie Dinmont terriers embody the "local color" Alyson Bardsley attributes to the fictional character that helped create the desire among tourists to visit "Scott country."[21] As trace of the authentic, originary background enabling the romantic story, Dandie and his dogs represent the lost ethnic authenticity to which Scott's claims of Spice's rarity and fragility refer. Thus the fictional character and his fictional dogs were read as references to a historical figure whose dogs would provide metonymic access to the lost pastoral of preindustrial Britain, and the need to preserve what remains of that pastoral—just as the Foxhound appeared as a need to be fulfilled. Farmer Dandie is one of those "romance figures" that Ian Duncan identifies as "occupying a separate mimetic space from that of the modern state." As such characters leave the urban world "to enter the natural world," Duncan says, they return to "archetypal being."[22] Dandie's authenticity, then, is signaled by his function as archetype of a premodern and indigenous regionality that, Duncan suggests, "can only be recognized through our own distance from it."[23] Distance foregrounds the loss itself, so that what is lost remains strategically nebulous, and at the same time necessitates the preservation of representatives of that very loss. The spuriousness of the modern representative of the loss is displaced by the physical fact of the representative—in this case, Spice, who changes from an individual little dog to authentic member of a rare breed. Her authenticity, as representative of the loss, the lack, provides the frame excluding any suspicion about her status, her purity, excluding any question about the violence of creating and maintaining any breed. She attains a living history, and one that would be corroborated by identifying the living model of the fictional Dandie.

Various contending claims over who the original model for Dandie might be were spawned by the huge popularity of the novel. The first edition of *Guy Mannering* sold out the day after publication, and two more editions sold out within three months.[24] Among the numerous claimants for the title of the original, James Anderson proved most able to exploit the popularity, solely because he had named all his terriers Mustard and Pepper—even though two years after the publication of *Guy Mannering*, Scott wrote that Anderson was "a man I never saw in my life before," and that "In truth, I knew nothing of the man, except his odd humours of having only two names for twenty dogs. But there are lines of general resemblance among all these hillmen, which there is no missing."[25] The modern editor of *Guy Mannering* lists four "real-life farming alternatives" to Anderson, affirming Scott's own view that Dandie was less an individual than a regional type, and as type could lay more claim to archetypal authenticity.[26] With so many contending claims to the title of the real Dandie, arguments over the origin of the Mustards and Peppers proliferated. Scott himself strategically fueled the controversy with characteristic claims that his own terriers were pure representatives of the spurious breed. Scott announced the arrival of Spice in a letter of August 1823 (nine years after the novel) to Lord Montagu: "Harden the Liddesdal[e] keeper has sent me a Dandie Dinmont terrier a real pepper which I take as a piece of great attention."[27] Six months later, Scott writes of Ginger, "a whelp of one of Dandie Dinmont's Mustard and Pepper terriers," and describes her as a "Liddesdale devil."[28] These letters connect the terriers that had popularly acquired the name of Dandie Dinmont by the early 1820s with Liddesdale, situating the dogs in the border landscape that had served as the regional model for the fictional Dandie's farm, Charlieshope. The breed thus attained a historical regionality that proleptically affirmed its ethnic authenticity. What would thenceforth be preserved and perpetuated is the breed, categorical signifier of nostalgia for a lost native Scottish pastoral. As Diana Donald states in her study of the changing perceptions of animals during the eighteenth and nineteenth centuries, "dogs took on an aura of history—a mythic history as opposed to the values of the modern world."[29] As representative of the indigenous archetype, the Dandie Dinmont terrier becomes an embodied history whose purity must be preserved, for "purity," with its threatened loss, reenacts the loss of that romantic past, which is romantic precisely because it has been lost—even if it never existed.

The other, fictional dogs that Scott described as characters participate in this same mythopoeic creation of authenticity that owes its "preservation" to vividly descriptive fictional narratives. To state this point baldly, the fictional dogs are promoted as representations of a romanticized past brought narratively and descriptively into the modern present in which

Sir William Allan, *Sir Walter Scott 1771–1832. Novelist and Poet*, 1844. Scottish National Gallery, Edinburgh.

Scott engages with his household dogs *as though* they were the originals of the fictional representations. Fictional dogs appear *as though* they were modern dogs transported into a romantic past, and the household dogs appear *as though* they were the descendants of romantically ancient dogs. This mimetic analogy turns the breed preserved by Scott into the sign of authenticity, enabling a dog lover to recognize a dog as the connection to a primordiality. The accounts of loyalty that Brown sees as the masculine counterpart to feminine expressions of affection limit the range of engagements between male and canine characters to those in which the dog represents lineal purity; loyalty bonds dogs to class and region as much as to a man. The problem of how to read a dog is resolved by subsuming individuality into breed. Illegible alterity is hidden behind the legibility of breed, which grants a dog the face that can be recognized and understood. Just as the original "proper" name of dogs was written into the modern taxonomic landscape by Buffon as the instinct to serve humans, so Scott's romances of canine regional indigeneity strategically conceal the technological enforcement of the landscape as though it were nature. Legibility consistently arises from the similitudes conditioned by a categorical framing around a loss or a need: a dog looks as though she intended to mean only what the human wants her to mean, just as her ancestors always did.

In *The Talisman*, the vividly detailed canine-human relationship is developed amidst a broad array of human-animal analogies, comparisons, and epithets. In addition, the novel is set in the Crusades, so that many of the analogies, comparisons, and epithets hold nationalist and racial referents. These linkages reach a complexity that makes the novel into a proving ground for the similitude between race and breed that I showed in chapter 1 to be instrumental in naturalizing eighteenth-century taxonomies. The confrontation in *The Talisman* between Europeans (clashing factions from Britain, the Holy Roman Empire, or Austria, and the Knights Templar) and Saracens (Arabs and Kurds, and one notable Ethiopian) becomes so intertwined with the animal-human comparisons that the mechanism of analogy itself becomes naturalized into visually descriptive identifications. The main character, a Scottish knight, identifies himself as "Kenneth of the Couching Leopard," and he has joined the Crusades to serve Richard Lionheart in his war against the Kurd, Saladin, who is referred to variably as "Lion of the Mountain" and "infidel dog."[30] Sir Kenneth has brought a single companion, Roswal, a large staghound commonly referred to in terms of his nobility.

The scene of the human and the canine characters facing off comes at a moment when the tension between the European factions threatens to break up the Christian coalition, culminating in an internecine intrigue to destroy Richard. The conniving Conrade, Marquis of Montserrat, has riled the drunken Austrian Archduke Leopold by maliciously claiming that the three lions passant of England, formerly said to be leopards but now "become lions at all points. . . . must take precedence of beast, fish, or fowl," which includes the Austrian eagle.[31] Conrade's immediate reference is the English banner that currently hangs at the center of the Christian camp, but obviously carries the broader intention of suggesting that the upstart English King Richard, "descendent of the Counts of Anjou," has wrongly asserted precedence over the Austrian archduke, descendent of emperors.[32] Leopold proclaims that he will not "yield ground one inch to the English bandog," and will "place the eagle of Austria where she shall float as high as ever floated the cognizance of king or Kaiser."[33] He then proceeds with his inebriated followers to pull down the English banner and to raise the Austrian standard. The hot-tempered Richard promptly responds by tearing down the Austrian flag, trampling on it, and reestablishing his own banner. Sir Kenneth is then called upon to stand guard over the English flag, to make sure no one defiles it or steals it in the night. When the expected happens and Kenneth is lured away by a false message purporting to be from his beloved Edith, he is riven between loyalty to Richard and loyalty to his lady, and tries to resolve his dilemma by leaving Roswal to guard the flag.

Kenneth says to Roswal, "Watch thou here, and let no one approach," and the response should be noted in full:

> The majestic dog looked in his master's face, as if to be sure that he understood his charge, then sat down beside the mantle, with ears erect and head raised, like a sentinel, understanding perfectly the purpose for which he was stationed there.[34]

This vivid description brings to bear many of the discursive forces of need that cement the loyalty and devotion of dogs as the basis for their relations with humans. Roswal is "majestic," and indeed he is described elsewhere in the novel as holding a pedigree as worthy as any of the humans, being "of the noblest Northern breed," as Sir Thomas De Vaux tells King Richard.[35] The "as if" qualifying the look Roswal directs at Kenneth, along with the simile, "like a sentinel," that turns the raised head and erect ears into indicators of perfect understanding, makes the "majestic dog" into a matrix of signifiers requiring proper reading. That Kenneth does understand his dog is indicated in the fact that it is he who has given the command leading to Roswal presenting himself as a legible sign of loyalty; the legibility itself constitutes loyalty. And, further, the pair hold the bond of their shared nobility and shared ties to non-Norman Scotland.

As a noble Northerner, and as a legal participant of the hunt (a detail the narrative spends some time on), Roswal acts precisely as he should, as he is expected to act by the noble humans who share class and regional identity with him. Like Kenneth, De Vaux is a Northerner (though English, and not Scottish), and therefore—in the logic of the narrative—capable of recognizing Roswal's own regional affiliation and authenticity, describing the hound as "a most perfect creature of Heaven . . . of the noblest Northern breed."[36] When Roswal looks "in his master's face, as if to be sure," he is performing the signification that is expected of him as a type, adhering to the categorical imperative governing natives of the North. In his actions, Roswal affirms his archetypal, regional character in the narrative, just as Kenneth affirms his when he acts as would be expected of a nobleman loyal to the Christian cause and to Richard, and as would be expected of a romantic hero with noble feelings for his lady love. In the regularity of his actions, Roswal attains a readable character that is fundamentally analogous to Kenneth's and those other humans, like De Vaux, who demonstrate the capacity to recognize the analogous relation between noble humans and noble hounds. Such recognition depends on the imputation of a humanlike interiority to Roswal, and—especially—of an interiority that can be recognized by other characters and readers through its signification of region and rank. Roswal's type—Northern and noble—holds meaning among all the epithets that identify the human characters as types. In this novel, *type* can be determined by rank—determined by pedigree—as well as regularity of action, or animal analogy. In this regard, the etymological sense of rank or epithet, "noble" becomes apparent in its derivation from the Latin *nobilis*, or "well-known." The quality of nobility is that of being known or knowable, of being present as the embodiment of a pedigree, of archetype, of heritage. Human pedigrees are naturalized in the same fashion as racial categories, through analogy with animals. Royalty are lions, eagles, falcons, and the racial enemies are unbaptized dogs. Roswal escapes the aspersion of being unbaptized by appearing *as if* he understands, as a noble—as knowable, since his pedigree makes him a peer of his human analogs.

The conditional "as if" sets Roswal into a mimetic relation with Kenneth in which the hound attains a face that reflects the man. The mimetic reflection between the two characters functions within the narrative of vividly described scenes and objects; the descriptions make the distant era and lands of the Crusades appear as if present. The narrator, who must be recognizable as being like us readers, projects his modern subjectivity onto the described objects, setting himself into a dialogue with them "as if" the elements structuring his own capacity for judgment served universally to structure all subjectivities. To complete the process of romanticizing hypotyposis, the characters within the narrative must recognize one another in the same way readers can recognize the distant time and place. Just as the fictional characters recognize one another as though they were lions facing eagles, hounds facing men, British mastiffs facing unbaptized dogs, so readers recognize the similitudes as though they were both modern and natural. In such ways, these novels rewrite the economimesis structuring the modern landscape as though it were a direct dialogue between the privileged aesthetic subject and the divine author of nature, as though the modern landscape were universal. Scott's romances, narrated as though they were factual histories, instruct readers in the effective recognition of breed dogs as metonymies of a romanticized pastoral preserved in the modern landscape.

In spite of Roswal's nobility and size, the evil Conrade manages to wound the hound and steal the banner. When word of the theft reaches Richard, he punishes Kenneth with banishment. Meanwhile, Roswal's wound is healed by El Hakim the "leech," who is actually Ildrahim "Lion of the Mountain" in disguise, who, in turn, is actually Saladin. As the Muslim physician prepares to treat Roswal, Kenneth says to him, "This patient, Hakim, is beyond thy help, . . . and, besides, he is, by thy law, an unclean animal."[37] The wise (and noble) Hakim transcends such parochial categorizations, and handles "Roswal's wound with as much care and attention as if he had been a human being," and in turn, "the animal all the while suffering him patiently to perform these kind offices, as if he had been aware of his kind intentions."[38] This exchange of conditional recognitions between physician and hound culminates in Hakim's pronouncement "The animal may be cured . . . if you will permit me to carry him to my tent, and treat him with the care which his nobleness deserves."[39] With this statement, Hakim-Saladin discloses that recognition of nobility crosses species and religious barriers when both parties share it. As Kenneth bids goodbye, he indulges in self-pity over having failed to defend the flag and hound: "I would . . . I could exchange conditions with that noble animal."[40] Kenneth and Roswal's shared Northern ethnicity makes them effectively kin, and—unlike the Norman Richard—indigenous to the British Isle. In addition, they are both noble, which has been recognized by the noble Saladin, who, in his disguise as Hakim, has penetrated Kenneth's disguise of a poor knight: Kenneth is actually David, Earl of Huntingdon and Prince Royal of Scotland.[41]

But Kenneth cannot reciprocate Saladin's perspicacity by recognizing a corresponding nobility in the Muslim. When Hakim tries offering him refuge in Saladin's army, Kenneth sneeringly rejects the kind gesture by saying he would rather face execution by the Christians, so that his "writhen features should blacken as they are like to do in this evening's setting sun."[42] In response, Hakim explains that numerous leaders of the quarreling Christian factions have proposed alliances with Saladin, and that Richard himself has negotiated a treaty centered around the proposed marriage of his cousin Edith to the Muslim king. Kenneth, who has his own hopes for marrying Edith, conceals his jealousy with the question "And what Christian . . . would sanction an union so unnatural, as that of a Christian maiden with an unbelieving Saracen?"[43] The question of miscegenation that Kenneth raises is complicated by the fact that he is Scottish, and Edith, as a Plantagenet, is a Norman; another way of saying this is that Kenneth is an authentic and original Brit, while Edith is not.

All the claims Kenneth makes to nobility on the basis of Northern identity, metonymized in Roswal, are diminished by his bigotry here. He has either failed to perceive Saladin's nobility through the medical disguise, or he refuses to acknowledge it out of racial and religious bias. The moral turn of the romantic plot requires that Kenneth learn to perceive nobility categorically across lesser categorical barriers in order to claim it for himself and to be worthy of marrying noble Edith. What amounts to a lesson in empathy comes when Saladin grants Kenneth's wish to exchange conditions with Roswal in order to make the bigoted Scotsman recognize what he shares with both noble hounds and noble Muslims. Literally enslaved into alterity by being transformed into a mute Nubian, Kenneth must struggle to have his nobility recognized through the conditionals qualifying any similitude between himself and the other white nobles, particularly Richard and Edith. The racial discourse governing Scott's romance divides Christian Europeans from Muslim Kurds and Arabs, through the same taxonomy dividing Scots from Normans. But it has also insisted that nobility remains recognizably constant through all the categorical variability. In his guise as the Nubian Zohauk, accompanied by "a large and noble staghound," Kenneth is described as having an appearance that is "highly interesting": "He was of superb stature and nobly formed, and his commanding features, although almost jet-black, showed nothing of negro descent."[44] The distinction between the Nubian and the Negro descent holds value in the race theory of Scott's day, which associated the Ethiopian "Nubian" with the Semitic peoples and the "Negro" with the people of central Africa who were still being transported to America as slaves. Zohauk strikes Richard as a well-formed man, and especially after indicating that he is not Muslim but Christian, which he does by crossing his forehead rather than by speaking, for "the Lord of Speech hath been stricken with silence betwixt the ivory walls of his palace"—or, as Richard puts it more bluntly, "A Nubian Christian . . . mutilated of the organ of speech by these heathen dogs."[45] Zohauk's appearance with the repeated qualifications of being "noble" depends on the all-important exclusion of "negro descent," which would disqualify the disguise. Since the Earl of Huntingdon is Scottish royalty, his quality must show through all disguises, from the impoverished Kenneth to the "jet-black" Nubian; and this same quality must appear in equal measure and with equal persistence in the metonymic Roswal, whose disguise consists of having no apparent name, being referred to as "a large and noble staghound," or "the large dog, which might be termed [Zohauk's] brother slave."[46] In the mythic landscape of legible nobility, Roswal's proper name cannot be erased through suppression of his individual given name. His proper name is nobility, the nebulous, mystical justice of the landscape. The metonymic connection between Roswal and Kenneth enables the hound not only to signify Kenneth's racially concealed nobility, but also to signify *for* the mute Nubian.

After saving Richard's life by killing the would-be assassin sent by Conrade, Zohauk pens an offer to the king to reveal the traitor who had stolen the banner (he had "seemed desirous to speak, but uttered only that imperfect sound proper to his melancholy condition"[47]). The offer is to have the leaders of all the different factions of the Christians appear before Richard, and "that if he who did the injury . . . shall be among the number, he may be made manifest in his iniquity, though it be hidden under seven veils."[48] Richard takes him up on the offer and has the entire Christian army parade before him. When Conrade approaches King Richard, "Roswal, uttering a furious and savage yell, [springs] forwards. . . . and seizing the Marquis by the throat, pull[s] him down from the saddle."[49] At this demonstration, Richard fully accepts Conrade's guilt and accuses the Marquis directly. When Philip of France attempts to intervene by objecting that "this is an unusual impeachment," that "the word of a knight and a prince" should prevail over "the barking of a cur," Richard counters that they should all "recollect that the Almighty, who gave the dog to be companion of our pleasures and our toils, hath invested him with a nature noble and incapable of deceit." The dog, Lionheart continues, "hath a share of man's intelligence, but no share of man's falsehood. . . . Murderers and robbers have been ere now convicted, and suffered death under such evidence, and men have said that the finger of God was in it."[50]

In this view, dogs are imbued with a divine authority, that of indicter in God's name. The "proper" name of dogs is woven into the texture of the romantic landscape to become one of the "encrypted signs, [the] figural writing set down in nature's production."[51] Roswal's attack on Conrade is a divine gift of revelation, for dogs are *incapable* of deceit." Having "a share of man's intelligence, but no share of man's falsehood," a dog would share and reflect the noble part of human subjectivity, that which remains legible even under seven veils, but only to those like Kenneth, De Vaux, and Richard who can recognize what they share because of their customary commerce, as nobles, with the divine author of their moral and social landscape. The noble intelligence is untainted by the other human quality of deception. *The* dog, Richard says, lacks human deception and shares human nobility, which, as demonstrated here, is the directly apprehensible expressiveness of mute God, nature, and law.

The sole character incapable of deception within this mimetic economy, Roswal cannot misdirect his signifying into any sort of catachresis. Although he possesses the interiority expressed in his legible face, he cannot disguise himself as many of the human characters do. The directness of this characterization attributes to Roswal the untwisted, undisguised, and fully present innocence of nature awaiting the sympathetic human reader. Derrida addresses the imputation of innocence to animal interiority when he responds to Lacan's claim, which is exactly in accord with that of Richard, that an animal cannot lie (or pretend to lie). The attribution of innocence to animals denies them the Adamically flawed knowledge of whether something is true or false. In this discourse, where animals live "anterior to the difference between good and evil," Derrida says, the animal is said to lack the very quality, the very lack, specific to humans, and that enables humans to manipulate what they signify.[52] Lacking the capacity for deceit (the human flaw of linguistic indirection), Roswal's place on the scale of class and race is that of a quasi-subject, one who can signify, who can make gestures and accusations that are recognizable by others, but who is without the auto-deixis that would also enable him to lie, or at least to signify indirectly. Incapable of lying or disguise, Roswal is both legibly noble and loyal, and without any unknowable feelings toward the humans; as a signifier, he is fully present, eager to be read categorically, as continuous with primordial connectivity. It is here that any conditionality grounding his significance is most conveniently concealed, making him fully legible, for his interiority—unlike that of human characters—is fully visible, exterior.

In this way Roswal embodies the great accomplishment of the English sportsmen who created the Foxhound in response to the lack in nature. As gestures of conditional meaning based on the structure of similitude, a good dog's actions signify a will to expression, waiting to be recognized by the human subject. This popular novel disseminates the rhetorical and aesthetic

Illustration from *The Talisman* in which Roswal passes judgment. Private Collection/The Stapleton Collection/Bridgeman Images.

alignments from the hunt literature—exemplified by Beckford and Taplin—to portray a human and a dog engaging in a friendship structured as the sublation of alterity into coagency through the mutual recognition of sameness, though the sameness is restricted to what the human requires to be knowable. This dog attains a recognizable interiority, to be sure, but one qualified as a lesser intentionality—because less disguisable—that requires human intervention to voice its mute revelation of divine law. And the lack signified by this muteness indicates the desire on the part of the dog to be recognized as being almost a subject, the desire to be completed by human recognition and friendship, to join into a coagency with noble humans to reveal divine justice. Every act of recognition in this novel, every time a character penetrates the disguise, or species difference, of another character by perceiving their nobility, the landscape of romance modernized as though it were history is reinforced. In the accounts of foxhunting, the frame consists of the aesthetic landscape in which legitimate participants attain a performative connectivity to the unified whole. In this novel the frame is delineated by the romance of the Crusades, where alterity is made into the emblem of the "dog" Saladin and the mute Nubian Zohauk, whose incomprehensibility is categorized through the animal correspondences and racial exclusion, while the dog Roswal sheds his through human racial correspondence of nobility. The frame of this novel, as with that of hunt literature, is the need to correct apparent lacks—Kenneth's bigotry, the conflicts among the Christian factions, among others—all taking the shape of uncertain alliances or relations that replicate the monstrous variety of an illegible landscape. Roswal's legibility expels that uncertainty, just as the breed taxonomies align canine illegibility, or misdirection, with the undefinable cur. In its illegibility, the cur holds no analogy, no similitude with any other being. Except that in this novel, the cur could be recognized in Conrade, the one character who bears no animal epithet, who holds no relation of analogy or similitude with any other character, and is therefore indicted by "the finger of God."

The context of animal correspondences generated throughout the narrative similarly resolves the racial alterity in the analogous structure that gives meaning to Roswal's expressive quasi-subjectivity as part of a visual discourse of recognitions. Richard the lion takes on a falcon glance to understand Kenneth the leopard. British island mastiffs ally themselves with the French eagle and the Austrian bear (an alliance threatened by the Templar wolves) to wage war against the unbaptized dogs of Islam. Saladin, also a lion, proves himself most capable of recognition, as demonstrated by his ability to recognize the nobility of Kenneth the leopard, by his respect for "Melech Ric," and—perhaps most importantly—by his admiration for both Edith Plantagenet (he recognizes beauty) and Roswal.

Harry Shaw argues that in *The Talisman* Kenneth's confrontation with the Other—Saladin—enables readers to "encounter the Other in ways that would lead to further understanding on something like equal terms."[53] This statement shows just how effective the institutionalized resolution of racial (and species) alterity in Scott's novel has continued to be. The "understanding" Shaw looks forward to is wholly dependent on the taxonomic alignment of animals and class, and of breed and race as a naturalized fact. The animal correspondences provide an Aesopian projection of the class and ethnic identities onto a romanticized historical setting that gives them the durability of universals. At the same time, the nobility linking Kenneth, Roswal, and Saladin gains an analogous, even attendant, universality. The racial-species categories, and the noble essence transcending the categorical divisions to make interspecies kinship possible, affirm and reaffirm one another cyclically. Shaw's "understanding" rests upon, and cannot exceed, the delineations of self and other that allow for—and even demand—the analogical economy that aligns individuals into kinship relations on the basis of shared origins, hence Shaw's "equal terms." This optimism reflects and extends the categories of race—and analogous breed—by accepting them as the definition and limit of alterity. Understanding simply entails, then, a recognition of noble similitude tempered by the category of race or species. And the consequence is that race and breed are reinforced as natural, universal categories, whereas alterity remains unexamined, excluded from the necessary discourse of optimistic fulfillment.

The complex animal identities make the similitude of a hound's gaze and a quasi-subjective expression into an event of nature (or the accusatory "finger of God") that transcends political alliances, religious belief, and ethnic or national identity. Roswal *almost* speaks, just as the mute Nubian Zohauk "seemed desirous to speak" when Richard offered to reward him if he could reveal the thief of the banner through some magic.[54] The parallel between the hound who yells and the Nubian who writes suggests mutual interiorities: inside the Nubian disguise is Kenneth, noble Scotsman (appointed by divine law to the Scottish throne), and inside the hound is a willing loyalty eager to express human justice and truth as natural law. Both racial and canine muteness signify an inner nobility that will find expression among those capable of recognizing it, provided the racial muteness is expunged of the "Negro" and the canine is expunged of the "cur" that King Philip accuses him of being.

The scenes aligning Zohauk's racialized muteness with Roswal's expression reveal the import of interspecies, interracial kinship for the modern landscape (and they demonstrate the working of the mechanisms that make them possible and necessary). Roswal, who becomes Zohauk's "brother slave,"[55] retains his noble dignity in servitude just as Kenneth does in being othered. The fraternity between Kenneth and Roswal enables one to stand in for the other, as when Kenneth-Zohauk's muteness is alleviated by Roswal's speech act identifying Conrade's treachery. Even when the man exchanges his Scottish identity for an Ethiopian one, the nobility that connects him and the hound persists. The nebulosity of nobility as an inherent quality facilitates its endurance through transformations across racial and species lines. And as a quality inherent in an individual, it is something that is apparent and recognizable from birth, even before. Thus, it is tied to origin, and to the history that makes an individual known and recognizable, but only through the obliteration of excess particularities—of particularity itself.

In his study of friendship, Derrida addresses the reconciliation among a fragmented Greek *polis* by noting that it "has no other cause than actual kinship, *suggénia*, on a solid and firm affinity (*bébaion*) stemming from birth, from native community."[56] Derrida is thinking of political reconciliation through the shared genealogy and culture of a political body; his observation applies to nobility as well, in that—as *The Talisman* makes repeatedly clear—nobility denotes not merely a rank but a birth that establishes a knowable and nebulous quality individuals retain through life and pass on to their offspring. As such, nobility aligns individuals into familial relatedness, kinship. Derrida goes on to say in this same passage,

> This kinship nurtures a constant and homophilial friendship (*philían bébaion kai omóphulon*) not only in words but in fact, in deeds (*ou lógō all' érgō*). In other words, the effectivity/actuality of the tie of friendship, that which assures constancy beyond discourses, is indeed real kinship, the reality of the tie of birth (*è tô onti suggéneia*). Provided that it is real—and not only spoken or set by convention—this syngenealogy durably guarantees the strength of the social bond in life and according to life.[57]

Social rank might be mere convention, but noble birth is "real" in the sense of participating in the "legal fiction" of genealogy.[58] Derrida focuses on the genealogical continuity again a few pages later when he observes—still in regard to Plato's *Menexenus*—that a noble birth makes obligatory "the search for an equality before the law *in conformity* with equality of birth." Such equality, Derrida goes on to say, "is founded firmly on the physio-ontological ground of what *is* in *nature*, revealing itself at birth."[59] Birth makes equality among nobles a necessity, which even the otherwise traditionally insurmountable barriers of race and species cannot dispel. Thus, the relation between Kenneth and Roswal goes beyond the aesthetic "connectivity" described in hunt literature to represent a genealogically necessary equality. Any denial of that equality would be nothing other than the bigotry Kenneth displays when he denies the same equality between Hakim-Saladin and himself—a bigotry he must rectify through experiencing that hostility directed at him, as one whose name has been written for him.

An equality, such as nobility, so rigorously enforced forms a "politics of fraternity," and "One can hardly see how a *perhaps* could ever stand a chance in such a politics."[60] This "perhaps" (which Derrida allows does perhaps have "a chance" in the simple fact of having been forgotten through the enforcement against it) has been expelled from Scott's nativist landscape of nobles, because knowability has expunged currish unconditionality. The nobility of the characters shines through any disguise, and in that way precludes any surprise on their part. Kenneth may anger Edith when he remains mute before her as she perceives his identity through his Nubian guise, but his loyalty to the oath he made to remain mute affirms his nobility all the more strongly (i.e., romantically). Roswal may let out a "savage yell" when he identifies Conrade as the villain who wounded him and defiled the English flag, but his savagery is in defense of his noble honor, and his yell proclaims that he will, after all, be known.[61] The equality among nobles ensures that their knowability will be preserved, and protected against any effort to obscure it by indirection or surprise, or by any violation of the romance that nobility has not been lost, but remains continuous even in the modern landscape. The equality, then, would seem to belong less to the individuals than to the knowable origin of nobility, so that any particularity of dog or man becomes forgettable when placed next to nobility, in the same way that disguise only seems to emphasize nobility.

This novel romanticizes the narrowly framed relation of kinship between humans and dogs by setting it amidst the chivalric plot of nobility; and with the same gesture it makes that relation seem natural, not only through the romantic story but through the apparent stability of racial identities and political alliances that transcend the cultural clash. The very next novel Scott wrote, *Woodstock*, also includes a dog, this one named Bevis, that performs as a good character—loyal, and with the desire to communicate. In contrast to the clarity of Roswal's expressions, Bevis's invoke confusion, and even fright; and in contrast to Roswal's unambiguous loyalty, Bevis's raises the specter of misinterpretation, unknowability. Just as in *The Talisman*, human and canine characters in *Woodstock* are aligned as family members, and through complementary scenes of speech acts and muteness; but in the later novel, human muteness results from the terror of the dog making a signifying gesture, and in contrast to Roswal, Bevis proves incomprehensible, exceeding the assertions of his loyalty by other characters and the narrator, and challenging the repeated assertions that his known origin and family membership give him a recognizable character. Through the misinterpretations and other narrative details showing that the human characters prevent themselves from understanding the canine character, *Woodstock* actually affirms the limits making human-canine relations possible and meaningful in the modern landscape. And through the same elements, the novel will provide a "perhaps," a possibility for human-canine friendships forgotten in the landscape of breed discourse.

Initially, Bevis plays a role in the plot of *Woodstock* similar to that of Roswal in *The Talisman*, providing a vital indicator of social standing of the aged Cavalier, Sir Henry Lee, and his family during the English Civil War, when families, class structures, religious and national allegiances have all been sundered. Most of the plot revolves around the need of Charles Stuart to escape from Cromwell after losing the battle of Worcester. The main human characters, Sir Henry and his daughter Alice, live in the royal Lodge of Woodstock, the aged Sir Henry serving in the office of Forest Ranger, protecting the royal interests of the forest. Father and daughter are diehard Royalists, as are their servants, Josceline Joliffe, the forester, and his sweetheart, Phoebe. One of the least trustworthy characters, Trusty Tomkins, is a fanatic who holds no allegiance to anyone, and who tries to play Royalists and Republicans off one another for his own gain. Bevis, the large dog described as staghound, wolfhound, and mastiff—the multiple categorization that for Scott seems simply to mean large and noble hound—has always lived at Woodstock as Sir Henry's loyal companion. Following Scott's compulsion to imply an extra-narrative realm through references to historical artifacts, the editors of the Edinburgh edition of *Woodstock* include a comment in their "Historical Note" that "there is still at Ditchley Park a portrait of Sir Henry with his Cheshire mastiff and ten lines of verse praising canine fidelity. The tradition is that 'one night when on retiring to rest Sir Henry ordered the dog out of the room, the faithful dog refused to go and soon after dragged from under the bed a man with a knife who had hidden himself there in order to kill the Knight.'"[62] This note is but one example of how the extra-narrative realm enforces the depiction of modern human-canine relations as the mode that has always existed. It also helps to authenticate the narrative's insistence that Bevis is unfailingly loyal to Sir Henry, a characterization that—as I shall show—is problematic.

The narrative insists on making the aged Sir Henry the primary focus for Bevis, identifying the old knight as the "master" to whom the hound is forever loyal. This position fits with Henry's role as patriarch within the family structure, and as a member of the old gentry. But Sir Henry is also repeatedly shown to have passed into his dotage, so that—as many critics have pointed out—his quotations of Shakespeare are inappropriate or even inaccurate, and he often makes blunders out of simple ignorance.[63] Sir Henry, we are told in the narrative, is "not a person of very quick apprehension," though his ignorance is often merely that of limited perspective.[64] One of the many oddities of this novel is that, despite the narrative insistence that Sir Henry is Bevis's "master," and that he is always attended by his loyal hound, very few scenes put the two of them together, and none sets them into the mutual facial recognition central to the depiction of Roswal and Sir Kenneth; there is a central scene in which Bevis performs a conditional approximation to speech, but Henry plays only an ancillary role in it. It is not just that Sir Henry is old and foolish, but that the social order that once sustained his capacity for judgment has been completely disrupted. His ignorance, his incapacity to judge soundly are indicative of the general confusion of factionalism during the Civil Wars, and establish that this human-dog relation is far removed from that in *The Talisman*, where similar conflicts did not disrupt the relations between Sir Kenneth and Roswal. Taken together, these two novels offer complementary representations of human-dog relations in the modern world: on the one hand, they romanticize these relations to make them seem natural, enduring from at least the Middle Ages into modernity, and on the other hand, they reveal that the naturalness of the relations depends on the conditional troping of the unknowable into conventions of recognizable loyalty—or legible legality.

THE

WAVERLEY NOVELS

VOL. XXXIX

WOODSTOCK

"BEVIS."

FORTY-EIGHT VOLUMES BOUND IN TWENTY-FOUR

Frontispiece from *Woodstock*, showing Bevis. Walter Scott, *Woodstock or the Cavalier*, ed. Andrew Lang (London: J. C. Nimmo, 1892).

The uncertainty permeating judgment and relations is made prominent early on in *Woodstock*, and specifically in regard to Sir Henry's reading of Bevis. In a scene that contributes directly to the linguistic confrontation between dog and human characters, Bevis leaves Sir Henry and Alice to follow Josceline and Trusty Tomkins, making Sir Henry feel jilted. Alice attempts to assuage her father's hurt feelings with the explanation that Bevis chose to follow Tomkins out of the sagacity that "saw in this man a stranger, whom he thought himself obliged to watch circumspectly."[65] Sir Henry, facing the loss of his position as Ranger of the royal estate, disagrees morosely, averring that "he leaves me because my fortunes have fled from me. There is a feeling in nature, affecting even the instinct, as it is called, of dumb animals, which teaches them to fly from misfortune." The subsequent exchange rehearses the modern explanation for the human-canine bond:

> "The dog leaves his own race [said Alice], to attach himself to ours; forsakes, for his master the company, food, and pleasure of his own kind; and surely the fidelity of such a devoted and voluntary servant as Bevis hath been in particular, ought not to be lightly suspected."
>
> "I am not angry with the dog, Alice; I am only sorry," replied her father. "I have read, in faithful chronicles, that when Richard II. and Henry of Bolingbroke were at Berkeley Castle, a dog of the same kind deserted the King, whom he had always attended upon, and attached himself to Henry, whom he then saw for the first time. Richard foretold, from the desertion of his favorite, his approaching deposition. The dog was afterwards kept at Woodstock, and Bevis is said to be of his breed, which was heedfully kept up. What I might foretell of mischief from his desertion, I cannot guess, but my mind assures me it bodes no good."[66]

The two interpretations are overt parallels, and they reflect the degree to which father and daughter both connect an individual with type; for Alice, Bevis replicates the qualities of a mythic "race," while for Sir Henry, Bevis replicates the actions of a family pedigree, or Woodstock "breed." The parallel reflects the Lees' royalist allegiance, and, as my analysis of the previous novel shows, it also perpetuates the analogy that makes canine breed and human race into naturalized proofs for one another, and that makes an individual like Bevis into the meaningful emblem of a taxon—breed, race, or, in this novel, religio-political faction. Both interpretations also focus on loyalty, as fidelity or faithfulness, as the defining quality of a dog's attachment to humans. Alice and Sir Henry attribute a willing intention to "the dog" (the category that for Alice categorically denotes the canine "race," and for Henry refers to the singular representative of a breed), but an intention limited to the desire to serve a human. To the Lees, Bevis's choice of following Josceline and Tomkins means either an act of loyalty to father and daughter or a shifting of loyalty from them, since the canine category is defined by its loyalty to the human category. What Sir Henry calls "the instinct . . . of dumb animals" refers to a categorical identity superseding any individual intentionality.

The interpretations merge together in their emphasis on loyalty, fidelity, and devotion to humans. Taken together, these two accounts of canine loyalty exemplify the writing of "the dog" in modern discourse. Alice recounts the originary moment of domestication identified by Buffon in terms of instinct; in this version, instinct is replaced by voluntariness, so that the myth of primordial union shifts from an event of mute and naive nature, replicated in Richard Lionheart's speech as a gift to man from God, to a willing indenture. Sir Henry, the character who supposedly knows Bevis best, and the one Bevis supposedly serves voluntarily, focuses not on the fidelity but on the voluntarism that turns Bevis into the agent capable of shifting his loyalty. This agency is itself a quality of the breed, however, which in turn belongs to the site of Woodstock. In their complementary alignment, the two accounts situate Bevis in the modern landscape as the inscription of the arche-dog's self-presence, a presence that entails a loss—the pleasure of the dog's "own kind," and the Plantagenet dynasty. The instinctual "feeling in nature" may be recast in the modern terms of voluntarism and agency, but it continues to invoke just such myths of primordial loss.

The most important aspect of this doubled interpretation is that, much later in the narrative, it is shown to be wrong, so that the Lees' histories of species, breed, and familial loyalties are retrospectively made into fabrications for covering their ignorance of their own dog. Even while the narrative insists that Bevis directs his loyalty wholly toward Sir Henry, it shows that the hound has experiences—participates in a world, events—well apart from the old Cavalier. Characters in this novel continually find their categorical certainty thrust back into the instability of inept readers trying to find a pattern of meaning in shifting variability, the bane of post-Enlightenment judgment. Sir Henry's wrong interpretation rests upon the hierarchical relations that the old knight had accepted as a fact of nature and that extend from the patriarchal king to his retainers, and from patriarchal human master to his canine retainers. Alice, who overinterprets the scene with the same abstract idealism she imposes on human characters, assures her father that the old order does persist as the nature that republicans have perverted; as long as there are those who serve their superiors voluntarily, there is the hope that Cromwell will fall and that the natural order of the Stuarts will return. In a curious fashion, the uncertainty pervading this novel dismantles the landscape of originary myths that Scott elsewhere sustains and even helps to institutionalize.

The pervasive uncertainty becomes insurmountable in the scene of Bevis's speech act. If seen as a simple parallel to Roswal's testimony, Bevis's action would constitute a similar irrefutable expression of truth. But in this troubled novel about troubled speech and troubled reading, Bevis's signifying gesture sparks no recognition, but only incomprehension, terror, and aphasia. Bevis's testimony cannot be said to have "the finger of God" in it, since its meaning remains inaccessible. The indeterminate gesture follows a pattern of overdetermined speech acts, beginning when Trusty Tomkins attempts to rape Josceline's sweetheart, Phoebe. Josceline, who has figured out that Tomkins is actually Phil Hazeldine, the poacher who tricked him years earlier, has kept a watch on him and leaps in to save Phoebe. When Tomkins shoots at him, Josceline deals the Independent a fatal blow with his quarterstaff while calling out, "Let ash answer iron."[67] Josceline's self-proclaimed speech act holds the very clear meaning of Tomkins's death; it is complicated, however, by the account Josceline immediately gives Phoebe of the relations the two men had years ago as both "pot-mates" and opponents when Josceline the forester caught Phil poaching. It is in this account that we learn for the first time that Tomkins, or Hazeldine, served at Woodstock before the war as "dog-leader," providing the simple explanation to Bevis's apparent disloyalty that had led both Alice and Sir Henry to their false interpretations. As Josceline recounts the personal history that complicates the ashy answer he gave to iron, he also reveals the complex of relations aligning himself, Tomkins, and Bevis in a way that no one else ever becomes aware of. As dog leader, Tomkins had a relation to Bevis that remains wholly beyond the descriptive field in which Sir Henry, Alice, and the others carry on the main plot. And, indeed, this detail, coming quite late in the narrative, completely reverses the sense of the first scene involving Bevis, making the breach of loyalty into a possible expression of welcome to his old trainer, Trusty Tomkins, who had once been both a willing servant to Sir Henry and a poacher in the forest Sir Henry protects.

When Alice and Sir Henry read Bevis's decision to follow Tomkins—whom they do not recognize—they create originary narratives based on a faith in their knowledge of Bevis as the representative of two archetypes, "the Dog" and the Woodstock breed. Both this archetypal reading, and the narrative's insistence on Bevis's unabated loyalty to Sir Henry are put into question with Josceline's revelation of the bond between Tomkins and Bevis. How far that bond extended and what shape it took remain unknowable, for it lies outside the narrative. Once that alternative relation is broached, every reference to Bevis's loyalty to Sir Henry is weighted with questions of how much the narrative itself knows of the canine character it describes, and whether it is perhaps challenging the archetypal terms of the man-dog relation cast as loyalty. So when Josceline refers to the earlier relation, the dependence of the descriptive narrative as a whole on an extra-narrative realm that remains undeterminable becomes troublingly evident. The evidence of the extra-narrative realm that should remain implicit and external becomes even more prominent in the following scenes with Bevis.

Back at the Lodge, after having killed Tomkins and left the body unburied, Josceline demurs when Sir Henry orders him back out into the night, fearing the ghost of his victim might do him harm. Angered by the hesitation, the old knight banishes the forester, a punishment in excess of the supposed crime, and made egregious by Henry's intemperate insults: "How? puppy, fool, and blockhead. . . . Out, hound!—get down to the kennel yonder instantly, or I will break the knave's pate of thee."[68] Cast into a canine muteness out of willing loyalty to the old knight, and because of his fear of ghosts, Josceline instinctively looks to Dr. Rochecliffe, the Divine, "with an eye of agony . . . as if entreating [Rochecliffe] to interfere in his behalf." Sir Henry's condemnation carries the force of making Josceline into a proper inhabitant of the kennel, compelled to rely on the conditional mute "eye of agony," to protect his master from knowledge of the ashy answer to iron. Just as Dr. Rochecliffe is on the verge of speaking up in response to Josceline's mute appeal, he is interrupted when "a most melancholy howling [arises] at the hall-door, and a dog [is] heard scratching for admittance." Sir Henry attempts to allay everyone's fear with the assurance that, on the basis of his privileged relation with Bevis and Bevis's ancestors, he knows how to interpret the howls: "It is no alarm, . . . for in such cases the dog's bark is short, sharp, and furious. These long howls are said to be ominous. It was even so that Bevis's grandsire bayed the whole livelong night on which my poor father died. If it comes now as a presage, God send it regard the old and useless, not the young, and those who may yet serve King and country!"[69] When the door is opened, however, it is not Sir Henry that Bevis seeks:

> Bevis advanced into the room where the company were assembled, bearing something in his mouth, and exhibiting, in an unusual degree, that sense of duty and interest which a dog seems to show when he thinks he has the charge of something important. He entered therefore, drooping his long tail, slouching his head and ears, and walking with the stately yet melancholy dignity of a warhorse at his master's funeral. In this manner he paced through the room, went straight up to Josceline, who had been regarding him with astonishment, and uttering a short and melancholy howl, laid at his feet the object which he bore in his mouth. Josceline stooped, and took from the floor a man's glove. . . . But Josceline had no sooner looked at what in itself was so common an object, than he dropped it from his hand, staggered backward, uttered a groan, and nearly fell to the ground.[70]

Bevis's proffer of the dead man's glove is the culmination of the difficulty all characters have in understanding each other (a difficulty taken to the extreme by Cromwell's insanely apocalyptic speeches that leave his listeners dumbfounded and terrified). By the time Bevis drops the glove at Josceline's feet, that difficulty has advanced to complete aphasia. Though Josceline has shown himself capable of bold speech acts—answering steel with ash—he can only respond to Bevis's act of dropping the glove with a groan of terror.

Bevis is described as "exhibiting, in an unusual degree, that sense of duty and interest which a dog *seems* to show when he *thinks* he has . . . something important." The qualification is that Bevis "seems to show" that he thinks; but *what* he thinks remains unstated, and strategically, so that the elision is easily forgotten in the rehearsal of the formula that a dog fulfills his "duty" *as though* he thinks. But though his actual thoughts are elided, his howls elicit immediate comprehension from doddering Sir Henry—who, out of ignorance of the facts on more than one level, has unjustly declared loyal Josceline to be a bad dog. In referring to Bevis's grandsire, Sir Henry inadvertently calls up his own earlier fear that the hound would replicate the betrayal of his ancestor; with this, Sir Henry underscores his ignorance of Bevis's connection to Tomkins. Sir Henry interprets Bevis's howl somewhat correctly as a speech act referring to death, but is unaware of the one that has already happened. Sir Henry replicates here his blind reliance on pedigree to read Bevis as being both *his* hound and his *loyal* hound. The old Cavalier is foolish because his claims to knowledge—categorical or particular—consistently reveal that he knows less than anyone.

Josceline, who alone knows of the early connection between Bevis and Tomkins, can only think the glove must be aligned with the "broken words" Tomkins uttered while dying: "Josceline—I am gone—but I forgive thee—Doctor Rochecliffe—I wish I had more—Oh!—the clergyman—the funeral service—."[71] The disjointed phrases of the dying Independent collate the confusion of the several incomprehensible speech acts, and they compel Josceline to struggle to find a meaning in them, just as he needs to determine the meaning behind Bevis bringing him the glove, and as the Lees had earlier tried to find meaning in Bevis leaving them. Convinced that Woodstock is already inhabited by ghosts, Josceline tells Rochecliffe of the "broken words," and says, "Methinks he sent Bevis with his glove to put me in mind of them." And when Rochecliffe dismisses Josceline's fears as the stuff of romance, the forester goes on: "I must say, Bevis took an interest in the man—if indeed it was not something worse in the shape of Bevis, for methought his eyes looked wild and fiery, as if he would have spoken."[72] The conditional "as if" is qualified by the subjunctive "would have spoken," making Bevis not just the mimetic reflection of subjectivity, but the conditional representation of a conditionality suggestive of unspeakable terror. For Josceline the possibility of a canine subjective interiority is virtually identical with the mute voice of death, or of an intention beyond the living. In other words, Josceline attempting to trace the significance of Bevis bringing him the glove can only extend the meaning from one mute indeterminacy to another. Josceline was unwillingly assimilated into the canine conditionality when Sir Henry banished him to the kennel and put him in the category of disloyal dog. Just as Sir Kenneth is muted when assimilated into a racial (though not class) otherness, Josceline troped into puppyhood by his master is forced to rely on the mute conditional, "as if entreating."[73] Through ocular similitude, Bevis, Tomkins, and Josceline become conditional analogs, fraught with broken words and illegible faces. Whereas other narrative texts—descriptions of foxhunting, natural histories—aver a linguistic landscape, legible as though it were a painting, in this narrative the hound's muteness, as well as his putatively signifying gestures of dropping the glove, walking in a certain posture, howling, only add to the confusion of what is signified, or even if there is any significance to these actions. The glove and Bevis, forged into a metonymy, signify for Josceline a determinacy demanding some secondary (indeterminate) determination. The gesture seems to carry a referential meaning, and intention, but only of something nebulous that eludes and interrupts speech. And, indeed, the signification comes not from a legible subject, as happened with Roswal and Kenneth, but from "something worse in the shape of Bevis"; it is the representation of something other than—that looks as if—would it could.

The conditional similitude in *The Talisman* gave Roswal and Kenneth faces with which each could recognize an analogous nobility in the other, because the similitude worked within the larger discourse of animal epithets generating analogies between race and breed as part of a natural order of birth. The narrative in *The Talisman* never suggests that Roswal has any life—inner or outer—apart from his willing loyalty to Kenneth: as fellow nobles, their mutual recognition transcends race and species, providing the pattern for later claims of human-canine similitude. That larger discourse of race is transposed in *Woodstock* into religious and political factionalism that has disrupted the alignments that had once made similitudes meaningful and legible. The similitudes aligning human and canine characters through the conditionality of birth, of heritage, or of continuity with a region are thus set amidst a discursive instability complicating them beyond the straightforward enactment of communication. In this novel the conditionals setting Bevis and the humans into a reflective exchange end up undercutting the descriptive historicity of conventionalized human-canine recognition. Any reenactment of that recognition becomes untenable as anything more than a conventional rehearsal favoring the perspicacity of the human involved. The landscape allowing for comprehensible human-canine confrontations is suddenly revealed as a set of formulations recounting an originary loss that never happened outside the discursive landscape. The aphasic terror Josceline feels when Bevis looks as if he would speak with a voice from beyond the living is the terror of encountering alterity, unpresentable in the discursive landscape of kinship and willing loyalty. This is the terror of encountering the landscape as a written discourse no longer represented as though it were the divine expression itself.

When Bevis brings Tomkins's glove to Josceline, the conditionals weight his action with both an intentionality and an incomprehensibility. The incomprehensible intentionality is in accord with his excessive character that runs beyond the narrative, implying a set of interstices that stretch from his swift departure out of one scene to his sudden and boisterous entrance into another. Set alongside the gesture with Tomkins's glove, Bevis's departures work as speech acts, iterations of turning away, of proclaiming his privacy. Where Bevis goes and where he comes from remain unstated. But, given his relation with Tomkins, his movements in and out of the scene of narratable action suggest a complex world of interactions that remains unknown, unnarratable, inconceivable, and illegible to the human characters.

Not only does Bevis have an inaccessible private life, but he has one that is at odds with the receptions given him by the human characters, and certainly with Roswal's reception throughout *The Talisman*. The conditional similitudes reinforce the supposition that a dog is wholly present in his loyalty, and thus accessible, when turning his gaze to a human; the supposition is that the dog is responding directly and wholly to the human. Thus, the human characters like Alice and Kenneth, and the nonfictional historians like Buffon and Taplin, read in the dog's gaze an intention to respond in a way parallel to "the dog's" willing departure from "his own race" in order "to attach himself to ours," an originary willingness, an instinct, to be legal and legible. Such a willingness implies a dependence on human recognition (such as the eighteenth-century recognition that animals can respond and not merely react).

And yet, the Lees' reading of Bevis works no differently from Kenneth and Lionheart's reading of Roswal. The readings of Roswal work within a system of human-animal, breed-race analogies that provide a naturalized grammar. The mute yet meaningful gestures of Roswal appear as though they were the same as the mute yet meaningful gestures of the Nubian, Zohauk. These analogies reify the similitudes pairing race and breed, man and dog conceptually so that the singular dog, Roswal, and the singular man, Kenneth/Zohauk, can both recognize one another and be recognized as members of the same (nobility) or analogous (Northern man, Northern hound) categories. Their mutual recognition would seem to affirm the archetypal reading of dogs choosing to become loyal servants to men.

In contrast, Bevis continually exceeds the category assigned him. He is Sir Henry's loyal dog, but chooses to go off with the poacher Tomkins. Where his loyalty lies, or whether his loyalty is confined to one human, are questions that remain suspended, just like the questions of what he does outside the narrated scenes before and after he rushes into them. There is no system of analogy in this novel comparable to that of *The Talisman*, and consequently claims about loyalty or legibility are twisted into ironic misreadings displaying a character's—and the narrator's—ignorance. The misreadings, along with Josceline's fearful incomprehension demonstrate the incompleteness of knowledge, engagement, or co-constitutionality, attainable in a dog's gaze, and the concealment of that incompleteness behind accounts of a dog's similitude to humans, of a dog's categorical identity that make an individual dog legible, as though he were wholly present in his instinct and without a private life. The cover-up facilitates the insouciance with which the novel overlooks the currish excess of Bevis's character, and with which claims of canine loyalty in general delimit the possibility of canine subjectivity and responsiveness. And, given the ending of this novel, "cover-up" is the only appropriate term.

Once the wars are over and "the ancient ties of kindred and friendship [regain] at least part of their former influence,"[74] Bevis again appears unambiguously the loyal and constant companion of Sir Henry. In the tableau drawn up of the Lee family attending Charles II's triumphant return to London—the ekphrastic quality of which Judith Wilt underscores by calling it "a sculpture group in a wayside bank"[75]—there is in addition to Alice, Sir Henry, and Josceline,

> one other remarkable figure . . . a gigantic dog, which bore the signs of being at the extremity of canine life. But though exhibiting the ruin of his former appearance . . . the noble hound had lost none of his instinctive fondness for his master. To lie by Sir Henry's feet in the summer or by the fire in the winter, to raise his head to look on him, to lick his withered hand or his shrivelled cheek from time to time, seemed now all that Bevis lived for.[76]

The indeterminacy that had dominated the characterization of Bevis throughout the narrative, setting him beyond the range of what the narrative could visually describe, is now apparently dispelled. The whole of Bevis as character, as willing and loyal servant to Sir Henry, can now be presented up in the phrase "instinctive fondness," which returns the human-canine relation to that where the dog serves fondly as mimetic reflection of human mastery. The possibilities raised by the anterior relations with Tomkins, that Bevis might have expressed fondness to others and in other ways, and even that what appears like devotion to one master might in fact entail other feelings altogether, have now been folded into this singular instinct for loyalty to one master, who is "now all that Bevis lives for." And it is just such a claim of a singular possible relation, and of complete legibility that enables a dog's face to be cast in a "sculpture group," presented as a wholly and immediately known character—or at least known in the sense that Henry knows Bevis.

A second gesture that conceals the indeterminacy occurs in the very last sentence of the narrative equating the death of the old knight with that of the noble hound: "I have only to add, that his faithful dog did not survive him many days; and that the image of Bevis lies carved at his Master's feet on the tomb which was erected to the Memory of Sir Henry Lee of Ditchley."[77] In another sculpture, Bevis on the tomb signifies in traditional fashion Sir Henry's station as loyal knight. And the tableau of canine fondness and faithfulness so great that life without a master cannot be sustained provides an emblem of a dog whose sole focus is on the privileged human. Following this sentence, Scott appended a footnote in the Magnum edition:

> It may interest some readers to know that Bevis, the gallant hound, one of the handsomest and active of the ancient Highland deer-hounds, had his prototype in a dog called Maida, the gift of the late Chief of Glengarry to the author. A beautiful sketch was made by Edwin Landseer, and afterwards engraved. I cannot suppress the avowal of some personal vanity when I mention that a friend, going though Munich, picked up a common snuff-box, such as are sold for one franc, on which was displayed the form of this veteran favorite, simply marked as Der lieblung hund von Walter Scott. Mr. Landseer's painting is at Blair-Adam, the property of my venerable friend, the Right Honorable Lord Chief Commissioner Adam.[78]

Within the frame of the narrative, Bevis is replicated in his death on Sir Henry's tomb. Scott then extends that replication beyond the narrative frame, and into the realm of historical anteriority, by pointing out that Bevis is the replication of his own loyal and noble Maida—and that Bevis's qualities as "one of the handsomest and most active of the ancient Highland deer-hounds" have their prototype in Scott's own hound. Maida was likewise replicated in the sketch by Landseer, and then the snuff boxes in Munich. What matters in this fourfold replication is simply the replication itself, that all the particularities, from the fictional Bevis to the mass-produced knickknacks, hold their value as representations of the originary being associated with a romanticized and regional primordiality.

Scott extends this replication of his beloved hound even further when he writes in a letter to Lady Abercorn, sometime in August or September of 1826, just after the publication of *Woodstock*, "I hope you had the last novel. . . . It has been eminently successful though written under disadvantageous circumstances & though I don't much like it except the picture of Bevis which is a large dog of my own his unpoetical name is Nimrod."[79] Nimrod was the hound sent to Scott by Glengarry upon hearing of Maida's death. Whether or not Scott committed a slip here is largely beside the point, for what matters is that Maida can be replicated in the dogs of the fictional narratives, in the tomb Scott had built for him, in the numerous portraits painted of him, the cheap knickknacks, and in the subsequent large dogs—including Bran, who joined the household in 1830.[80] Replicability certainly offers some balm for Scott's grief on losing Maida, and it helps to resolve a much greater tension as well, for it quells the deep anxiety over the variability—the incomprehensible alterity, the currishness—that exceeds the legible grammar of the landscape, and that is epitomized by dogs who might engage in wholly different landscapes. Much of the replicability emanates from the extra-narrative frame of Scott's novels that are paralleled by his epistolary references to Highland chieftains and their canine gifts. The prototype is no more determinable, presentable, than Bevis beyond the ekphrastic narrative scene. The replicability is what comforts Scott as the portrait signifying canine loyalty with certainty, again and again. Bevis—or Maida, or Nimrod, or Bran—frozen into determinable form works just as do the hounds killed by Colonel Thornton so they could be posed in lifelike positions, as a guaranteed signifier of a determinable relationship—man's best friend, who will always present the face of legible similitude.

The threat Bevis's privacy poses extends beyond this novel—and Scott's connection of Bevis to Maida shows that the effort to suppress the threat extends equally far. Any accounts of companionship will only have the value of the conventional accounts offered by Alice and Henry. They all cover up the ignorance of canine life beyond the human, beyond the character

SIR WALTER SCOTT'S DEERHOUND MAIDA :
FROM MONUMENT AT ABBOTSFORD.

Last Page from *Woodstock*.

granted within a closed economy of predetermined relations. To grant a dog a face—another way of saying that a dog is seen through its breed—is to conceal a dog's incomprehensible alterity behind categorical legibility. The lack corrected by the necessary Foxhound has become the frame excluding from view the currish illegibility in which a dog lives apart from its breed-assigned identity. The direct, vivid descriptions of scene and action that make a dog recognizable as a conventional character, such as Roswal, Bevis, or Colonel Thornton's hounds, conceal everything nonhuman about the particular dog, in order to establish the replicable similitude readable as loyalty, affection to one person, unity of the landscape, instinct, and even the finger of God. And they conceal the one fact established by the revelation that Bevis had a relationship with Tomkins, and that is that when a dog departs the scene it does not mean he has ceased responding, but that he is responding elsewhere, otherwise.

The depictions of Bevis as an active hound undercut the tableaux of dogs as loyally recognizable characters. His departures from and dramatic entries into scenes—along with Henry's and Alice's misinterpretations of the first departure—enact the experience of a trace that cannot be grasped except in its absence. Bevis's character can best be described as the dog whose absence is made to seem *as though* it were loyalty, *as though* it were a presence with a recognizable face. In this regard, *Woodstock* can be read as the deconstructive reenactment of *The Talisman*. The canine disappearance performed by Bevis puts in question the legibility of Roswal, and it discloses the way interpretations of a canine trace can support a structure of breed, racial, and species alignments and divisions that make the enmities and allegiances of war appear naturalized into necessities. Just as Henry interprets the barking that precedes Bevis's entry with the empty glove, so a canine trace can be interpreted to seem *as if* a human knows what a dog's action means. The complex animal epithets in *The Talisman* acquire their effectiveness as putative signifiers in just such an interpretation; that is, they enable a reader (or the characters) to read the human-animal associations *as though* they could be read meaningfully, *as though* they imparted some essential quality of the characters, justifying their political and racial alignments.

What makes *Woodstock* so curious a novel in its depiction of a canine character, especially when set beside the racial muteness and breed expressivity of *The Talisman*, is that the narrative itself plays the role of mute, interdicted from commenting on possibilities it has itself raised. Repeatedly emphasizing that Bevis exceeds the descriptive scenes as he runs out of them or has relations with other characters prior to any of these scenes, the narrative cannot comment on or describe anything about him beyond the narrow frame of his character as loyal hound. Repeatedly, the narrative emphasizes that Bevis challenges any easy account of his character, as when Sir Henry replies to a rhetorical question by saying, "I could as soon undertake to tell you the reason why Bevis turns around three times before he lies down."[81] When the narrative insists, at the end, that Bevis represents the category of "instinctive fondness," genetically programmed loyalty to one master, it has already ensured that that infinitely reproduceable representation appears specious. It takes on the quality of a fable told to keep the non-anthropocentric possibilities at bay. These are the possibilities that when a dog looks at us he thinks otherwise than as a human would, that she sees us otherwise than as the focus of her loyalty, or that the world can be experienced and read otherwise than as mute nature waiting to be categorized into an expressively recognizable face.

When Derrida sees his cat looking at him, he wonders what it means to be seen by this cat. And—if it is fair to draw an analogy between a philosopher's account of being seen by a cat and a dog lover's fictional description of an inarticulate man watching a dog approach with the glove of a murdered man, as if there were a similitude between philosophy and fiction, between cat lovers and dog lovers, between cats and dogs—it is this wonder raised by the narrative of Bevis, said by the author to represent the dog already mythologized prior to the novel, that raises the question of what it means to be approached, to be noticed by a dog. What does Bevis represent of Sir Walter's dog? A friendship centered around specious claims of loyalty and fabricated nobility? Or the unknowable? Bevis appearing with the glove is incomprehensible, because he offers no legible sign of what it should mean, or if it has any meaning within the human economy. There is no finger of God in this scene, but only an empty glove: no pointing, no indicting.

Scott stands as far from Pope in his relations with dogs as we do, for Pope lies beyond the divide drawn by the eighteenth century. The vividness of Scott's descriptions, the recognizably three-dimensional characters that move through his descriptive scenes, and the dependence on a mythic primordiality that gives his modern characters the authenticity of indigeneity, all work together to make the canine characters as believable as the human characters, as though they express something of Scott and his dogs. And they are believable because they present a face made legible through the descriptive conventions of realist narrative, dependent on hypotyposis, which makes temporally or spatially distant places and characters seem present through visually detailed rhetoric. Roswal does indeed meet the criteria of a modern dog: he belongs to a clearly defined class, which gives him the status of a proto-breed; he presents a face that makes his intentions immediately and fully present—in other words, he is both legal and legible. But Bevis compels a reconsideration of the modern claim of canine legibility. The modern reading mythologizes dogs as much as Scott does Maida, Spice, and the others, connecting them to a romantic pastoral of work—exemplified by Dandie's dogs—and assigning them a loyalty that effectively confines them to the role of willing servant to a human. Just as Pope's accounts of dogs raise the possibility of modes of caring, responsive relations that do not demand that dogs present recognizable faces, so Scott's Bevis raises a possibility within modernity of a human-canine friendship without presence, framed by incomprehensibility.

Throughout the nineteenth century, dogs became commodified as pets bought and sold for their metonymic representation of the lost native landscape. Dogs as companions, in sharp contrast to the hounds or other dogs used in the field, came increasingly to serve not just as an appendage, the signifier of a person's status or character, but as a direct reflection of the person's own interiority, and as the being of alterity with whom the person had a particular, albeit predetermined, exchange. The aesthetic link between human and nature provided by the Foxhound in the eighteenth century became more indirect—but nonetheless effective—as breeds like the Dandie were sold as pets. The historical narratives necessarily establish the pet dog as having once had a specific function in the preindustrial countryside very like that of the Foxhound or Dandie's Mustard and Peppers. These histories stressing both indigenous origin and practical function of the dogs give particular value to a breed, investing it, in Diana Donald's words, with "historical glamour" by making the breed that is always under threat of being lost into a relic "of more plain-living, arduous or heroic times"—times that are under threat of being forgotten.[82] Such a romance also serves the more vital function of concealing the imposition of a legible character onto an individual, insisting that she choose to attach herself loyally to us.

Cynical Friendships
Anthro-Canine Relations Today

In the interview with Jean-Luc Nancy "Eating Well," Derrida comments on
the responsibility he insists is a key element in the deconstructive project: "Responsibility
carries within it, and must do so, an essential excessiveness. It regulates itself neither on the
principle of reason nor on any sort of accountancy. To put it rather abruptly, I would say
that among other things, the subject is also a principle of calculability. . . . I believe there is
no responsibility, no ethico-political decision that must not pass through the proofs of the
incalculable or the undecidable. Otherwise, everything would be reducible to calculation,
program, causality, and, at best, 'hypothetical imperative.'"[1] Commenting on this passage,
Kelly Oliver says, "For Derrida, an ethics that remains open to surprise or open to the other
requires giving up moral habits along with the notion that morality is a matter of habit."[2] In
this chapter I turn to twenty-first-century narratives of human-dog relations to ask whether
surprise is a possibility, or if it has been domesticated into calculability by the dominance of
breed. Two hundred years after the Foxhound was finally shaped into its recognizable character, breed virtually always precedes the encounters we have with dogs. "What *kind* of dog
is that?" is the question people ask when meeting a dog they don't recognize as anything other
than a dog. People get breed dogs as signifiers of their projected identity (Iain Sinclair says
that among entry-level drug dealers in London's East End, "it's a toss up between a first-time
pit bull and a BMW with 40,000 miles on the clock"[3]), or with expectation of a particular
predetermined relationship that very often begins in a mimesis (President Obama's "mutt").
Two questions arise concerning the force of breed to affect the responsive relations we have
with dogs. First, how does the dominance of breed discourse affect human responses to dogs
today? I begin with the assumption that it does so by shaping our responses to dogs into cal-
culations, so that we face a pit bull differently than we do a Westie or a mutt. And second, is
there a possibility of turning from that dominating habit of calculation instituted over two
centuries to respond to a dog with surprise? I avoid proclaiming anything like a "post-breed"
discourse or ethics, because such a gesture carries the implicit claim of transcendence, or of
"improvement," that is very much a part of the modern subject whose interrogation must
always intertwine itself with these questions. But I do wish to hold out the possibility that,
within the breed discourse that still regulates responses to dogs and the responses we expect to
elicit from them, surprises can happen. Or, to use the terms of Derrida's statement from "Eating Well," the decisions that we make about possible interactions with dogs, even with breed
discourse, must pass through some proof or phase of the incalculable; it is in this phase where

the habits ingrained by two hundred years of the regulative, mimetic discourse of breed might be surprised with unsuspected or forgotten possibilities. The force of the preceding chapters leads me to consider one possibility in particular, one that also arises in the discourse of ethics, finding an expected analogy in animal studies, and that begins from the encounter with the other's gaze; this encounter, I believe, takes only the first step, however, by opening the possibility of surprise, and one that has been presented so frequently among animal theorists as to acquire conventions that obscure the risks of the incalculable. This possibility persists, overlooked and devalued, in terms that appeared in literary works about dogs two and three centuries ago, and that I have emphasized already in my discussion. These terms introduce an indirect or oblique possibility similar to the engagements Pope had with his unnamed dogs, and that builds on the incalculable private life of dogs suggested by Scott's portrayal of Bevis; this possibility resists habituation by eluding the need for facial recognition or claims of commonality that rely on breed conformation to enforce calculability.

The obliquity of this possibility occurs as a turning away from a face, from the requirement of a face, and from the requirement that a dog meet our look *as though* he understood us the way we imagine. Such a turn entails recoiling from the need for a categorization that assigns an essentializing "as such" to dogs, giving them a recognizable and legal presence. It entails letting go the linguistic requirements that entrap a dog in the series of conditional similitudes that make him or her reflect us as a diminished subjectivity incapable of expressing the hopes and disappointments of a canine agency. And it begins with letting go the privilege on which we humans have based our economies of techno-science, aesthetics, and ethical engagements—particularly, in the case of dogs, friendship, or at least the form described as mutually willing.

My thinking is aided by a wide range of discussions that have interrogated the binary structure of human-animal relations from different perspectives. And it is particularly facilitated by two accounts of humans responding not to *animals* or to *the* animal, but to dogs. It is these two accounts—both of which are at once autobiography and critical reflection—that occupy most of my discussion in this chapter for the obvious reason that they make real efforts to account for an ethics of dog-human relations—a "cynical friendship," if you will. But there is also the reason, which I cannot fully explore here, that the designation "human-animal" has already been shown to be too broad, for my responses to the dog sitting next to me are vastly—even abyssally—different from my responses to the foxes, skunks, hawks, snakes, tarantulas, deer, and other beasts (my neighbor the pharmacist!) that regularly pass through my backyard.

The cumulative accounts of the preceding chapters, I hope, will make plain that the view of dogs inherited by us living in the twenty-first-century West took shape about two hundred years ago, and that any possibility of being surprised in our relations with dogs will have to account for this inheritance. By turning back to the eighteenth century when institutions and discourses of regulation and manipulation of animals attained their modern form, I have set the stage for showing that the accounts of direct engagements by twenty-first-century humans with their canine companions perpetuate those institutions and discourses. Ultimately and even inadvertently these accounts privilege humans even while trying not to. By following the different attempts to overcome or twist free of anthropocentrism, I hope to open other possibilities, ones that do not try so much to overcome a difference between humans and dogs, as to begin interrogating the difference itself. It is in finally allowing that dogs are not humans, admitting that the analogies formed between them and humans require prompt qualification (both are mortal, both are responsive, though in profoundly different manners) that we dog lovers might respond to a dog with an allowance for the surprise necessary to allowing her to perform as an individual rather than as the reproduceable representation of an archetype. I do not think a simple return to Pope's indirect friendship of three centuries ago is possible, or even desirable; it stands out simply as a different mode of possible friendship whose difference is marked in it having become incomprehensible, illegible to us now. Whatever the actual tenor of those friendships, they were by no means—for Pope and his dogs living in them, or for us looking at them as an alien, irretrievable possibility—innocent, Edenic, or pastoral, for they took place in a different writing, a different landscape. Nonetheless, I do hold that we might begin rethinking our responses to animals by involving some of the terms of indirection, by letting go the need for description, for visualization conducted as hypotyposis, ekphrasis, or deixis. My hope is that by taking up the determinations of human-canine relations, and how they epitomize the broader human-animal relations, and by considering how and where the discourse of breed persists, we might find alternative futures for dogs and humans together that can allow for intimacy within difference.

The question of a "cynical friendship" is complicated by the fact that dogs hold a double status in today's discourse on human-animal relations, and wholly because of the dominance of breed. On the one hand, *malgré* Levinas, breed has given dogs a recognizable face, but one that enables them to be responded to only as something like bastard citizens, in that they are possessed of a quasi-subjectivity sustained by breed histories and by the structures of conditional similitude. On the other hand, when they cannot serve any mimetic function, they remain the bothersome cur that is sacrificed to facilitate the citizenship of breed dogs. This double status is unique among nonhumans; while other domesticated animals have been subjected to breed technology, none of their mixed-breed or unpapered varieties receive the opprobrium of the cur, which is not just impure, but also improper. The cur is the non-category of dog. As such, the cur complicates the question of human-animal relations by compelling us to ask if "animal" covers both breed dog and cur in the same way (and this complication leads to the further question of whether "animal" can refer to horses, cats, or cows in the same way as snakes, hawks, or fleas).[4] In order to engage with that complication, I shall ground consideration of a friendship of indirection or obliquity in the present by examining twenty-first-century accounts of human relations with breed dogs.

The narratives by Alice Kuzniar and Donna Haraway of their relations with dogs. These accounts stand out because they are both by scholars—albeit in very different fields—aware of trends in animal studies or critical thinking, and they both describe in detail the ways that relations with dogs can facilitate a less violent response to other nonhumans. Kuzniar is trained as a literary theorist, while Haraway is trained as a scientist. Kuzniar writes of her dogs in repose, as domestic companions and pets, while Haraway engages with her dogs performatively in competitive agility trials. In examining these two works, I shall bear in mind the question of whether and to what extent human-canine relations in the twenty-first century have wrested free of the breed discourse that took shape in eighteenth-century Britain and that I have shown to be a prime enforcer of the regulation and manipulation of dogs. These present-day canine celebrations fulfill the modern conventions of human-dog relations so completely as to demand consideration of other possibilities, perhaps and at least that of engaging with dogs obliquely, building from the face-to-face encounter that has made dogs legible in expected ways and at the same time has become a paradigm for challenging human privilege. This is a possibility that has been raised by suggestions—made in response to Haraway's narrative—of just letting go of the abyssal divide between humans and animals; I contend that such suggestions simply displace the divide behind the face-to-face encounters with breed dogs, with categorical identification rather than individual surprise. An oblique encounter might rather "let go" the desire for a canine face that constructs a canine subjectivity through conditional similitudes. This possibility has been raised—though not in reference to dogs or their double status—by thinkers seeking an ethical discourse that would align humans and animals with less privilege on one side and less violence toward the other. If these latter suggestions do not forgo an abyssal division, they do open abyssal avenues for interrogating our responses to the dogs we share our lives with. The cynical friendship I propose begins at the abyssal divide, admitting that multiple divisions yawn between modern humans and modern dogs, and suggesting that relations, and even friendships, can develop within that divide.

Among twenty-first-century writers on dogs, there are two different responses to the historical fact that breed has contributed to the existence of almost any dog in the West. The first leaves unquestioned the history of breed and its consequential effect on the human capacity, or willingness, to engage with a dog. This is the response that identifies individual dogs by breeds, accepting their breed characteristics as what makes them preferable to other dogs. In this response, it is the breed, not individuals, that provides the representation supportive of the subject-formation of the human-canine engagement—and in this response, the engagement necessarily retains this hyphenated form. This response appears in the work of Alice Kuzniar, below. The second response is aware of the effects of taxonomizing animals, of regulating them through various laws, designations, narratives, and breeding technologies; and with such awareness, this response either attempts to evade the technological dominance by embracing mutts—as President Obama would have liked to do—or it embraces breeds and their technological preservation. This embrace can entail the justification that technology has benefited dogs through regulated breeding, or it can put forth the argument that technology is an inescapable quality of the modern landscape in which dogs and humans alike are shaped by powers of "improvement," and can come together today, more than before, in a coevolution of mutual improvement. This second response is epitomized by the work of Donna Haraway.

Beyond these accounts dealing with dogs, there is also a body of theoretical and philosophical writing that has focused particularly on the questions concerning human-animal difference. Many of these works take their cue from Derrida's animal essays, or from developments in post-humanist thinking and in feminist theory. Inevitably, then, these works situate the questions of human-animal relations alongside efforts to rethink, in one way or another, the dominance of "Man" (the carnophallogocentric subject) in the modern world. Together, at least some of these works offer a way of reorienting our thinking about animals that could lead us from the reliance on breed. These suggestions raise a possibility not necessarily of punctuating humanism but of bending the discourse on interactions between beings away from oppositional dichotomies.

MELANCHOLIC WHIPPETS AND JOYFUL AUSSIES

In my view, Alice Kuzniar's study of her relation with her two whippets, *Melancholia's Dog*, stands at the vanguard of animal studies, and is probably the most important book written in the past fifteen years on human-dog relations. This is because Kuzniar brings her training in critical theory to bear on her study to make it considerably more than a personal account; she rigorously pursues the thinking that begins at the abyssal limit between humans and animals by wondering at the "mute intimacy that can arise between" two beings so profoundly divided.[5] Her rigor compels her to qualify her thinking from the start with the question "how can we presume to know [a dog] can be so attuned to our feelings?"[6] This uncertainty, this unwillingness to impose an understanding on her canine friends, overarches most of her thinking. It is because this is a serious effort to think critically about the relations between a modern human and her modern dogs that the book warrants serious reading.

Framing the consideration of human-canine relations within a psychoanalytic discourse of melancholy enables Kuzniar to focus on the reticence of dogs to join us in our babbling, our incessant chatter that she calls by the term, from Walter Benjamin, *Überbenennung*. In this sense, canine reticence becomes other than dumbness—which compels humans to denigrate dogs or to idealize them;[7] it becomes rather a "sovereign reserve" that calls for "an attentive listening" from the humans who care to engage with dogs apart from domination. Through her serious and rigorous effort at "attentive listening," Kuzniar opens a way for human-canine relations that lies apart from the privileged subject and all that entails, for she can avoid the pitfalls of claiming a sameness as an admission to animality within ourselves. The point she returns to repeatedly is the ambivalent recognition that she stands in an "uncertainty and unbridgeable distance from the pet that is otherwise so close"; this recognition, in fact, constitutes the central point of her reflections, for it is "our resignation to the fact of this separation," she says, "that renders us bereft."[8] Instead of claiming to know, of claiming to perceive what is there in its presence, Kuzniar orients her attentiveness as a subject that finds itself alone, removed from what it most wants to know, what it feels close to at the same time that it finds its capacity to listen interrupted.

It is this non-privileged—let's say unprivileged—subject Kuzniar introduces that would offer an opportunity of engaging with dogs without subjugating them or without admitting them into our company as lesser, dumb beings. This possibility returns us to the suggestion by Matthew Calarco that we look to the animal "*as if* we have missed or misinterpreted the Other's trace."[9] Such a possibility, it would seem, could bypass the assumption that privileged knowledge entails the capacity to improve the object, to make it closer to its "as such," and could avoid the accompanying gestures of conditional similitude and analogy that forever set a dog in the relation of mimetic representation calling for historicization. More importantly, the similitude between human and dog would be conditioned by an uncertainty that opens relations onto possibilities other than privilege, perhaps even an utterly surprising—or frightening—possibility.

In this same direction, Kuzniar pursues an identification with her dogs in terms, again, of psychoanalytic accounts of melancholy. Considering the experience of having one of her dogs die, she observes that "the inability to articulate or measure one's bereavement is why one grieves so intensely for departed pets. . . . In her inability to abandon mourning, the melancholic person is faithful to the lost object, so faithful, as if she were . . . a dog herself: she wishes, in her mourning, to be as faithful to the pet as it was to her in life."[10] Her emulation of canine ethics subjects Kuzniar to a conditional similitude in which she would be a dog if she could. And before she gets to the point where she could say what the canine ethics, *as such*, would be, she finds herself up against the experience of having "missed or misinterpreted the Other's trace," unable to know anything beyond the dog's absence. Thus, she defines "melancholia" in terms of canine companionship: "However close we are to the canine pet, that closeness can never be enough and we are always conscious of the obliqueness and imperfection that govern our communion with it and, hence, of a fundamental muteness."[11] The "muteness" here belongs to the human whose attentive closeness to a dog leads to the desire for greater closeness, greater understanding, undercut by the constant recognition that little more than chatter—*Überbenennung*—can be offered to the ever-reticent dog. Such attentive muteness, which puts Kuzniar in the role of confronting her grief *as if* she were a reticent dog, holds the possibility of dissolving the frame that presents a landscape as a known totality, and of obviating the requisite "as such" demanded of every being in the landscape. This obliqueness intruding on her communion compels her to renounce a claim to knowledge. Needless to say, this is Kuzniar's most radical insight, and one that warrants far more examination in animal studies than it has received.

And the reason it has not been taken up by others, perhaps, is that it is a difficult stance to maintain. To be *as if* one were a dog develops a responsiveness to alterity that turns away from a face-to-face encounter. This oblique response turns away from privileging itself as the singular consciousness and mode of knowing; it would, perhaps, allow the engagement between self and other to occur as an event in which knowing—understood in its modern, dominating, mode—would not necessarily arise, or be sought. Such a response would begin from a subject that is already other in itself, that casts itself in an "as if" precluding the "as such" of self-presence, of the "proper name." The bereavement Kuzniar feels for her dead canine friend extends itself into a sense of being bereft of subjective knowing. The oblique response Kuzniar describes here begins not from a privileged, knowing perspective, but from that of reticence, holding oneself back. In Kuzniar's psychoanalytic terms, such reticence is figured as a loss; and taken to its fullest extent, such bereavement would effectively deprivilege the responsiveness a human would bear toward her dogs and perhaps dispossess her from the framed landscape. Instead of a governing subject based on privilege, Kuzniar raises the possibility of another subject, allowing for other ways of responding to dogs: this possibility begins with bereavement, being dispossessed, the experience of loss.

Kuzniar addresses this loss directly in order to account for the ways we moderns signify our relations with dogs. For the melancholic, "representation is allowed on the condition of denying loss, which it amply papers over," Kuzniar says; and the language of melancholy is characterized by "its proliferation of signs and a signifying exaltation," which is motivated by the compensation linguistic production provides for the sense of loss.[12] On the one hand, this proliferation could be understood simply as the dog lover's tendency to talk about dogs too much; but on the other hand, and more to Kuzniar's point, it is found in "dog collectibles," such as "porcelain figurines, even handsome coffee table books on dogs." These "metonymic, fetishistic signs," Kuzniar contends, "evoke a pleasurable but imprecise nostalgia"; the endlessness of their production is driven by their compensatory function.[13] Making her point directly, Kuzniar provides this formulation: "The pet dog in today's culture is granted the extravagant, intense value that marks it as compensatory for an originary loss. . . . As the metonymy of pleasure, the dog serves as a replacement for the archaic Thing, which Kristeva locates in the maternal."[14]

As an explanation for the deep feelings people have for dogs, this seems perfectly feasible. And it seems just on the verge of engaging the abyssal fear of an un-represented relation between her and a dog. But it also has the effect of making "the" dog into a function. As a metonymy, a dog would fulfill a role that would make any one dog replaceable not just by collectibles, but by another dog. In this formulation, the dog can make up for the human's sense of loss. But the question arises, would a canine subject also experience such a loss? Or would this be the sort of flaw Derrida writes of that, yet again, privileges the human by sparking specifically *human* self-consciousness, or, in Kuzniar's terms, "a proliferation of signs" into a discourse about dogs, but in which dogs serve as referents not for the lost presence shared with a human but of the loss experienced by a human? Kuzniar here has sidestepped the "unbridgeable distance" she has recognized lying between her and the dogs "otherwise so close" by troping "the" dog into a "replacement for the archaic Thing." Her dogs, which she represents to herself through their breed—whippets—ensure her a continual compensation for the "originary loss"; they provide her with a "replacement" both for the "thing" she mourns melancholically as well as for each other. Through their breed they provide a sustained making-present that Derrida questions in representation. On the one hand, he says, "to render present would be to bring to presence, into presence to cause or allow to come by presenting. On the other hand . . . to render present, like all 'rendering' and like all restitution, would be to repeat, to be able to repeat." In this sense, a sustainable *re*-presenting "marks the repetition, *in*, *for*, and *by* the subject, *a parti subjecti* of a presence that otherwise would present itself to the subject without depending on it."[15] The returning present, Derrida goes on to say, doubtless "already had the form of what is for and before the subject but was not at its disposition in this preposition itself." It is in the *re*-presentation that the subject installs the idea of the present before it, at its disposal; and, Derrida continues, "this putting at one's disposal is the very thing that constitutes the subject as a subject."[16] Derrida's comments, made in regard to Heidegger's thinking of *Vorstellen* as "the mark of modernity,"[17] have far-reaching implications, to which I will return below. For now, they raise a strong suggestion about seeing a dog through the representation of a breed: in looking at her dogs as whippets, Kuzniar turns them collectively into the singular representation whose categorical referent, "whippet," precedes her sufficiently to constitute her as a subject who can then engage with them in conventional (representational) ways. Reticence becomes a signifier in the discourse on human feelings for dogs, rather than the holding back from *Überbenennung*.

As I have shown in two previous chapters, a common gesture in breed discourse has been to ground the putative history of a breed in a romanticized pastoralism that has been lost, instituted by Buffon in the primordial dog choosing to befriend humans. Accounts of the Foxhound strategically obscure the rigors of breeding manipulation to create the sense that the modern hound was a natural development of necessity, while accounts of foxhunting make the sport into the extension of ancient modes of human engagement with nature that likewise seeks the coagency with humans. And the romances of Walter Scott turn his fictionalized canine characters as well as the real dogs he kept into indigenous elements of the native regional landscape. Especially in Scott's account, we can see the effect of this nostalgia, as the dogs embody the Scotland that is perennially under threat by the modern world of unified Britain. Kuzniar's nostalgia replicates those earlier manifestations, bridging the gap between her and her whippets by turning them into the representation of something lost, a *re*-presenting of an originariness that facilitates a discourse of subjective completeness, the "proper name" that cannot be pronounced but that must be preserved as loss. The dog who chooses, in the self-presence of pastoral (or maternal) naïveté, to befriend her can never be recalled, and that friendship can now only be represented in the mourning for its loss that constitutes, for Kuzniar, the subject choosing, as if she were a dog, the dogs she will befriend.

Kuzniar's psychoanalytic explanation for the affection people feel for their canine companions, then, cannot get away from the discourse of breed, because Kuzniar herself embraces

Photograph of a Whippet. Photograph by Marcin Błaszkowski, Wikimedia Commons, 2009.

that discourse as a natural—or unexamined—component of dogs. And because it is the representational function of breed that facilitates her capacity as subject to represent herself as a dog. Just how overwhelmingly breed discourse governs the reflections Kuzniar offers becomes apparent in the references she makes to particular dogs—both to her own whippets and the dogs she looks at in photographs and writings. The particularity that she finds in the photographs trouble and embarrass her, interrupting the representational service provided by breed. One detail to keep in mind while reading the way Kuzniar describes these dogs, however, is that the honesty with which she writes of her embarrassment raises the distinct possibility that she is intentionally performing *as if* she were the modern subject dependent on breed.

Kuzniar clearly loves her whippets. As she turns her discussion to photographs of dogs, she suggests that "Our fascination with canine photography, especially of a breed that we love, . . . derives from this desire to wrest a secret from the animal being. . . . To gaze at my whippets, too, is to sweep my eyes over their smooth fur, to study them in their perfection, namely, to dwell with their muteness."[18] The "secret" Kuzniar desires to discover is contained in the whippets' muteness that she dwells with, and her desire is an aspect of the nostalgia and melancholy that she has explored in the pages just before this statement. The photographs she discusses as "works that meditate on silence" and "point to what lies beyond signification—an ephemerality, an expectancy of what is about to happen, an elsewhere that intimates a realm beyond the human senses, and even a self-contained wholeness in the dog that has no need of words."[19] It is not so much what the photographs depict that Kuzniar wants to consider, but the experience of encountering a photograph's "resistance to signification," which replicates her experience of looking at her quiet dogs.[20] As representations, the photographs have already put the imaged dogs at the disposal of the viewing subject, however, framing the "expectancy" into a modern engagement in which the representation is placed before, and at the disposal of, the subject, who is constituted as the viewing and *re*-presenting subject. These whippets who embody the "perfection" that compensates for the melancholy stemming from the originary loss are similarly *re*-presented in Kuzniar's loving gaze that sets them in a "self-contained wholeness" beyond her grasp. Yearning for the secret "realm beyond the human senses," Kuzniar represents her dogs as silent yet visible, framed in their breed perfection that can be experienced by her only in its withdrawal. In the directness of her viewing, and perhaps even in her yearning to engage in that realm beyond, Kuzniar sets up her photographic readings as representations of her engagement with her breed dogs. Melancholically aware of the restrictions and impositions of the modern mode, she rehearses the modern engagement of representing a dog as being at her disposal, as sadly and mutely sharing her melancholy.

The perfection Kuzniar studies in her whippets is equivalent to the bondedness she has developed with them by dwelling "with their muteness," for it is this that sustains the loss that lies at the root of the nostalgia. At an early point in her discussion on shame, which "is constitutive of the subjective experience of selfhood,"[21] she refers generally to her whippets' demonstrations of shame when they transgress their "sense of etiquette and cleanliness." And she adds this comment: "It is my own belief, though my reasons for it are merely based on living attentively with female whippets, that isolation from community, which is what shame is about, is much feared by dogs."[22] Certainly anyone who has lived "attentively" with dogs—or horses, or birds, or other animals—would agree with Kuzniar's belief along with the openly unscientific basis for that belief. My question is how "community" and "muteness"—which seem to hold a strong relation to the dogs' "perfection"—work within Kuzniar's personal account of her oblique and reticent relations with her "female whippets."

The frankness of this account makes it possible to mark the limits to the communal muteness Kuzniar constructs out of the melancholic recognition that the dogs who are so close to her also stand at an unbridgeable remove. The photographs that she looks to as an equally ambivalent experience of anticipating a reticence in fact reveal her dependence on breed discourse. For in stark contrast to the perfection of her whippets are the photographs she discusses by Walter Schels, who "eschews both beauty and approachability." These photographs

> are of repulsive curs, made even less attractive by being photographed close to the muzzle and at low angle. Although the collection begins with a shar-pei—with its disconcertingly strange facial folds—most dogs appear to be of the bulldog and pit bull variety, though without any purebred lines. They have drooping jowls, irregular bites, graying muzzles, and puss [*sic*] collected under their eyes. In some photos, the close-up makes the wet, shiny nostrils or tongue look disturbingly foreign and obscenely large. By sheer virtue of this focus on the ugly face, Schels raises the question of shame.[23]

The particular photograph Kuzniar includes as an example of Schels's collection is entitled "Dog, English Bulldog." It is worth noting that the photographic subject identified with a breed name is transposed by Kuzniar into the more nebulous "bulldog and pit bull variety." These are the dogs Kuzniar categorizes as "ugly," "repulsive," and "disconcerting"—in short, they are curs; regardless of their breeding, Kuzniar makes them curs by expelling them from her community. Their ugliness is wholly synonymous with their being curs and with their expulsion. Her attention to the physical details of the dogs photographed emphasizes the disgust she experiences in contrast to the perfection she studies in her whippets—dogs she identifies consistently by breed. Whereas she has built a community of oblique and reticent attentiveness with her whippets, in looking at Schels's pictures, she says, "the ugliness of the dogs makes looking at the portraits seem invasive."[24] Instead of community, the experience is of shame—but not a shame she imputes to the curs themselves, but to herself, because "in the excess of [the cur's] deformities," she finds that the dog "cannot be made to signify." The "invasive probing" she blames herself for stems from her repulsion. These dogs are shame itself, as she indicates when she says, "Their look is profoundly sad, as if they knew that they were unwanted dogs."[25] Their sadness resembles that of her dogs, but on the condition of delineating the frame to her melancholic community: she and her whippets do not want these ugly dogs, whose shame is that they do in fact bring her to the realm she had longed for, beyond the human. Her repulsion comes from their non-significance; they hold no representational status, and no relation to the nostalgia that frames the community Kuzniar has developed with her whippets. She does not *want* the "disturbingly foreign" dogs that are "disconcerting," "irregular," "obscene," and "ugly," because they represent no traceable origin that can be desired as the unpronounceable "proper name." In the terms of her own discourse, these ugly dogs lie outside of the community of mute representations of perfection. Their "sad" look of being "unwanted dogs" marks, and very plainly, the limit of the community that Kuzniar has established with her perfect female whippets. It is only by sacrificing the ugly dogs—keeping them (and, as Sydenham Edwards might add, their incessant barking) at bay—that Kuzniar's community of muteness can maintain itself.

For Kant "one kind of ugliness alone cannot be represented . . . without destroying all aesthetical delight, and consequently artistic beauty, namely, that which excites *disgust*."[26] As Derrida comments in "Economimesis," disgust is "the absolute excluded," and its exclusion is from the landscape in which the privileged aesthetic subject represents itself in a dialogue with mute nature. Disgust, he says, "is unrepresentable. And at the same time it is unnameable in its singularity. If one could name it or represent it, it would begin to enter into the auto-affective circle of mastery or reappropriation. An economy would be possible. The disgusting X [is] . . . the absolute other of the system."[27] The ugly, repulsive curs disgust Kuzniar precisely because of their singularity. And their singularity stems from their breedlessness, the fact that Kuzniar cannot, or will not, give them a name or make them into representations of a breed standard with a narratable history. "Shar-pei" and "English bull-dog" are certainly breed names, but Kuzniar turns from them to focus wholly on the "disconcertingly strange" and "disturbingly foreign" particulars of these non-whippets. And, in spite of her claim that they "cannot be made to signify," that their eyes are "unreadable," she does in fact "read" them when she applies the conditional, "as if they knew," that imputes to them a subjectivity framed in their incapacity to provide the representation necessary for the human subject who cares about beautiful relations with dogs.[28] Unlike the originary breed dogs who "instinctively" want to be our friend, who always look as though they want to be called by us, these curs have no name, no origin, no history that enables them to perform the replaceability, to be called. With this gesture, Kuzniar, who is genuinely capable of finding a way to engage with her whippets apart from the privileged subject, has imputed the conditional similitude of shameful knowledge to the curs, which she then makes into her own experience by way of empathizing with them for their shame in being disgusting. They have no place in the economimesis she has constructed with her female whippets because they hold no representative status of breed—or at least a breed she recognizes. Could it be that the shame she attributes to herself for intruding on the curs' ugliness is in fact not her own melancholic isolation—for she has a community—but a deflective gesture to obscure the sacrifice of unnameable individuality necessary to framing the economimesis of her aesthetic relations with whippets?

This question persists as Kuzniar turns from photographs of curs to those by William Wegman, whose subjects are not "unwanted" or disgusting. Kuzniar locates the "empathetic shame" experienced on looking at Wegman's dogs thus: "Instead of the viewer being unsettled because confronted with the ugliness of the animal, here uneasiness arises . . . from one's lurking sense that one's curiosity comes at the expense of the dog subjugated to strange poses."[29] The dogs themselves are not shameful, and they are not individualized, but clearly and notably, for Kuzniar, a definite breed. She says, "The breed that Wegman has selected as his signature is not incidental."[30] In these photographs, the dogs give up their disgusting individuality to attain the identity of a selected breed that serves as the signature of the artist. There is no ugliness in these pictures for Kuzniar, because there are no individual dogs to threaten her interpretive ability. Here the disconcerting ethical confrontation with the possibility of having missed the trace of the other, as Calarco pinpoints it, has been bypassed in favor of the less disgusting interpretive engagement with a signature, the representation of the artist.

Photograph of Three Shar-Pei Dogs in a Car. Wikimedia Commons, 2005.

The uneasiness Kuzniar feels in seeing the Weimaraners comes from the fact that they are someone else's dogs, engaged in relations and in a signed landscape beyond her own that could provide an affirming analogy to her own aesthetic community.

Moving from the confrontation with disgusting canine individuality, Kuzniar explores the experience of "empathetic shame" arising from curiosity. Wegman's signature Weimaraners appear within the economimetic writing that supports the "empathetic shame," so that Kuzniar does not succumb to interpretive failure. The photographs of the Weimaraners wearing wigs and human clothes come close to challenging Kuzniar, leading her to use some of the same qualifiers with which she expelled the ugly curs. "Often the discrepancy of the canine body peeking out from under human dress makes this body all too visible," she says, "as if they were trying to hide." She views them interpretatively through a conditional similitude very like that she used with the bulldog; just after taking the sense of embarrassment onto herself, she finds it reflected in the Weimaraners, who display a self-dividing shame. But empathizing with the shame poses a problem, one that gets right to the heart of the process of economimesis. To recognize the Weimaraners' shame compels Kuzniar to feel her own shame, her own self-division, which interrupts the connectedness she finds with her whippets in her own landscape of beauty, which, as a landscape, now appears in its written quality. So she says, "Particularly disconcerting are the shots where human hands appear from out of the dress, emphasizing the oddity of the dog's face."[31] The doggishness of the Weimaraners threatens to break out of the costume, to become, as she says, naked. And it is the possibility of nakedness that Kuzniar has associated with shame. Here, though, that nakedness is the doggishness that arouses the interpretive act of signing the Weimaraners with the conditional similitude expressing the shame that can be empathized with. Even with their purebred lines, Wegman's subjects become shameful when they threaten Kuzniar's aesthetic subject with excessively visible doggishness: their human clothes draw attention to the physicality of the dogs, making too apparent the empathetically subjective act of imputing human-like qualities to them through narratives of breed history, or through seeing them as signatures, or through gestures of conditional similitude. These canine signatures are anything but reticent, as they signify the process of conditional similitude itself, of trying to pass *as if* they were the ones empathizing with shameful humans. The shame Kuzniar describes feeling while indulging in a curiosity about the dogs' appearance comes out of an excessively obvious gesture of conditional similitude, in which the conditionality peeks out and becomes "all too visible." In wearing human clothes, Wegman's Weimaraners overdetermine the feeling of empathy that can only be expressed toward dogs who are recognizable through being seen as becoming almost human. In drawing them toward representational human subjectivity, the empathetic human tries to hide the conditionality of the similitude. The condition of similitude is that we forget that a dog has qualities that are not human, and wherever those canine qualities are too visible, they become disconcerting—just as did the Shar-pei's "strange facial folds" in Schels's picture—to emphasize "the oddity of the dog's face."

Kuzniar is far too honest and thoughtful—attentive—simply to allow herself to construct a canine interiority analogous to the human's. What makes her book worth taking seriously is her refusal to do just that, for she insistently reminds us and herself of a dog's inaccessibility. As she says, in concluding the discussion of Schels's and Wegman's pictures, the human clothes worn by the Weimaraners "externalize that which blocks approach to the animal psyche and reflect the impossibility of photography to access that which—even in the age of postmodernity—we long for it to reveal."[32] Kuzniar's "Reflections on our Animal Kinship" is more than a critical study of literary and visual accounts. It discloses Kuzniar's own shame in struggling—and failing—to uncover the mystery of the dogs whose proximity underscores the "unbridgeable distance" between them and the woman who loves them. It "denudes," disconcertingly, the writing of the aesthetic and empathetic subject who can only represent herself within the landscape always already grammatized as breed. The capacity for letting her shame show, without knowing whether or not it will find empathy or disgust, spurs thought about human-canine relations in a fertile direction by questioning the capacity of this human subject to know, and by demonstrating the dependence of even the postmodern or post-humanist thinker on the economimesis maintained by breed discourse. For the longing Kuzniar feels for a revelation of canine subjectivity is itself perpetuated by her dependence on breed identity, and the sacrificial expulsion of dogs that cannot signify, that hold no representational status that would allow them to be reproduced as "fetishist signs" replacing "the archaic Thing."[33] The visual perfection evoked by a recognized breed eliminates the excess of chatter, but at the cost of instituting the economimesis that demands as sacrifice the expulsion of the ugly, disgustingly individual dog, the cur. Because of this sacrifice, because of its modern necessity, and because Kuzniar cannot but feel discomfiture at the sight of dogs violating the grammar of conditional similitude—making the conditionality too overt—her postmodern longing does not quite open itself, cannot open itself, to surprise, instead protecting itself from the disgust of anything incalculable, unpredictable. But while breed remains a necessity for Kuzniar as the standard of beauty, she does make disconcertingly naked the writing of the loss structuring the subject seeking to love a dog. In doing so, she raises possibilities for an oblique engagement from a position of being bereft, a "perhaps" that has been ignored, suppressed by the conditionality of similitude. This "perhaps" will be something I return to after considering a twenty-first-century claim of direct engagement.

Donna Haraway embraces the technological mode of knowing her canine partner, and asserts that such an embrace makes possible the move beyond humanist discourses. Haraway situates her relation with her dog, Cayenne, within the performative events of training as a team for competitive agility trials. Thinking in terms of coactivity, of the coordination between teammates, Haraway can reorient subjectivity to an interactive engagement rather than the domination of objects. So, she situates the account of her engagement with Cayenne within a Marxist-feminist perspective as she suggests that "we might nurture responsibility with and for other animals better by plumbing the category of labor more than the category of rights, with its inevitable preoccupation with similarity, analogy, calculation, and honorary membership in the expanded abstraction of the Human."[34] With this, Haraway bypasses the debate over valuations of self and other by casting the subject wholly in terms of labor, for "in the idiom of labor, animals are working subjects, not just worked objects."[35] In this sense, the human subject would seem to lose the privilege granted it in the techno-aesthetic modernity in which it is delineated as the knowing, judging being that can and should manage the landscape. With the emphasis on labor, the "subject" becomes the performative coordination of two (or more) agents, rather than the dominant human who perceives the dog as a necessary element in the aesthetically unified, and legally exclusive, landscape. The subject would be neither Haraway nor Cayenne individually, then, but the event of their training that incorporates them both into an active engagement enduring through the agility run. In their training they attain a "copresence," which Haraway describes as the play "that makes us new, that makes us into something that is neither one nor two." She goes on to say this:

> The power of language is purported to be its potentially infinite inventiveness. . . . however, the inventive potency of play redoes beings in ways that should not be called language but that deserve their own names. Besides, it is not potentially *infinite* expressiveness that is interesting for play partners but, rather, unexpected and nonteleological inventions that can take mortal shape only within the finite and dissimilar naturalcultural [*sic*] repertoires of companion species. Another name for those sorts of inventions is joy.[36]

The "redoing" of beings that Haraway attends to throughout her book is what makes her account so promising to the prospect of a posthumanist animal studies, since it leaves behind the concept of a statically framed ethos whose knowledge is cumulative. With this performative subject, Haraway can describe—though as she says early on, she is "needy for ways to specify these matters in non-humanist terms"[37]—her relations not just in terms of what she feels or wonders *about* Cayenne, but in terms of their interactions together.

Since training for Haraway occurs as a joyful "redoing" of the partners engaged in their mutual interaction, the event forsakes the limits of teleology or meaning outside of the playful training event, to allow a "coming into being of something unexpected." The unexpected quality of what comes into being is what makes it joyful, and its performative temporariness, its temporality, is what places it outside of the manageable frame of humanist discourse. "Training," Haraway says, "requires calculation, method, discipline, science, but training is for opening up what is not known to be possible, but might be, for all the intra-acting partners."[38] Such openness to possibility, to the as yet unknown, makes these performative engagements powerfully fertile for an as yet unknown thinking about human-animal relations. And the power lies precisely in the openness, the potentiality offered in each event in itself, rather than as an event that contributes categorically to a static organization outside itself.

In this regard, one of the most potent moments in the event of reading this book comes when Haraway says that "the question between animals and humans here is, Who are you? and so, Who are we?" And she goes on to insist that this remain a question: "*Who* is not a relative pronoun in the co-constitutive relationships called training; it is an interrogative one. . . . *who* refers to partners-in-the-making through the active relations of coshaping, not to possessive human or animal individuals whose boundaries and natures are set in advance of the entanglements of becoming together."[39] As long as the entanglements occur as interrogatives, it would seem, the ways humans and dogs come together would cease to require regulation, management, or lead to improvement of one partner or the other. And as long as the interrogative could occur as an event for itself, the coshaping could continually raise possibilities for more than new ways of talking about the human-dog event, but also new ways of dwelling in the world. Such is the potency of Haraway's account of this coshaping performative entanglement that it would seem, along with Kuzniar's oblique reticence, to cast the modern subject down from its representational privilege and into an engagement with dogs opened otherwise than through similitudes conditioned by the imputation that a dog wishes to approximate the human. Such engagement would seem to obviate both privilege and similitude because of its non-teleological, active performativity. As long as the question reaches no answer, the performance would be oriented toward no telos, and the performers could respond to one another apart from any face that would connote an ethos—or breed identity.

But Haraway cannot resist answering the question posed by "the co-constitutive relationships called training."[40] Her answers derive from a need to assert her knowledge, and the way she asserts her ability to know is telling, for it reflects a prominent strain in her account that goes well beyond the sections detailing her involvement with Cayenne. In the entanglement of companionship and partnership that Haraway finds in training, subjectivity comes into being as the active working partners respond to one another. When Haraway sets this performative, coshaping subject in terms of actual training, however, she intermixes references to this posthumanist subject with references to the privileged subject of the humanist tradition. In the context of detailing some of the governing principles of responsive training, Haraway states categorically,

> The philosophic and literary conceit that all we have is representations and no access to what animals think and feel is wrong. Human beings do, or can, know more than we used to know, and the right to gauge that knowledge is rooted in historical, flawed, generative cross species practices. . . . To claim not to be able to communicate with and to know one another and other critters, however imperfectly, is a denial of mortal entanglements (the open) for which we are all responsible and in which we respond. . . . Response is comprehending that subject-making is real. Response is face-to-face in the contact zone of an entangled relationship. Response is the open.[41]

In this passage, Haraway makes a strong case for the potency of responsiveness. But in order to make her case, she must assert that response is knowing, and not the qualified knowing that Kuzniar describes, or the ethical experience that Calarco derives from his reading of Levinas. Haraway seems to be at odds with herself here, since knowing holds considerable importance for her—she *must* know—so that response, which she does say "is irreducible to calculation," entails at least a good bit of knowing in the traditional scientific sense relying on a subjective self-presence, and with the attendant promise of an evolutionary expansion of gaugeable knowledge. If knowledge can be measured through its accumulation, then it maintains a historical continuity that reinvokes a Hegelian subject; in this regard, the coshaping performances of interactive individuals become data-gathering exercises. Knowledge becomes the overarching factor for Haraway, making communication into the exchange of information between self-present individuals. Response in this passage occurs in "face-to-face" encounters, and so only in the occasions when each partner comes with a face that can allow for a recognizable and acceptable response, and that can allow for the directness that matters for Haraway.

In order to achieve this directness, Haraway must denounce a "philosophical and literary conceit." What she denounces—the notion "that all we have is representations"—would be the conceptual framework, or literary imagery that interferes with direct "face-to-face" encounters. Much of Haraway's discussion in this book consists of efforts to clear away the humanist conceits of philosophy and literature that intrude into the openness of response and interrupt the coshaping of performative subjects. There are, it seems to me, two problems at work here that Haraway leaves unexamined, and necessarily so. First is the assumption that "face-to-face" encounters are free of conceits, of representations. Second is her dependence on an opposition between knowing gained through face-to-face encounters and the conceits of philosophy and literature. I shall consider each of these problems in turn.

The face-to-face encounter works, for Haraway, as the event of two beings coming into each other's presence to create a new kinship. She stresses "kin making and family membership," she says, because her concern lies with opening new possibilities of subjectivity that will be found in the responsive encounters between companion species. But the promise and possibility of trans-species encounters cannot be approached, she says, "if the fleshly historical reality of face-to-face, body-to-body subject making across species is denied or forgotten in the humanist doctrine that holds only humans to be true subjects with real histories."[42] Much of what makes Haraway's discussion compelling is this suggestion of a performative subjectivity that is not necessarily replicable and that needs no resolution but remains an unanswered question. But her questions of "who are we?" resolve themselves along determinate lines in these same comments. Setting the coshaping as a kinship puts the performative engagement into the delimiting set of a category that allows for recognizable presence. And a category of "kin" or "family" imposes a set of conditions on both partners that limit the possibilities by which they present themselves to the other. Kinship establishes an exclusionary limit outside of which the unrecognizable, unrelated are kept. Admission within the limit requires a knowable history as well as a recognizable presence, which is to say a face.

The face Haraway responds to comes with a history that intermingles with her own personal history. "That's why I have to tell these stories," she says, "to tease out the personal and collective response required now, not centuries ago."[43] And so she tells her own history, as the scientifically trained daughter of a sportswriter, and that of Cayenne. In a subchapter entitled "Breed Stories: Australian Shepherds," Haraway recounts the narrative of Cayenne's breed, which she says should rather be called "the United States western ranch dog" since it is not from Australia. Haraway begins by rejecting the "Romantic-origin stories" that have Basque immigrants bringing their herding dogs to the western United States by way of Australia. Instead she relates the exploitation of indigenous Americans, first by the Spanish invaders who brought European sheep into the Southwestern desert, and then by the U.S. Army, who slaughtered the descendants of the Spanish sheep who had been adapted by the Navajo to the local environment and culture. And "at some point," despite, she says, the lack of references to herding dogs in official histories of the Spanish conquest and Navajo sheep culture, "the Navajo did enlist the work of dogs for their sheep, mostly for protection from predators who surely came from the same motley of dogs in the West, both English and Iberian in lineage and imaginably even some preconquest dogs, who contributed to Australian shepherds."[44] With her grounding in Marxist feminism, Haraway ends the breed narrative with the statement that "The bedrock test of an Australian shepherd . . . remains the ability to herd with consummate skill. If 'versatility' does not start there, the working breed will not survive."[45] Her interest in this breed comes from its focus on performance as a herding dog, as a working subject. And she is frank about her interest in preserving the breed as a breed of working subjects with histories. She says, "Living in response to these histories is not about guilt and its resultant exterminationist nonsolutions, such as shutting down all stock ranching, encouraging only vegan diets, and working against the deliberate breeding of herding, pet, and show dogs."[46] Unlike Kuzniar, Haraway feels neither guilt nor shame, because the histories, along with the ability to retell them, are necessary to her capacity for response. And without guilt or shame her response is direct, and self-present.

The history Haraway relates is curious not only for its culmination in guiltlessness—what could even be called a reactionary guiltlessness—but also for its corrective function. Rejecting "Romantic-origin stories," as a humanist conceit, she relates an origin story that adheres closely to the conventions of breed narratives. As with the histories of the Foxhound, her narrative connects Australian shepherds to a landscape, which, if not primordial, at least involves indigenous people plying their craftwork. The sheep herded by Cayenne's ancestors, Haraway tells us, continue to provide the wool "spun and woven into the Southwest Indians' exquisite textiles."[47] And to dispel any supposition that these dogs have not played a role in the modern Southwestern United States as necessary as that played by the Foxhound in England, Haraway relates how "a rodeo performer from Idaho named Jay Sisler is part of the story of molding a kind of dog into a contemporary breed."[48] She includes a photograph of Sisler, decked out in his showy cowboy garb, posing with his "performing canine partners,"[49] thus proving with an artifact that such an originary figure really did exist.[50] Haraway's history does not go so far as Buffon's to point to a primordial sheepdog *choosing* to work with a primordial shepherd. Her account bypasses any mythic pastoral naiveté by referring to depredations by the Spanish, then the U.S. Army. And yet, her narrative adheres to the conventions of breed histories that emphasize work and the demands placed on work by the regional environment. Historical verifiability consistently ends with indigenous laborers interacting with the land alongside dogs. No less than in Buffon's account, this interaction—Haraway shifts from "instinct" to saying "the Navajo did *enlist* the work of dogs"—inscribes the breed's proper name that gives it grounding within her landscape of posthumanist truth. And she does this by supplanting humanist myth with historical accuracy. Historical verifiability, work, and regionalism are all motifs in the literary mode of breed-origin narratives that Haraway rejects in order to tell her nonliterary breed-origin narrative: she rejects the mode in order to replicate the genre.

The putative aim of this very conventional anti-Romantic originary narrative is to assert the lack of guilt or embarrassment Haraway feels in embracing breed technology and aesthetics. Toward that end, she presents her encounter with the breed as an apostasy growing from an innocent dalliance. When she was "tempted" to take up the sport of agility training to help her "Aussie-chow cross mutt, Roland" socialize, she turned from the unathletic mutt to look for "a great agility prospect, a.k.a., a high-drive, purpose-bred, puppy athlete."[51] The search, which resulted in her coshaping partnership with Cayenne, involved other face-to-face encounters with people in the Australian-shepherd and agility-training communities. One of these encounters she relates in detail, and says that she approached it with her "alibi as a science studies scholar and look-alike anthropologist."[52] At the moment of her revelatory apostasy, Haraway entered a responsive collaboration in a guise, with her face made into an alibi, perhaps with a touch of shame. But she threw off her alibi to discover her genuine self.

The initial concealment of her self, *as such*, stems from the unease with which she first fell into the breed discourse, and this part of her narrative is very much an apology to make the apostasy work as a productive event. "In the beginning of everything that led to this book," she says in the non-Romantic confession of her revelation, "I was pure at heart, at least in relation to dog breeds." Her purity entailed the naive view that breeds were "the embodiment of animalizing racist eugenics, everything that represents modern people's misuse of other sentient beings for their own instrumental ends."[53] It is such "purity" that she falls from, which is to say, if we catch her irony, the delusional self-righteousness of the "progressive, American middle-class, white bubble . . . the Church of the Shelter Dog, that ideal victim and scapegoat." According to the dogma of this church, breeds are bad and mutts are "good as long as they [are] sterilized; trained to a low standard—lest human control play too big a role . . . and off leash in every possible situation." It is this church that Haraway broke from, as she "fell in love with kinds as well as with individuals."[54] Once she has freed herself of this cloying dogma, Haraway can look for her "purpose-bred" partner who can be highly trained—seemingly unlike Roland the mutt—to present a face with which Haraway herself—no longer disguised in a shame-hiding alibi, but herself *as such*—can work in a performative coshaping.

Except that much of the shaping has already taken place. The account of her acceptance of breeds as a fall from the dogma of political correctness casts her love of kinds as a liberation from the conceits that she rejects in literature and philosophy. The "Church of the Shelter Dog" can thrive, it seems, only in the "white bubble," where progressives are insulated against actual face-to-face working encounters. Outside the bubble are the working people—sheep ranchers, herding-dog breeders, and the agility community—who engage in coshaping relations with dogs. And these people work in the landscape, a written and conventional landscape that comes to be represented in the agility course where Haraway and Cayenne perform their coshaping. In order to be able to present the breed history of Australian shepherds as anything more than a conventional originary narrative—the romanticizing strategies of which Haraway contemns—she must expunge from the history of breeds its discursive conceits to make her telling into a factual account of the meeting of two individuals, a meeting that takes on much the same quality of destiny, of filling a lack, that played such a role in the accounts of the Foxhound. But in the face-to-face encounter, the destiny has governed the canine partner who was "purpose-bred" to have a face that could be recognized and engaged with in the sport the human partner desired to participate in. As an Australian shepherd, Cayenne was bred purposely to perform as a "working subject," and to a degree that the purposeless mutt Roland can attain with only "modest success."[55] Cayenne's only choice can be "enlistment" to fill the lack; this is her socially and morally recognizable proper name in the conventional landscape of work represented in agility training. What Haraway can recognize in her scientifically trained discourse of labor is that because Cayenne comes with an already recognizable face, she is the one Haraway can know; the "prospect" Cayenne offers is of a self-presence that Haraway can interact with directly, without alibis or middle-class romanticizing. Belonging to a working breed, Cayenne offers Marxist Haraway the prospect of an engagement between workers as such, and with more than "modest success."

Haraway insists that she knows her coworker, Cayenne, directly, free from humanist conceits. This insistence is as necessary to her representational account of the coshaping performative subjectivity as are her narratives of her father, her email exchanges with other agility competitors, and her history of the Australian shepherd breed. All these interlocking accounts together portray the face-to-face interactions that create subjectivities through work, and these subjectivities are constituted by the performances in which multiple beings are involved with one another. Haraway thinks through the myriad analogical modes of work through which humans and dogs are intertwined, and she insists on actual intertwinings rather than those of conceits generated discursively. Thus she gives more credence to the relations between human ranchers and their herding dogs, and lab technicians working with hemophiliac dogs, than to philosophers who describe their nonhuman companions without naming them or situating them in working roles, or relating their breed history. It is the failure, she says, "to come face-to-face with animals" that has perpetuated the Cartesian dichotomy seeing animals only as bodies "whose *reactions* are of interest but who have no *presence*, no *face* that demands recognition."[56] A dog's presence or face, she asserts, provides the human with the knowledge that allows both partners to respond when one drops her guise of shame and the other has been technologically made by other humans into a prosthetic representation of a worker.

A notable example Haraway provides of a face-to-face responsive knowing, and prosthetic, relationship is set in the laboratory studying hemophilia with canine subjects. Laboratories

A Blue Merle Australian Shepherd at the Spring 2007 Helena Montana Kennel Club Agility Trial. Courtesy of Ron Armstrong.

provide the workplace where dogs "labor as research models both for their own and for human conditions."[57] In the research project Haraway describes, a litter of Irish setter puppies that had been found to have hemophilia "had to become patients if they were to become technologies and models. The entire labor organization of the laboratory addressed the priority of treating the dogs before anything else. . . . Lab staff could not function as researchers if they did not function as caregivers. Dogs could not work as models if they did not work as patients."[58]

The particular laboratory Haraway refers to is the Francis Owen Blood Research Laboratory at the University of North Carolina, Chapel Hill. The research began in 1947 when two female Irish setters that had been diagnosed with hemophilia A were both purposely bred to produce litters of hemophiliac puppies. Descendants of these setters continue to serve as patient-workers in this laboratory, as the caregiving technicians also serve as techno-breeders who use software to determine the amount of inbreeding necessary to maintain the characteristic of hemophilia, and the amount of outbreeding to exclude unwanted traits. Timothy Nichols, director of the laboratory, says, "All of our breeding is for a purpose—to maintain the germ lines. Researchers design their experiments with planned breeding in mind, to have enough dogs for their studies."[59] These dogs do indeed produce a knowledge, specifically of the drugs that treat hemophilia in humans, for they provide the analogy that enables researchers to determine whether a treatment is safe for humans or not: potential treatments—or products—that were safe for dogs were also deemed safe for humans, and, according to Nichols, "products that were not well tolerated by the dogs were either shelved or reformulated until they were tolerated." So, certainly the dogs are laborers, as Haraway says, in that they produce something; but to say that they are "laboring subjects," or that their face-to-face engagement with the human technicians arises as an "*opportunity* of participating in scientific research"[60] obscures the fact that they are themselves technological products who may engage with humans only so long as they "maintain the germ lines." These dogs effectively stopped being Irish setters many generations ago, for their dominant breed characteristic is the disease hemophilia, regulated by a computer program; if they were to be given a breed name, it would have to be something like "Owen Laboratory Hemophiliac." In this particular coshaping engagement, the answer to Haraway's question "Who are you?" would be simple: the dog created to serve as a hemophiliac, whose face is "known" only in terms of whether or not a drug can be "tolerated." This breed has been created as infinitely replicable victims to enable the researchers "to have enough dogs for their studies." The knowledge produced in the laboratory could be termed "coshaping" only with the allowance that the shaping is heavily weighted in one direction and for the sole benefit of humans. The knowledge gained in this laboratory is anything but posthumanist: not only does it preserve the human privilege, it also rests on the representational function of making the hemophiliac dogs serve as stand-ins for humans, concealing the forced enlistment behind the "opportunity" for participation. And the knowledge has always been predetermined and regulated by the discourse—the landscape—of hemophilia treatment and academic research. It is unashamedly technological, and the dogs serve a singularly prosthetic function, namely, that of representing human hemophiliacs. Any coshaping would consist entirely of the human accumulation of knowledge about an infinitely replicable breed created specifically to serve as laboratory specimens, as representations, or humanist conceits.

Haraway asserts, in this same context, that "dogs have not been passive raw material to the action of others. . . . dogs have not been unchangeable animals confined to the supposedly ahistorical order of nature. . . . dogs and people are emergent as historical beings, as subjects and objects to each other, precisely through the verbs of their relating."[61] This characteristic statement still holds a good deal of truth, that dogs share a cultural discourse with humans; but if this non-romantic history that Haraway wants to tell entails "verbs" that form a dog into a hemophiliac analog of humans, then the suggestion that such dogs have been anything but "passive raw material" depends on a narrative that continues to sustain human privilege. Haraway's Marxist-feminist stance enables a clear scrutiny of the force of history in shaping relations and subjectivities. But as a trained scientist, Haraway cannot give up her faith—which is no less metaphysical than the humanist conceits she seeks to move beyond as the apostate—that empirical knowledge gained through "face-to-face, body-to-body"[62] encounters somehow transcends the inability of philosophers to see directly, an inability that arouses her "pity."[63]

Faith in cumulative and communicable knowledge has guided the modern form of human subjectivity that grants itself an absolute privilege over all other animals. Leonard Lawlor says, with a compelling bluntness: "Humans believe they have the right to dominate the animals because humans believe they possess a special kind of subjectivity."[64] The privilege granted to human subjectivity by itself is fully established, in Lawlor's synopsis, when Kant extends the Cartesian cogito into an autonomy arising out of auto-affection, or "pure self presence [that] gives humans a dignity that far surpasses that of animals . . . [and] justifies the human right to domination."[65] Derrida points out that for Kant as well as Heidegger—in other words, for modern philosophy—such self-presence has provided "the condition for experience of what is 'as such.'"[66] The human claim to know a dog's face, and to discern from that face what a dog knows or feels arises from the certainty afforded by self-presence. The self-present subject is the one who asserts its power to know other beings directly, without the conceits of humanist ideology, discourse, or tradition. The knowledge acquired by such a subject attains its privileged status by its claim to directness. Lawlor identifies the privilege the human subject grants itself as the violence of enclosing other species in service to itself. The human justifies its violence by its self-purity, its complete self-presence, a similitude of which it grants to animals only as representations of its self-presence. The purity and completeness of self-presence for the modern human subject becomes the standard by which humans measure animals' capacity to engage in the world and—particularly—with humans.

Since at least Buffon, dogs have been granted faces that express, in conditional terms, an interiority analogous to that of humans. But a real consequence of the enclosure Lawlor describes as "globalization," and that I have called the framed landscape, is that canine interiority can exist only in the presence of a human. Canine subjectivity—a dog's face that compels humans to identify a sameness capable of dispelling abyssal alterity—can be recognized or even allowed only as a representational analog to the human. What self-presence, or "agency," means to a dog when its enlistment in coagency meets with only "modest success," when it engages in a world away from the humanly framed one, or simply when it ventures away from humans, remains inconceivable within the modern discourses privileging the calculable human engagement as the only legitimate possibility. This is the reason Derrida poses the almost impossible charge that to relate to something as it is in itself means relating to it "as it is in my absence."[67] The questions of what or who a dog is apart from me raise the possibility of a landscape unframed, or at least framed differently—a world without the techno-aesthetic subject, without any need for such a subject. That world would not *lack* language or knowledge or connectedness, since these would not be necessary. Granting the aptitude for subjectivity to a dog in these terms seriously challenges the dialectical sameness on which Haraway's assertion of knowing Cayenne depends. "The problems begin," Derrida says, at the point where one attributes "to the animal in general" (or we might say to a dog in particular) an aptitude "of *autobiographing* itself."[68] It is not just that in the canine autobiography humans might encounter something they could not read, but that they might encounter only marginal references, or even no recognizable references to themselves at all.

The discursive elements of breed, which allow humans to construct a dog's biography, preclude a dog "autobiographing itself," and thus relieve the human of having to confront the abyssal fear of not mattering, of not being the privileged being. In the biographies that humans write, dogs tacitly *want* to be born as hemophiliacs, to be considered a prospect for training, and are mutely thankful not to be "passive raw material." These biographies follow the archetypal pattern of the histories that Walter Scott's Alice and Sir Henry Lee tell one another to account for Bevis choosing to walk away from them: in these narratives, dogs need humans to make their lives complete, through humans speaking for them, through service, through joyful connectivity. In these biographies, the human leads, the dog follows, bearing the facial representation of the originary dog asking to be enlisted as a coworker. The technological violence of regulating dogs as breeds is only a part of the autobiography of the modern subject, as is the insistence that dogs have freely and actively participated in their own technological regulation, or that nature *needed* the Foxhound to become complete. The biography of breed dogs has been told and retold these past two centuries by the humans who need a canine face to represent the happy complicity of dogs—and the world generally—in their own manipulation. For dogs to have been technologized means that they have been shaped by humans specifically to have a face that humans might bond with.

In restricting knowledge, as the mode of engaging with another being, to the direct form reliant on self-presence, Haraway sustains—unashamedly embraces—the privileged subject of the modern humanism she claims to reject. If her caring responsiveness accepts breed as a historical fact analogous to being the daughter of a sportswriter, then it strategically blinds itself to her dependence on a discursive tradition that orients responsiveness even before the actual encounter by setting human and dog up as mutual analogs, similitudes conditioned by their inclusion within a framed performance. Accepting breed as one fact among others is to write Cayenne's biography for her, and to make Cayenne, agility training, and the coshaping relations into a representation of the humanist bonding with the landscape that Haraway must deny in order to narrate the aesthetic experience of bonding with a canine other. Together, the representational status of the agility arena, of Cayenne as a breed dog, and of Haraway's narrative of her apostasy all frame the performative event into a prosopopoeia, a mutual recognition of faces. The conceit of representation alone is what makes these performances into the discovery of what Derrida describes as otherness without alterity. The representation alone is what makes these performances seem to obviate the abyssal alterity, which always raises the frightening possibility of human irrelevance. Once again the question comes down to this: outside of the humanist frame of laboratory research or interactive sports like agility training, could Haraway recognize an unhistoricized dog? Could she see a face to respond to in a cur?

There is no room for these questions in Haraway's account, since it depends on the knowledge gained from framed, prearranged encounters. These questions are excluded from the narratives Haraway constructs, for they mark the limit that makes her coshaping encounter possible. Cayenne remains the representation that Haraway claims her empiricist approach has eliminated: whether the technologically created dog who enters the agility ring is encountered as a prosthesis within the prosthetic arena, or as the conscious being whose regulated pedigree has made her a promising prospect for conventional communication within the discourse of a sport, she still "works" in the role of the mimetic reflection that has sustained the humanist subject since the Enlightenment.

And in taking the stance that, as a scientist who rejects philosophical and literary conceits, she has moved beyond humanism, Haraway replicates a key humanist gesture. She embraces the modern humanist claim—prominent both in the Enlightenment and in the Romantic turn from the Enlightenment—to correct previous beliefs, discourses, philosophies, or modes of knowing, reading, interpreting. This amounts to a claim of transcendence, to have gone beyond the limiting frame of the humanist landscape, to have attained a higher, more privileged perspective. It is nothing other than the modern form of humanism, and as such is underscored in the obvious parallel between Haraway's assertion that she has freed herself from conceits in her engagements with Cayenne and Wordsworth's identical claim to have freed himself from allegories in his poetry.[69] Her apostasy from humanist conceits has freed Haraway from the self-dividing shame that is very much a part of Kuzniar's account, and that situates a conditional similitude—a fault, Derrida says—at the origin of self-presence and knowledge.[70] In telling of her approach to Cayenne, Haraway must assert her lack of shame, her self-presence, and her privileged capacity to know another's autobiography, to pronounce another's "proper name" without the catachresis of writing through conventions.

THE CYNICAL FRIEND'S REFUSAL

It seems beyond question that we allow for the two-way genuine affection, care, and responsiveness that characterizes most relations between humans and dogs. This fact is evident in both Kuzniar's and Haraway's accounts, even if those accounts adhere to the generic conventions of breed, and even if they carry the legacy of dogs being manipulated across generations into categorical guarantees of reproducible friendships. My concern is not to dismiss the possibilities of friendships between humans and dogs—for I, too, have loved dogs, and have mourned their deaths. It is from learning repeatedly that our canine friends affect us, even without always bothering to ask, by making us caring, loving, and responsive, that I wish to inquire into other possibilities of friendship.

To begin, I would like to pick up from Kuzniar's account of an oblique encounter with a realm beyond the human that might let go the need for a sameness by letting go the requirement that a performative engagement between responsive beings occur as faces recognizing one another, or even meeting each other's gaze. If Kuzniar's obliquity could be matched with Derrida's critique of categorical thinking that works along with the account of responsibility, then we might find a way to relate to dogs without demanding a face, or similitude conditioned by human primacy—in short, without requiring dogs to represent our projected subjectivity. Perhaps we could think about the possibility for a friendship arising when we "call the friend by a name which is no longer that of the near one or the neighbor."[71]

J. M. W. Turner, *Dawn after the Wreck*, 1841. © Samuel Courtauld Trust, The Courtauld Gallery, London, UK/Bridgeman Images.

My primary motive in attempting to work out a non-facial engagement comes from the simple fact—which my previous chapters have made clear—that modern dogs' faces have been shaped into legible categories by two hundred years of human intervention. Dogs have been categorized far more extensively than any other modern domestic animal, even those, like horses and cows, that have also been subjected to "improvement." My attempt at a non-facial engagement is motivated secondly by the overwhelming consequences of Derrida's thinking on the mode governing the modern subject's engagement with other beings. I have referred to the critiques of representation, Kantian aesthetics, the law, friendship, and human-animal relations at different stages of this study, because they all compel the reexamination of the relations we moderns take for granted with modern dogs, whom we designate our best friends, and whom we admire aesthetically while restricting them biologically. Such a reexamination, I believe, does not necessarily have to aim for some ideal as a truer or more humane engagement. Certainly, on an individual level, the engagements described by Kuzniar and Haraway exemplify the most humane degree imaginable. But this kind of humaneness, beginning with appreciation of beauty and the prospect of athletic bondedness, is reached at the cost of voiding surprise to ensure that the canine friend will respond to us in an expected way, with the familiar look of a breed face.

To explore the possibility of an oblique, unexpectable engagement, I return to the discussions on animal relations by Derrida, who distinguishes two types of discourse on animals. The second he says is that of "poets or prophets . . . who admit to taking upon themselves the address that an animal addresses to them, before even having the time or the power to take themselves off." Of taking upon oneself of an address from an animal, he says, he knows "of no *statutory representative* of it, that is to say, no subject who does so as theoretical, philosophical, or juridical man, or even as a citizen," though it is where he wants to think.[72] The other sort of discourse, which he describes first, has been conducted by "people who have no doubt seen, observed, analyzed, and reflected on the animal," and this type includes the vast majority of commentaries on animals generally, and, I will add, on dogs in particular. This kind of discourse belongs wholly to the modern subject I have characterized throughout this study as the one privileging itself, and claiming a comprehensive vision. It is not merely anthropocentric, but moderno-centric. This is the subject whose claim to privilege depends on its simultaneous privileging of direct vision. Derrida goes on to make the most significant distinction of this dominant discourse on animals, saying that these observers and analysts of animals

> have never been *seen seen* by the animal. Their gaze has never intersected with that of an animal directed at them (forget about their being naked). If, indeed, they did happen to be seen seen furtively by the animal one day, they took no (thematic, theoretical, or philosophical) account of it. They neither wanted nor had the capacity to draw any systematic consequence from the fact that an animal could, facing them, look at them, clothed or naked, and in a word, without a word, *address them*. They have taken no account of the fact that what they call "animal" could *look* at them, and *address* them from down there, from a wholly other origin.[73]

Derrida's account of being "seen seen" naked by a cat has become a paradigm of the human finding his privileged vision interrupted as he is made into the object of another's deprivileging vision. This paradigm Derrida adopts from that established by Emmanuel Levinas as the basis of his ethics.[74]

Levinas lays out the key elements of the "face-to-face" in this passage:

It is my responsibility before a face looking at me as absolutely foreign (and the epiphany of the face coincides with these two moments) that constitutes the original fact of fraternity. Paternity is not a causality, but the establishment of a unicity with which the unicity of the father does and does not coincide. The non-coincidence consists, concretely, in my position as brother; it implies other unicities at my side. Thus my unicity qua I contains both self-sufficiency of being and my partialness, my position before the other as a face. In this welcoming of the face (which is already my responsibility in his regard, and where accordingly he approaches me from a dimension of height and dominates me) equality is founded. Equality is produced where the other commands the same and reveals himself to the same in responsibility; otherwise it is but an abstract idea and a word. It cannot be detached from the welcoming of the face of which it is a moment.[75]

This paradigm establishes an ethics of responsibility to the other, and has been echoed by Levinas in his account of the dog Bobby: "For a few short weeks, before the sentinels chased him away, a wandering dog entered our lives. . . . He would appear at morning assembly and was waiting for us as we returned, jumping up and down and barking in delight. For him, there was no doubt that we were men."[76] As Derrida points out, this touching story does not indicate a capacity in Levinas to see a face looking at him from a dog; in fact, Derrida states bluntly, "The animal has neither face nor even skin in the sense Levinas has taught us to give to those words."[77] From here, Derrida goes on to recount a report from John Llewelyn, who asked Levinas whether an animal could be seen to have a face, and received the response "'The human face is completely different and only afterwards do we discover the face of an animal. I don't know if a snake has a face. I can't answer that question.'"[78] Because of Levinas's insistence "on the originary, paradigmatic, 'prototypical' character of ethics as human," Derrida reorients the face-to-face paradigm radically by allowing the possibility of being looked at not by another man, his brother, or a Kantian (or a Derridian), but by a cat, "from a wholly other origin."[79]

Levinas limits his ethics severely when he allows that the face of the Other could only be human, even a fraternal human. Calarco justly comments on this reorientation that "Today philosophy finds itself *faced by animals*, a sharp reversal of the classical philosophical gaze. What philosophy is now encountering, and what Levinas's philosophy tried desperately but unsuccessfully to block or dissimulate, is the simple fact that we know neither what animals can do nor what they might become."[80] When Bobby looks at Levinas, it is to recognize the humanity of the Jewish prisoners in a way the Germans had refused to do; and so Derrida dismisses the account of Bobby with the comment that "This allegorical dog is an other without alterity, without logos, without ethics. It can witness to us only for us, being too other to be brother or neighbor."[81] In being seen to "witness only for us," a Levinasian dog can only affirm the anthropocentric hierarchy that understands difference categorically, and thus precludes—blocks and dissumilates, in Calarco's terms—the possibility of encountering a dog as a particular being raising unanticipated possibilities for engagement.

In the same essay on Levinas, Derrida asks "whether a logic of the wholly other . . . is sufficient, by itself, to remove the anthropocentric prejudice that comes down from Descartes."[82] His answer, as he forewarns, "will be 'no,'" as Levinas allows only for a human ethics. In reorienting the face-to-face paradigm to allow for a cat to gaze at him within an ethical moment, Derrida extends the basis of ethics—the edict, you shall commit no murder, evoked by Llewelyn's question to Levinas—to nonhumans, and he extends the possibility that an animal can die, that the privacy of living, suffering, and dying as an unrepeatable individual is not limited to humans. In this same immediate context, Derrida opens the possibility that animals possess the capacity to proclaim, "Here I am," because—and this is the point I shall pursue—in depriving animals of that autodeictic gesture, Levinasian ethics deprives them of responsibility, of the power of response. In this traditional ethics, according to Derrida, an animal's "nonresponse cannot be compared to the nonresponse . . . understood as the death of the face of the other human."[83] Because an animal is said to lack the capacity of autodeixis, proclaiming itself to exist and to look at us, its silence can never indicate anything other than incapacity. "Thus," Derrida says, "at one and the same time the animal is deprived of the power and the right to respond, of course, and therefore of responsibility (and hence of the law, etc.), yet it is also deprived of nonresponse, of the right of nonresponse that is accorded the human face by means of secrecy or in death."[84] With this, Derrida opens the way toward accepting not only that animals feel, that they possess "auto-affection or auto-motion, hence the self of that relation to the self,"[85] but that they have private lives, and that their privacy functions apart from humans; with private lives, animals would be accorded the same right of summons Levinas accords humans when he says, "The face is present in its refusal to be contained."[86]

In his discussion of Levinas, Calarco comes to a similar moment of tension arising from the exclusion of nonhumans from ethics. Quite usefully, he defines ethics after Levinas as "an interruption of my egoism coming from the face of Other that transforms my being in the direction of generosity."[87] He then raises the possibility of extending this ethics perhaps even to an interruption of anthropocentrism when he states, "There are any number of ways in which my egoism might be interrupted, any number of kinds of entities that might disrupt me and any number of ways I might be transformed by such encounters."[88] The possibility that an interruption of egoism transforms a subject—a subject that has privileged itself to judging whether or not a being belongs in the landscape—has the potential for opening unanticipated questions about humans' relations with animals. And Calarco gives this potential even more force when he states, "Sometimes an ethical response might involve simply leaving the Other alone."[89] The shock of seeing an Other look at us as though we were Other, the shock of being "seen seen," could transform us toward the generosity of accepting an animal's privacy, with all the unforeseeable implications, that a dog, for example, might wish for something other than to be enlisted by us.

The generosity of allowing a dog to go in private comes from an ethics of incalculability, from well outside the modern landscape of representation through racial and breed categorization. In "Envoi," Derrida says, "It is in the direction of the *incalculable* that the limits of representation can be overrun."[90] The incalculable, the surprising is generally held at bay by the techno-aesthetic landscape that has structured and regulated modern engagements through various devices, and particularly through categorical delineations that obscure individuality and possibilities of other landscapes, other grammars. In our engagements with dogs, such calculability works through the breed discourse that makes whippets and Australian shepherds into representations of "perfection" and productivity. But in our encounters with unidentifiable, unhistoricized—which is to say, uncategorizable—dogs, calculability gives way to shame, confessions of inauthenticity, interpellations of not being wanted, for such encounters share with shock the disorientation of encountering something defying the limits giving it meaning and place within the landscape.

The shock and embarrassment Derrida experiences in being seen by a cat cannot be so easily transmuted in turn to an encounter with a modern dog in order to take on an incalculable address. The force of breed discourse determines the meaning of a dog's looking so effectively as to deflect the shock of contemplating that "wholly other origin" as part of the conditionality on which the similitude depends. Our dogs have long been clothed through the biological programming, and the legal transmutation into metonymic signification (reflected in coshaping performance) that molds them into a legible form. To take on an incalculable address, we need to divest them of their breed, or rather divest ourselves of their breed. Certainly Kuzniar attests to an embarrassment at seeing ugly dogs and the dogs who serve as someone else's signature, but that response only compels her to turn away. What remains challenging is to renew the shock of encountering a wholly other origin that would make the modern reliance on representation discomfitingly apparent in order to suspend the breed discourse making our engagements with dogs comfortably predictable. I would therefore like to extend Derrida's thinking on the animal gaze not so much through another account of seeing a dog's face seeing me, but rather by considering a possibility that would introduce a shock of illegibility, an interruption of my egoism, privilege, and reliance on categories. Dogs' faces have been made too calculable through the categorical *bêtise* of breed: as Derrida states in *Beast and the Sovereign*, "the category is a signature of *bêtise*."[91] The certainty Derrida has that when his cat responds "in its name, . . . it doesn't do so as the exemplar of a species called 'cat,'" and "that what we have here is an existence that refuses to be conceptualized," does not carry over so easily to dogs, who carry their history of breed distinctions as the faces we have literally shaped and historicized to see us from a conveniently familiar origin.[92] The possibility of taking on the address of a modern dog, therefore, must allow the chance of a different surprise, maybe the disappointment of seeing a dog choosing not to see me, to leave in order to engage in a world in which humans are poor in the Heideggerian sense, to interrupt or ruin—currishly—my prepared responsiveness, my anticipated questions. This is the most ordinary, everyday possibility of a dog having seen me before I see him, of already having determined that I did not merit his response once I did notice him, of addressing me by way of withdrawal. This might be someone else's dog, or no one's dog.

Following the question of whether animals dream, in "But as for Me, Who Am I (Following)?," Derrida poses numerous other questions about animals and their experiences, such as "'Does the animal produce representations?' a self, imagination, a relation to the future as such? Does the animal have not only signs but a language, and what language?"[93] He ends with a question about the questions: "How can the gamut of questions on the being of what would be proper to the animal be changed?"[94] The great challenge of changing the questions about dogs has been forestalled by breed discourse. Such discourse appears to allow for canine differences, variability, but—as I have shown—only within taxonomized limits. Modern dogs may be different from one another, as a Doberman differs from a retriever, but these differences reinforce the calculability of breed itself. Breed supplants one variable category—dog—for another, enforceable, category that allows for narrative reenactments of an originary history that fills a lack, thereafter framing our friendship without overtly appearing in it. These narratives obscure the risk of a dog turning away—choosing, perhaps, to allow for only "modest success" in a coagency, or perhaps not to return—by instituting infinitely replicable representations as the fable of human-dog companionship, the fable of falling "in love with kinds as well as individuals," as Haraway recounts doing.[95]

How can the gamut of questions be changed? Perhaps by asking questions that violate the genre of interrogatives already and ineluctably posed to dogs; perhaps by asking questions whose answers are not known in advance, whose answers are not contained in or calculated by the question. The performative question Haraway poses would need to be asked over and again, and outside of the "prospect" of performing well and according to the rules of a sport. In such an unguarded, unlimited space, the performance would perhaps open another question directed at ourselves, such as: Whom do you call? What if you get no answer? What call has yours drowned out? Have you precluded surprise? But such questions remain inadequate when directed at the dog refusing a face. Perhaps the gamut of questions can be changed only when we stop asking in order to accept the address of a dog that we have obscured with our conventional interrogations. The questions we have not heard might come from the incalculable dog refusing to be my friend.

By starting from the point where a dog has already chosen to turn away, I hope to open a non-narratable, nondescriptive possibility of receiving a dog's address. And one step toward hearing a different—or hitherto illegible—gamut of questions might take place in the disappointment of not being seen, not being recognized as the interesting person I am, by this dog. Any attempt I would make to describe this disappointment is overwhelmed by my canine world poverty, an impoverishment that is generally masked behind the breed narratives that consistently gather dogs into historical functions in my world, making them eternally loyal to me and my family, as well as to their infinitely repeatable face. These narratives not only drown out any address from an incalculability, but they do so by writing the biography of a dog in such a conventional way that she is always responding to my address. An unfaceable dog will stay outside any narrative I could construct from analogies—those conditional similitudes that have dogs looking at me *as if* they wanted nothing more than to be liked by me and *as if* their worlds were very like mine, though filled with ranker smells, louder noises, and dreams of chasing the cat out of the bathroom. Refusing to enter my autobiography, this dog never becomes grammatically present, and especially does not become present *again*, as a re-presenting.

By starting from the point at which a dog responsively turns away, I hope to recall something of the nondescriptive engagement of Pope walking quietly with his surly companion transmuted by reflections on what it means to have already missed the other's trace. This is the moment when any account of a dog no longer holds central reference to me, privileging me as the focus of the dog's gaze, which is too, too easy to read as fidelity. This moment raises the temptation of speculating about what a dog might experience, what worlds of engagements he might encounter, what transformative events he might live through on his own, what might surprise or bore him. But such speculation would still project my vision over his world, transforming a world in which I am poor into a wealth of descriptive and explanatory resources for something like the *new* order of engagements that even the best commentators hold out as a promise, and that, as a promise, is already calculated. To consider this dog responding apart from me, I have to relinquish the *bêtise* that has governed engagements with dogs—even such caring and thoughtful ones like Kuzniar's—that has ensured that most of the surprises I have would be that he demonstrated an intelligence or responsiveness in his world recognizable to me as analogs of human qualities. I would have to relinquish the habitual certainty that my world—the framed landscape of my aesthetic and ethical judgment—is the only possibility, and that a dog's intelligence and autobiography would be shaped within the frame shaping mine. Relinquishing *bêtise* can entail letting go numerous categorical identifications, and it could be surprising how many have to be given up and how difficult it can be to let them go, as the structures of conditional similitude and analogy depend on categorical identification, beginning with breed and moving through race, ethnicity, and history. In letting these go, I would be letting go the structure of knowing that relies on description and demonstration, on pointing to a being such as a dog and claiming a recognition based on the loyally replicable face I can describe as being presented to me. And I would be letting go the persistent anthropocentrism that limits my surprise to admissions that a dog does show signs of recognizable intelligence, sociability, or mourning (for the fact that these qualities should continue to be surprising is in itself disappointing). Only by letting all this go can I begin to consider what a "wholly other origin" might entail, how an alterity might surprise me with questions I had never imagined.

In turning away, a dog ceases to have a face for me; and in withdrawing his face, he erases the representational system through which I had made him enough like me that I could believe he was presenting himself to me in the desire for me to know him—as if he would speak to me of his appreciation for my understanding of him. He belies the fables constructed to explain him categorically, so that my accounts of canine loyalty or of "the dog" choosing to leave the wild for the security, or necessity, or joy, of companionship with humans appear as fanciful and subject to refutation as the explanations that Henry Lee and Alice offer each other for Bevis's decision to leave them behind. The breed histories of this dog who turns from me hold no relevance to the view he takes of his world exclusive of me—a world that Heidegger could not allow and that the eighteenth-century parliamentarians would have found both illegal and illegible, but that is not any more comprehensible to me who wants to experience it. The explanations I construct on the basis of informed understanding of dogs as either the singular category of "the dog," an animal favoring some senses over others, or as a breed whose fabled history provides the *telos* for my descriptions and coshaping partnerships, meet the limit of their validity the moment this one dog engages in a world without me. As this dog turns away, our friendship turns from an analog of fraternity to an indescribable event of obliquity in which a concord of friends aims for no kind of connectivity.

Had the dog I wanted to befriend shown me a face, my response would have begun too easily with the preamble "We are friends so long as you're my dog, so long as you remain tethered to the biography I've written for you." Precluding such an interpellation, this dog becomes an incalculable cur, leaving me suspended in the moment Derrida refers to as the "perhaps," the moment of expectation of a future that is undecidable and unreliable, the event of what may happen, or not.[96] This moment calls out the undecidability of the cur's world—if she does engage in something akin to Heideggerian gathering, or if she instead interrupts, breaks up such worlds—and the decision that I am not the one she had expected, and even the possibility that she, unlike me, had not expected or sought anyone. This "perhaps" to which I have responded carries the possibility, the risk, that this cur's call was for me *not* to expect a friendship, *not* to recognize her in any way that would lead to a shared knowledge or understanding, but instead to anticipate that she will run away to a world apart from me, to which I have no access—that she will never be my dog, or even *our* dog, a member of the economy framed by breed expectations.

The different (but perhaps not so new) gamut of questions can be heard only by ceasing to ask the old ones, those that consistently revolve around recognizability and loyalty, and those that privilege modernity with claims of improved care and greater knowledge. Canine loyalty is a reference that ensures a dog will appear to me as representative of a category, breed. In several contexts, Derrida suggests that a noncategorical acceptance of the other's address takes place prior to any reference to loyalty, or prior to any recognition of a face, or any enforcement of an economy of mimesis. The responsive acceptance he refers to would occur in the surprise that cannot be anticipated. Thus, in "Eating Well," he says that "there neither can be nor ever should be any concept adequate to what we call responsibility."[97] This responsive surprise occurs as "that yes-yes that answers before even being able to formulate a question," a question such as who are you? or who are we?[98] Such a responsive surprise would also take place before the question of what kind of dog you are. Before a tail can be seen to wag, or teeth seen to be bared, before I can recognize you as Sheltie, Sealy, or Pug, is where that responsiveness happens. And that means it takes place prior to any possible formulation of aesthetic connectivity, any discourses of improvement or legalization that supposedly answer the necessity of nature. In fact this is the responsive surprise that precedes either question or answer, just as it precedes the deictic pointing of stating, that is a dog.

In "I Don't Know Why We Are Doing This," the final chapter of *The Animal That Therefore I Am*, Derrida refers, through Heidegger's text *On the Essence of Ground*, to an account of a non-apophantic moment that isn't declarative, enunciative, "which doesn't show anything, which in a certain way 'doesn't say anything.'"[99] Derrida connects this moment with the performativity of prayer, of which he asks in *The Beast and the Sovereign*, "Is there not some implicit prayer in every address to the other? And is there not an implicit address to the other in every statement, however constative it look . . . ?" This performatively implicit address works as a "listen to me, I say to you."[100] In this performative moment when nothing is being pointed to or made present or vivid through description, Derrida suggests, one could possibly engage in that "fundamental muteness" Kuzniar drew from mourning her lost friend.[101] For Kuzniar the muteness is associated with an obliqueness that stands for imperfection in knowing her friend, in misinterpreting the friend in her absence; but I would suggest that this obliqueness does not have to relate to a flaw, which could too easily frame another discourse of improvement, as the need for the Foxhound did in the eighteenth century. The dog who turns away instills an obliqueness in our friendship by withdrawing her face so that I can no longer point to, describe, or declare anything about that face. Before my offered face, the cur performs a trope of responsive non-apophansis, less tainted by religious flirtation than prayer, but, like any catachresis, subject to the risks of misapprehension as unresponsiveness, or incapacity, or inappropriateness. It performatively turns any similitude, hope or expectation of a relation, into dissimilitude and disproportion. And, as a turn from an offer—even an offer that has yet to express anything—this cur's response might be heard (appropriately or inappropriately) *as though* it were an offer in turn, perhaps, of a friendship of a sort I have yet to imagine, that might exclude me. To hear what is *like* an offer of something that might be *like* a friendship in a gesture that could also indicate a refusal of any friendship could take a step into the "abyssal difference" in which Derrida says he wants to think about being "seen seen," and from which a gamut of new, non-apophantic questions might be posed.

This difference, in my view, is not abyssal simply as an uncrossable barrier, for breeds ensure legible friendships between humans and dogs, perhaps allowing humans to read themselves as looking like their dogs. This difference is not simply that imposed and enforced by anthropocentrism in so many ways, such as the gestures of commonality, connectivity, and coagency that reinforce the limits of "the human" by enlisting dogs, by granting them faces dependent on the conditionality of similitude. The difference encountered when the faceless dog turns away is abyssal in that any condition on which to ground a similitude has been refused. The abyss opened by the unknowable dog turning away does not occur as a "frontier" or barrier between me and the cur, so that questions of capacity, or hierarchies of ability, or states of evolution lose as much relevance as the categories of breed. This is the unlandscaped abyss of framelessness, the *Ungrund*, in which two beings have nothing between them.

Friendship, Derrida suggests in one context, "would be *unheimlich*," unhomely, houseless, or, in the translation he renders into Greek, "*atópos*: outside all place or placeless, without family, or familiarity, outside of self, expatriate, extraordinary, extravagant, absurd, or mad, unsuitable, strange, but also 'a stranger to.'"[102] Any ground of legibility, loyalty, recognition, narratable history, and anything that can be shared, falls away in that moment of the uncertain turn. And there, what looks *as though* it were a rejection, and yet is *perhaps* similar to a responsive offer in return (a similitude of a responsive offer made on condition of not leading to a relation), hangs illegibly, in the indeterminacy between the cur's world in which I am poor and my world from which the cur has already turned.[103]

The disruptive cur has ruined the paradigmatic encounter of a gaze from a wholly other origin by responding with her defacializing turn. Unable to address her gaze, I am left suspended in the moment of inarticulacy, of having nothing to offer her, to ask her, to call her by, or to call out to her, to entice her to me. This moment arises even apart from the "perhaps" of the friend turning into the enemy, for the cur was never either friend or enemy to begin with, but merely a cur, nameless, not mine, ours, or anyone's. The moment arises when this cur, who had stood close enough perhaps to bite my hand, turns from my reach or the sound of my call or the focus of my gaze without caring whether I am a Kantian or a cynic, humanist or scientist, worker or sportsman.

For the duration of this moment, in the space of wordlessness, this cur—whose gender I do not know—and I houselessly and abyssally stand without any orientation that would bring us together. Her turn, which I have read so far *as though* it were the troping of a non-apophantic response to a non-apophantic call or prayer, could in fact be the refusal of response, and the refusal of me, impoverished and outside her currish world. Having turned away from the appeal to share my world, she holds her world aloof and impenetrable, leaving me without the names to call someone who has turned away from friendship but not necessarily in enmity. In referring to this dog as "cur," or even "dog," I am admittedly pointing and describing, but not to some relatable or categorical quality from which I might build her biography: not only am I not able to ask, "whose dog are you?," I am also stymied from asking, "who are you?," or Haraway's "who are we?" The inability to ask that question, or that series of questions, hinges on the turn from my offer, or non-apophantic plea—for in turning away, this cur has made me bear the failure of language, even one that attempts to put a nonlanguage to work. A non-apophantic plea, which addresses someone in a response rather than describing them, might have sustained the "perhaps" of a non-"phratrocentric" relationship,[104] of a relation ungathered into a category, perhaps the category of uncategorizables, the category of curs, but only to prepare for this linguistic and categorial collapse. This faceless response to the undeclared interrogation does not show anything, but—as Derrida suggests over and over in passages on non-apophantic moments—it might, perhaps, *do* something.

In pursuing his hypothesis that an aneconomic friendship opened through a dyssymmetrical offer[105] would be "perhaps of the order neither of the common nor of its opposite," Derrida says further that it would also not be something like "a community without community," for "The aporia requiring the unceasing neutralization of one predicate by another," such as relation without relatedness, "calls on significations altogether different from those of the part shared or held in common."[106] A call for altogether different signification arises in and as an abyssal event, for which no category is ever adequate—how, Derrida asks in what we might hear as an effort to change "the gamut of questions," "can you name an event?"[107] Without making the autodeictic gesture of saying, "I," the dog turning away shows herself "capable of doing it," as Derrida says in yet another context, and thus affirming "its *responsibility*, its power to respond, to answer for itself, before others and before the law."[108] The old gamut of modern questions still revolve around that of whether animals respond or suffer.[109] Perhaps, then, one gamut of atopic, nongeneric questions can begin with that of the canine address that we have yet to hear, yet to be able to hear: the cur ruining the preconceived categories, her incessant barking interrupting my heartfelt, ready-made questions. The instability of this friendship gives rise to the breed histories that correct a flaw, improve on the unframed, un-representable possibility of engagements by naturalizing categories into the unsurprising relations of man's best friend choosing to remain loyal.

As Derrida asserts toward the end of the longest chapter in *The Animal That Therefore I Am*, humans depriving animals of the power and right to respond also deprive them of "the right of non-response that is accorded to the human face by means of privacy or in death."[110] Such deprivation of the right to privacy pinpoints the need for changing the gamut of questions we ask about animals and that we ask to animals. Perhaps we could change the gamut of questions by dispensing first with all the variations of interrogatory "whose dog are you?"—all those questions that anticipate a certain kind of response, and that have already imposed a recognizable face on a dog. Perhaps the gamut of questions might begin not with what I ask, but with the appeal contained in a dog's refusal to answer. If that refusal can be taken as something other than its traditional indication of lack or inability, then the most responsible questions would have to begin with respect, with the wish not to intrude. The anthropocentric view is that dogs have no private life because they perform acts in humans' public that humans would rather keep private. This view allows for only a narrow view of privacy, and ignores the fact that humans often perform acts in front of dogs that dogs might prefer they kept private. To allow not only that a dog can suffer as well as feel joy, but that she can do so in private opens a gamut of questions that we can yet only formulate crudely and provisionally. If a dog turns her face away, the questions I need to learn to ask would begin with the acknowledgment that I have already violated her privacy by wanting to recognize her breed. The change I would hope for, then, would be in the direction of the questioning: instead of asking, do you respond to my call? or even, how should I respond to your call?—since both of these look for the "fraternal friendship" that Derrida says Levinas limits himself to[111]—one would ask for neither similitude nor conditionality that would require audible, visible, tactile, olfactory, or spiritual presentation. And one would allow oneself to be questioned, one's humanness to be questioned, which would require much more attentiveness than we have hitherto given to our friends. If I cannot replicate Pope's graciousness in finding a concord in discord—a friendship of surly unlikeness—I can perhaps look to the quietness of a friendship in which two beings run together for a time, diverge, and possibly reconverge without passing over old ground, and without anticipating the ground to come.

Reorienting aesthetics of connectivity or discovered sameness into the obliqueness of surprise would allow that a dog's subjective experience lies beyond one's own. In being with this dog, I do not know her *as if* she were me. With that admission, perhaps I can appreciate her different style of being and of questioning. With that, we dog lovers can step back into the world, no longer demanding total comprehension of ourselves as the represented landscape, or subjugation of our canine companions. We might orient our relations with dogs in an active way growing out of our dissimilar singularities: we might find surprising joy in our different styles of being. As occasional and unnecessary participants in an unmapped, unnarrated world, we interact otherwise than by gazing aggressively into a body troped as a face, perhaps by turning to walk quietly side by side, "to live the gentle rigour of friendship," as Derrida suggests hopefully, "in absolute separation."[112] Such would be the oblique ethics of no face and no place. Giving up our face would also and at the same time let go the demand for a canine face cast in conditional similitude; letting go the modern demand for total knowledge, for legality and legibility, we would let go the frame that makes space into a totality. And, finally, letting go the frame, we could let go the sacrifice that excludes from our consciousness the ugly, unwanted, unnarratable curs. Such a hope will always already be written in a landscape, neither post-human nor new, but possibly open to abyssally different kinds of friendships, and many, many dogs.

Bounce.

Notes

INTRODUCTION

1. Fram, "Mutts Like Me"; Rhee, "Chewing over Obama's 'Mutt' Reference."
2. As Meisha Rosenberg has astutely observed, President Obama's eventual choice of Bo, a Portuguese water dog, "reads . . . as an acceptance of pedigree and all it implies," and at the same time serves "to cloak as much as to reveal race politics" ("Golden Retrievers Are White, Pit Bulls Are Black, and Chihuahuas Are Hispanic: Representations of Breeds of Dog and Issues of Race in Popular Culture," 114).
3. See Scott, *A Singular Woman*, 13.
4. Kuzniar, *Melancholia's Dog*.
5. Ritvo, *The Animal Estate*, 96. For other historical accounts on the creation of breeds, see Ritvo, "Race, Breed, and Myths of Origin"; Ritvo, *The Platypus and the Mermaid*; Derry, *Bred for Perfection*; Russell, *Like Engend'ring Like*; and Landry, *Noble Brutes*.
6. Foucault, *The History of Sexuality*, 136, 139; emphasis in the original. Needless to say, Foucault's thinking on biopower has facilitated some rich discussions in animal studies, two of the most prominent being Seshadri, *HumAnimal*, and Wolfe, *Before the Law*.
7. Derrida, *Of Grammatology*, 112. The point of nature being always already technologized is made by Toadvine, "Life beyond Biologism," among others.
8. Wolfe, *What Is Posthumanism*, xxix.
9. Donna Landry has explored the cultural effects of the hunt culture, and in particular the effect that the creation of the Thoroughbred had on the English countryside, in *Noble Brutes*. When she poses the challenging question "Might not horses have had some effect on human culture as well as the other way around?" she strikes just the right note, in my view (14). But her reduction of "animal studies as a field [that] has emphasized cruelty to animals as a way of unpacking the history of human-animal relations" (10) not only obscures the breadth of this burgeoning field, it also comes close to a reactionism born out of her oft-proclaimed membership in the English hunt culture.
10. Laurie Shannon conveys a sense of how these organizational principles work when she says, "The multiple criteria by which animals are said to vary in early modern classificatory thinking display an additive, cumulative, or inventorying sense of diversity"; *The Accommodated Animal*, 108.
11. Pope, "Lines on Bounce," *Minor Poems*, 405.
12. See Nash, "Animal Nomenclature," 109. Norman Ault discusses both sides of the question, allowing at most, however, that there might have been two Bounces (see *New Light on Pope*, 341). I do not wholly accept the multiple Bounce argument; Pope refers multiple times to dogs living for two decades, and he only mourns Bounce once.
13. Cummings, *Windsor Forest*, 70.
14. Cummings, *Windsor Forest*, 66; Cummings identifies his characterization as a paraphrase of Politian.

15. Cummings, *Windsor Forest*, 66.

16. Paulson, *Emblem and Expression*, 22.

17. Wasserman, *The Subtler Language*. Wasserman gives the fullest account of *concordia discors* in the chapter on John Denham's *Cooper's Hill*.

18. Wasserman, *The Subtler Language*, 111; emphasis mine.

19. Wall, *The Prose of Things*, 39.

20. Pope, *The Correspondence of Alexander Pope*.

21. Pope, *The Correspondence of Alexander Pope*, 1:74.

22. Tobit, 5:16.

23. Tobit, 11:4.

24. Pope, *The Correspondence of Alexander Pope*, 1:74.

25. Fabricant, "Defining Self and Others," 524.

26. Fabricant, "Defining Self and Others," 519. Crippled and as misshapen as his surly little dog, Pope was probably very aware of how he was seen.

27. Doody, *The Daring Muse*, 15.

28. Helsinger, "Land and National Representation in Britain," 17.

29. Helsinger, "Land and National Representation in Britain," 17.

30. Helsinger, "Land and National Representation in Britain," 17.

31. Kant, *Critique of Judgement*, 187.

32. Kant, *Critique of Judgement*, 182, 181.

33. Rodolphe Gasché argues convincingly that the equation of beauty and the good requires such a tour de force that Kant briefly has to abandon *Darstellung* in favor of the rhetorical device of hypotyposis, which is used to make something seem vividly present to the mind (see Gasché, *The Idea of Form*, 209). Gasché's careful and insightful discussion on this trope in Kant's aesthetics has contributed significantly to my understanding of the dependence on visual rhetoric after Pope.

34. Kant, *Critique of Judgement*, 180.

35. Barrell, "The Public Prospect and the Private View," 29; and for a more detailed version of this point, see Barrell, *The Political Theory of Painting*.

36. Wordsworth, "Preface" to *Lyrical Ballads*, 426.

37. Coleridge, "On the Principles of Genial Criticism," 558.

38. Kant, *Critique of Judgement*, 82.

39. Kant, *Critique of Judgement*, 135.

40. Derrida, "Economimesis," 9; italics in the original.

41. Derrida, "Economimesis," 15.

42. Kant, *Critique of Judgement*, 22.

43. Schelling, *Philosophical Inquiries*, 92.

44. Carrie Rohman suggests that "The onset of modernism coincides with the proliferation of Darwin's story of human origins, which indicates that the human being can be understood as a highly evolved animal," in *Stalking the Subject*, 22. This intriguing connection extends the techno-aesthetico-legal privilege established in the eighteenth century into biological terms.

45. Drayton, *Nature's Government*, 52.

46. Kant, *Critique of Judgement*, 23.

47. Ladelle McWhorter has usefully addressed the conjunction of sex and race in terms of biopower, noting that "the modern concept of race and the institutions and practices that developed and deployed that concept arose within the same networks of disciplinary normalization and biopower that gave us the modern concept of sex" ("Sex, Race, and Biopower," 30). Those very "networks

of disciplinary normalization and biopower" also and at the same time generated breed, a creative event that could be described in the Foucauldian formulation McWhorter applies to race as the biopolitical analog to sex: "a 'fictitious unity' that serves as a linchpin to hold together a disparate set of theories, institutions, practices, and relationships" (47; and see Foucault, *The History of Sexuality*, 154). I take up the elements of this disparate set in the following chapters.

48. Heidegger, "The Question Concerning Technology," in *The Question Concerning Technology and Other Essays*, 17.

49. Heidegger, "The Question Concerning Technology," in *The Question Concerning Technology and Other Essays*, 15.

50. Heidegger, "The Question Concerning Technology," in *The Question Concerning Technology and Other Essays*, 21.

51. Heidegger, "The Question Concerning Technology," in *The Question Concerning Technology and Other Essays*, 21.

52. Heidegger, "The Question Concerning Technology," in *The Question Concerning Technology and Other Essays*, 27.

53. There is also the somewhat nebulous category of vermin, which would include rats, skunks, and foxes. This last member holds a curious status in that it was an "unprotected" animal according to the Game Laws, which meant that traditionally it could be hunted by anyone; but when foxhunting exploded in the nineteenth century, foxes became a resource to be protected and managed, as well as a pest. Hunt rhetoric still tries to claim that it protects the resource and manages the pest.

54. Kant, *Critique of Judgement*, 141.

55. Heidegger, *An Introduction to Metaphysics*, 45.

56. Derrida, *Of Spirit*, 64, 65.

57. Not surprisingly, Derrida examines Heidegger's spiritual nostalgia—or reactionism—in far more detail that I have suggested here. In particular, Derrida pushes the definition of world as spirit through the distinction between world-forming (*weltbildend*) Man and the world-poor (*weltarm*) animal. He makes the point that Heidegger's formulation does not leave an animal deprived of world, that "if it is poor in world, the animal must certainly have some world, and thus some spirit" (*Of Spirit*, 48). The difference for Heidegger remains, however, one of essence, not degree. And so, Derrida says, "the world of the animal—and if the animal is poor in world, and therefore in spirit, one *must* be able to talk about a world of the animal and therefore of a spiritual world—is not a species of the human world. . . . it is not that the animal has a lesser relationship, a more limited access to entities, it has an *other* relationship" (*Of Spirit*, 49). Derrida finds the tension troubling Heidegger's logic to stem from two incompatible values: "that of lack and that of alterity" (*Of Spirit*, 49). This tension, Derrida says, compels Heidegger "to reintroduce the measure of man by the very route it claimed to be withdrawing from that measure—this meaning of lack or privation"; and such a meaning, he continues, can appear "only from a non-animal world, and from *our* point of view" (*Of Spirit*, 49–50; emphasis in the original). This important critique of the anthropocentric tenor of efforts to develop a post-humanism—even when, like Heidegger, they attempt to counter the anthropocentrically technological landscape—will orient my final chapter.

58. Derrida, "The Animal That Therefore I Am (More to Follow)," in *The Animal That Therefore I Am*, 13.

59. Derrida, "The Animal That Therefore I Am (More to Follow)," in *The Animal That Therefore I Am*, 25.

60. Derrida, "The Animal That Therefore I Am (More to Follow)," in *The Animal That Therefore I Am*, 31.

61. Derrida, "The Animal That Therefore I Am (More to Follow)," in *The Animal That Therefore I Am*, 24, 29.

62. Kant, *Critique of Judgement*, 22.

63. Kant, *Critique of Judgement*, 25.

64. Derrida, "The Animal That Therefore I Am (More to Follow)," in *The Animal That Therefore I Am*, 25.

65. See McGann, *The Poetics of Sensibility*, 15.

66. Kean, *Animal Rights*. See also Carr, *English Fox Hunting*, 195–212.

67. Fudge, *Animal*, 101.

68. Fudge, *Animal*, 103.

69. Fudge, *Animal*, 77.

70. Fudge, *Animal*, 76.

71. Heidegger, *Fundamental Concepts*, 210.

72. Derrida, "I Don't Know Why We Are Doing This," in *The Animal That Therefore I Am*, 160.

73. Heidegger, *Fundamental Concepts*, 287.

74. See, for example, Donna Haraway, *When Species Meet*; Anat Pick, for whom "contact with the flesh and blood vulnerability of beings is the nexus" shaping her readings (*Creaturely Poetics*, 17); and Rohman, who says, "The animal is the paradigmatic victim because it lacks even the possibility to name its injuries with humanist parlance" (*Stalking the Subject*, 17).

75. Lawlor, *This Is Not Sufficient*, 72.

76. Derrida, "Economimesis," 15.

77. Derrida, "The Animal That Therefore I Am (More to Follow)," in *The Animal That Therefore I Am*, 19.

78. Calarco, *Zoographies*, 140.

79. Calarco, *Zoographies*, 73.

80. Donald, *Picturing Animals in Britain*, 138.

CHAPTER 1. LEGAL AND LEGIBLE: BREED REGULATION IN LAW AND SCIENCE

1. The arrest itself, the charge of poaching, and the consequences for Pope and the Racketts have been discussed from different perspectives by Thompson, *Whigs and Hunters*, 278–94; Rogers, *Eighteenth-Century Encounters*, 75–92; Cruickshank and Erskine-Hill, "The Waltham Black Act and Jacobitism"; and Mack, *Alexander Pope*, 402–5.

2. Diana Donald discusses several of these portraits in *Picturing Animals in Britain*, 111, 119.

3. Blackstone, *Commentaries on the Laws of England*, 418.

4. Munsche, *Gentlemen and Poachers*, 3.

5. Munsche, *Gentlemen and Poachers*, 21.

6. Munsche, *Gentlemen and Poachers*, 6.

7. Derrida, "The Force of Law," 22.

8. Derrida, "The Force of Law," 22.

9. Derrida, "The Force of Law," 23.

10. Derrida, "The Force of Law," 22.
11. Williamson and Bellamy, *Property and Landscape*, 124.
12. Derrida, "The Force of Law," 18.
13. Derrida, "The Force of Law," 18.
14. Quoted in Munsche, *Gentlemen and Poachers*, 82.
15. Lapdogs have attracted a fair amount of attention over the past decade, generally for their associations with women and their possible role as the earliest modern dogs kept for reasons other than utility, which is to say as pets. See, for example, Wyett, "The Lap of Luxury"; Braunschneider, "The Lady and the Lapdog"; Brown, *Homeless Dogs and Melancholy Apes*; and Ellis, "Suffering Things." Kari Weil has a sophisticated discussion of Virginia Woolf's *Flush*, which explores how the biography searches "for an androgynous and mongrelized reality outside the cultural conventions that restrict what we know of such creatures as women and dogs," in *Thinking Animals*, 84.
16. Kant, *Critique of Judgement*, 180.
17. Brown, *Homeless Dogs and Melancholy Apes*, 65; and see Ellis, "Suffering Things," 98, and Wyett, "The Lap of Luxury," 282.
18. Thompson, *Whigs and Hunters*, 23.
19. Munsche, *Gentlemen and Poachers*, 107.
20. Thompson, *Whigs and Hunters*, 63.
21. Douglas Hay recounts an extended conflict in the 1760s between the gamekeepers of the Tory Lord Uxbridge and the sportsmen whose hounds and spaniels were repeatedly shot in "Poaching and the Game Laws."
22. Derrida, "The Force of Law," 13.
23. Derrida, "The Force of Law," 23.
24. Derrida, "Economimesis," 9.
25. King, *Reasons and Proposals for Laying a Tax upon Dogs*.
26. Munsche, *Gentlemen and Poachers*, 83.
27. Clark, *An Address to Both Houses of Parliament*, 6.
28. King, *Reasons and Proposals for Laying a Tax upon Dogs*, 8–11.
29. Woodfall, *An Impartial Report on the Debates That Occur in the Two Houses of Parliament*, 4:199.
30. John D. Blaisdell traces the several outbreaks of rabies in England and connects them to periods of accepted slaughter of dogs and to the support for a dog tax in "The Rise of Man's Best Friend."
31. Clark, *An Address to Both Houses of Parliament*, 9.
32. Ritvo, *The Animal Estate*, 170.
33. King, *Reasons and Proposals for Laying a Tax upon Dogs*, 13.
34. Linda Kalof points out, "As a direct consequence of the 1796 licensing law, thousands of unlicensed dogs were slaughtered throughout England," in *Looking at Animals in Human History*, 118.
35. King, *Reasons and Proposals for Laying a Tax upon Dogs*, 15.
36. King, *Reasons and Proposals for Laying a Tax upon Dogs*, 15.
37. King, *Reasons and Proposals for Laying a Tax upon Dogs*, 21.
38. Clark, *An Address to Both Houses of Parliament*, 13.
39. Clark, *An Address to Both Houses of Parliament*, 12.
40. Derrida, "The Force of Law," 19.
41. Derrida, "Economimesis," 9.
42. Clark, *An Address to Both Houses of Parliament*, 14.

43. Barry, *On the Necessity of Adopting Some Measures*, 7.

44. Barry, *On the Necessity of Adopting Some Measures*, 7.

45. Tague, "Eighteenth-Century English Debates."

46. Brindle, *The Dog's Plea*, 2.

47. Brindle, *The Dog's Plea*, 19.

48. Festa, "Person, Animal, Thing," 15; Festa quotes from *The Statutes at Large, from the Thirty-Fifth Year of the Reign of King George the Third, to the Thirty-Eighth year of the Reign of King George* (London, 1798), 17:415.

49. Festa, "Person, Animal, Thing," 5.

50. Festa, "Person, Animal, Thing," 30.

51. Tague, "Eighteenth-Century English Debates," 902.

52. Derrida, "The Force of Law," 13.

53. Peterson, *Bestial Traces*, 8.

54. See Rohman, *Stalking the Subject*. Rohman's argument is, of course, more complex than it appears in this simple summary; still, she does privilege animality as the corporeal bond humans can find with nonhumans.

55. Rohman, *Stalking the Subject*, 15.

56. Lemm, *Nietzsche's Animal Philosophy*, 11.

57. Derrida, *Of Grammatology*, 112.

58. Oliver, *Animal Lessons*, 62.

59. Kant, *Critique of Pure Reason*, A: 104.

60. Kant, *Critique of Pure Reason*, B: 103–4.

61. Nietzsche, "On Truth and Lies," 83.

62. Derrida, "Economimesis," 13.

63. Ritvo, *The Animal Estate*, 96.

64. Banton, *Racial Theories*, 24.

65. Sloan, "The Idea of Racial Degeneracy," 310.

66. Bernasconi, *Race*, 3.

67. Fenves, "What 'Progresses' Has Race-Theory Made," 12.

68. Kant, "Of the Different Human Races," 8.

69. Kant, "Of the Different Human Races," 14.

70. Shell, "Kant's Conception of a Human Race," 58.

71. Shell, "Kant's Conception of a Human Race," 60.

72. Blane, *Cynegetica*, 84–85.

73. Blane, *Cynegetica*, 86.

74. Heidegger, "The Question Concerning Technology," 21.

75. See Hudson, "From 'Nation' to 'Race,'" 258.

76. Patricia Fara identifies three theories on human variation, positioning that of John Locke between the traditional opposition of monogenism of Buffon and the polygenism of Isaac La Peyrère—which was largely rejected until the late eighteenth century: Locke also began with a monogenist account, but instead of climate identified activity as the determining factor in creating racial differences (*Sex, Botany and Empire*, 100). Activity, cast as occupation, such as hunting, certainly figured largely in explanations of the origins of canine breeds.

77. Buffon, *Natural History*, 4:11. On Buffon's topographical explanation of the human races, see Popkin, "The Philosophical Basis of Eighteenth-Century Racism," 251.

78. Buffon, *Natural History*, 4:344.

79. Buffon, *Natural History*, 4:337. Derrida points out that Descartes's criticism of accounts of animals focuses not so much on external similarities between animals and humans, but on "the passage from outside to inside, belief in the possibility of inducing from this *exterior* resemblance an *interior* analogy, namely the presence in the animal of a soul, of sentiments and passions like our own" ("But as for Me, Who Am I (Following)?" in *The Animal That Therefore I Am*, 79). Derrida draws out this characteristic from Descartes's anthropocentric thinking as though to distinguish the philosophical tradition from the tradition of writings on dogs (rather than on "the animal"), including Buffon, hunt writers, and novelists and poets. Since at least the eighteenth century, dogs have been made legible by being given faces that signify an analogous interiority. And this has happened through breed. But that interiority—which makes dogs loyal, man's best friend—has not yet been seen to entail a private or secret life, but an interiority that is directly legible through a legally defined breed face with its history. So the step I am working toward—at least in regard to relations between humans and dogs—will be not merely to assert an interiority but to accept the possibility of a *private*, unknowable, illegible interiority.

80. Kant, *Critique of Judgement*, 180.

81. Goldsmith, *A History of the Earth and Animated Nature*, 2:127; Edwards, *Cynographia Britannica*, 4–5.

82. McNeill, "Life beyond the Organism," 213.

83. Buffon, *Natural History*, 4:346.

84. Buffon, *Natural History*, 4:360.

85. Blane, *Cynegetica*, 87. Johann Friedrich Blumenbach, in describing the varieties of color among humans, associates whiteness with northern regions and other colors with southern latitudes, and provides analogies with several animals: "wolves, dogs, hares, cattle, crows, the chaffinch, etc." (*On the Natural Varieties of Mankind*, 108).

86. Quoted in Shaw, *The Illustrated Book of the Dog*, 2.

87. Caius, *Of Englishe Dogges*, 2.

88. See Secord, *A Breed Apart*, 60.

89. Edwards, *Cynographia Britannica*, 1.

90. Edwards, *Cynographia Britannica*, 4.

91. Edwards, *Cynographia Britannica*, 7–8.

92. Derrida, *Of Grammatology*, 112.

93. Taplin, *The Sportsman's Cabinet*, 1:7.

94. Taplin, *The Sportsman's Cabinet*, 1:22.

95. Taplin, *The Sportsman's Cabinet*, 1:125.

96. Edwards, *Cynographia Britannica*, 5.

97. Kant, "Of the Different Human Races," 14.

98. Buffon, *Natural History*, 4:358.

99. Buffon, *Natural History*, 4:359.

100. Derrida, *Of Grammatology*, 112; emphasis in the original.

101. Buffon, *Natural History*, 4:359.

102. Buffon, *Natural History*, 4:341.

103. Buffon, *Natural History*, 4:340–41.

104. Bindman, *Ape to Apollo*, 180.

105. Taplin, *The Sportsman's Cabinet*, 1:25.

106. Taplin, *The Sportsman's Cabinet*, 1:81.

107. Taplin, *The Sportsman's Cabinet*, 2:102.

108. Taplin, *The Sportsman's Cabinet*, 2:102–3.
109. Edwards, *Cynographia Britannica*, art: "The Drover's Dog, or Cur."
110. Derrida, "Economimesis," 22.
111. Kant, *Critique of Judgement*, 23.
112. Wood, "*Comment ne pas manger*—Deconstruction and Humanism," 33.
113. Lee, *A History and Description of the Modern Dogs*, 17.
114. Edwards, *Cynographia Britannica*, art: "Terrier."
115. Ritchie, *The British Dog*, 118.
116. Ritvo, *The Animal Estate*, 93.
117. Derrida, "The Force of Law," 36.
118. Kant, "Of the Different Human Races," 13n; emphasis mine.
119. Gorkom, "*What If*," 130.
120. Fabricant, "Defining Self and Others," 524.

CHAPTER 2. THE MODERN LANDSCAPE OF SPORT: REPRESENTATIONS OF THE FOXHOUND

1. Derrida, *The Truth in Painting*, 42.
2. Derrida, *The Truth in Painting*, 42.
3. Derrida, *The Truth in Painting*, 54.
4. Kant, *Critique of Judgement*, 57.
5. Derrida, *The Truth in Painting*, 59.
6. Derrida, *The Truth in Painting*, 61.
7. Derrida, *The Truth in Painting*, 63.
8. Derrida, *The Truth in Painting*, 73.
9. Overton, *Agricultural Revolution in England*, 197.
10. Blane, *Cynegetica*, 84–85.
11. Blaine, *An Encyclopædia of Rural Sports*, §1383.
12. Blaine, *An Encyclopædia of Rural Sports*, §1390. In like fashion, the Reverend William Daniel asserts "that the Hounds procured from England should degenerate in another Climate," and then backs up his patriotic fervor with a passage from Sommerville: "In thee alone, fair land of Liberty, / Is bred the perfect Hound, in Scent and Speed, / As yet unrivalled, while in other Climes / Their virtue fails, a weak degen'rate Race" (*Rural Sports*, 64–65). Conversely, when English foxhounds were imported into America in the early nineteenth century, they were found completely unsuited to the landscape and style of hunting in Virginia, as "their noses were not cold enough and they were too fast and too silent"; as a result they were used to chase deer instead of foxes (Mackay-Smith, *The American Foxhound*, 24). I thank Gordon Smith for sending me to this source in the National Sporting Library.
13. Quoted in Gilbey, *Hounds in Old Days*, 93.
14. See Nicholas Russell, *Like Engend'ring Like*, 12–13; and see Ritvo, "Barring the Cross," 45.
15. Blane, *Cynegetica*, 89–90.
16. Dale, *The Eighth Duke*, 74.
17. Dale, *The Eighth Duke*, 77.
18. Stephen Deuchar has made this mythic connection plain in his reading of George Stubbs's *The*

Grosvenor Hunt (1762), in *Sporting Art in Eighteenth-Century England*, 107–8. Gilbey points out as well that the old Southern hounds had been used to hunt stag (*Hounds in Old Days*, 75).

19. Dale, *The History of the Belvoir Hunt*, 2.
20. Derrida, *The Truth in Painting*, 59.
21. Edwards, *Cynographia Britannica*, n.p., art: "Beagle."
22. Dale, *The History of the Belvoir Hunt*, 2.
23. Buchanan-Jardine, *Hounds of the World*, 138–39.
24. Buchanan-Jardine, *Hounds of the World*, 102.
25. Buchanan-Jardine, *Hounds of the World*, 138.
26. Buchanan-Jardine, *Hounds of the World*, 103.
27. Vyner, *Notitia Venatica*, 12–13.
28. Dale, *The History of the Belvoir Hunt*, 31.
29. Boswell refers to Meynell on several occasions being in Johnson's company. See, for example, *The Life of Samuel Johnson*, 3:404. And for the connection to Walpole, see Ellis, *Leicestershire and the Quorn Hunt*, 8–12.
30. Barrell, "The Public Prospect," 24.
31. In discussing an example of resistance to industrial breeding practice, Cary Wolfe argues that cattle are included "as coconstitutive with human beings in resisting the articulations of a biopolitical *dispositif* in and through the body." He then draws this distinction: "Why specifically 'bio*political*' and not just 'bio*power*'? Because such practices involve not just the insertion of animal bodies into farming assemblages involving technologies, human beings, land, architectural spaces, and so for the purposes of changing and maximizing individuals and populations as the bearers of particular traits to suit the particular ends of capitalist enterprise" (*Before the Law*, 35–36). In much of the thinking inflected by biopolitical resistance, co-constitutionality, coagency, coevolution all play crucial roles, which I critique below.
32. Vyner, *Notitia Venatica*, 3.
33. Russell, *Like Engend'ring Like*, 198. Not surprisingly for an unabashed admirer of Meynell, Ellis also urges this line of influence.
34. Derry, *Bred for Perfection*, 3.
35. Pawson, *Robert Bakewell*, 9n.
36. Dale, *The History of the Belvoir Hunt*, 12. Buchanan-Jardine also refers to the precedence of Yarborough's and Beaufort's hounds (*Hounds of the World*, 140).
37. Dale, *The History of the Belvoir Hunt*, 73–74.
38. Hawkes, *The Meynellian Science*, 4, 7.
39. Taplin, *The Sportsman's Cabinet*, 2:180.
40. Longrigg, *The History of Foxhunting*, 87.
41. Derrida, "Economimesis," 5.
42. Beckford, *Thoughts on Hunting*, 273.
43. Daniel, *Rural Sports*, 212.
44. Fountain and Gates, *Stubbs' Dogs*, 40.
45. Moore, for example, says, "Ringwood might well have come out of any modern kennel," in *Foxhounds*, 16.
46. Carr, *English Foxhunting*, 50.
47. Burns, *The Final Report*, 1.
48. In his encomium to foxhunting, the Duke of Beaufort states an opinion that sets him in a continuous line with his ancestors in the eighteenth century whose regulation of the landscape was

driven by overt class bias: "Human beings do have latent aggressive tendencies that in ancient times were satisfied by war and the constant need for self-defence and preservation. Better surely that those tendencies should be directed into a sport that is so exhilarating and carries with it goodwill and comradeship of the best kind, than that it should vent itself in soccer hooliganism and the sort of violence that makes the streets of our cities unsafe for both young and old" (*Fox-hunting*, 190). In this view, foxhunting provides the uniting force that keeps civilization from collapsing into anarchy.

49. Marvin, "A Passionate Pursuit," 58.
50. Beckford, *Thoughts on Hunting*, 140.
51. Cuthbert Bede recounts a tradition that the bells of Peckleton Church in Leicester were donated by Thomas Boothby, "and that he had them so pitched and tuned as to resemble the cry of a pack of hounds." Quite notably, in this context, Bede adds that "the said bells are of a very melodious and cheery kind in their music" ("Tally-ho Notes," 207).
52. Barrell, "The Public Prospect," 25.
53. Taplin, *Sportsman's Cabinet*, 2:275.
54. Kant, *Critique of Judgement*, 135.
55. Kant, *Critique of Judgement*, 135–36; emphasis in the original.
56. Derrida, "The Animal That Therefore I Am (More to Follow)," in *The Animal That Therefore I Am*, 26.
57. Derrida, "Economimesis," 5, and *The Truth in Painting*, 73.
58. This painting was popular enough that Gilpin reproduced it several times. One of the later versions hangs in the same collection—of Samuel Whitbread—as that praised by Taplin, and several others are housed in the Courtauld Institute of Art.
59. Derrida, *Of Grammatology*, 112; emphasis in the original.
60. In accord with this necessity, Diana Donald, despite describing Thornton as a "fanatical sportsman" and as being "ruthless . . . in his demand for veracity" from Gilpin, finds the painting to hold a transcendent meaning when she concludes, "The fox's fate is, by implication, not attributable to human agency alone: it is part of a cycle of life and death which embraces the whole of nature" (*Picturing Animals in Britain*, 256–57).
61. Landry, *The Invention of the Countryside*, 112, 42.
62. Landry, *The Invention of the Countryside*, 53.
63. Landry, *The Invention of the Countryside*, 112.
64. Derrida, *The Truth in Painting*, 63.
65. Tory foxhunters, who opposed the American and French Revolutions and supported the slave trade, found their parliamentary opponent in Charles James Fox, proponent of democracy and opponent of servitude. Tories called their vulpine victim "Charlie" to add greater delight in the repeated slaughter, turning their blood sport into the execution of the Whig leader in effigy.
66. Beaufort, *Foxhunting*, 209.

CHAPTER 3. SIGNIFYING DOGS: POPULARIZED BREEDS IN THE ROMANCES OF WALTER SCOTT

1. Scott, *Ivanhoe*, 14.
2. Scott, *Ivanhoe*, 549–50.

3. Scott, *Waverley*, 75.

4. Wilt, *Secret Leaves*, 161, 162.

5. Ferris, *The Achievement of Literary Authority*, 205.

6. Wall, *The Prose of Things*, 42.

7. Brown, *Homeless Dogs and Melancholy Apes*, 65.

8. Brown, *Homeless Dogs and Melancholy Apes*, 72.

9. Brown, *Homeless Dogs and Melancholy Apes*, 77.

10. Thomas, *Man and the Natural World*.

11. Scott, *The Letters*, 4:180.

12. Scott, *The Letters*, 11:366.

13. Scott, *The Letters*, 4:206.

14. Scott, *The Letters*, 4:246.

15. McCracken-Flesher, *Possible Scotlands*, 13.

16. McCracken-Flesher, *Possible Scotlands*, 14.

17. Scott, *The Letters*, 10:283.

18. Scott, *The Letters*, 10:211.

19. Yoon Sun Lee explores in detail the ways that "the practice of antiquarianism made manifest the latent resemblance between historical value and market value: both were contingent on the relation between scarcity and a generalized demand" ("A Divided Inheritance," 548). This connection could hold relevance to canine commodification, though Lee confines her examination to one novel, *The Antiquary*, however, and makes no reference to the ways Scott generates the values that make a national British character desirable.

20. Maxwell, "Inundations of Time," 451.

21. Bardsley, "In and around the Borders," 397.

22. Duncan, *Modern Romance and Transformations*, 114. George G. Dekker comments in this regard that Dandie represents "the strong suggestion of an atavistic return to the savage origins of mankind" in *The Fictions of Romantic Tourism*, 179. And James Reed sees such a strong synecdochic connection between the region and the character, that he suggests Dandie's surname refers to one of the "place names which commemorate local history and personalities," and that is "Dinmontclair Knowe, to the east of Neecastleton in Liddesdale" (*Walter Scott*, 85–86).

23. Duncan, *Modern Romance and Transformations*, 112.

24. Johnson, *Sir Walter Scott*, 1:468.

25. Scott, *The Letters*, 4:216–17.

26. Scott, *Guy Mannering*, "Historical Note," 506. Scott's son-in-law and first biographer, John Gibson Lockhart, citing a memorandum from the son of Robert Shortreed—Scott's guide through the Border country during his so-called "raids" during the 1790s looking for artifacts and old ballads—describes how the pair stayed at a farmhouse as the guests of Willie Elliot, who kept "half a dozen dogs of all degrees" (*Memoirs of the Life of Sir Walter Scott*, 1:177). Shortreed *fils* puts forth this account in the effort to identify the original of Dandie Dinmont, but Lockhart himself looks to Scott's lifelong friend William Laidlaw and his wife as the models for Dandie and Ailie.

27. Scott, *The Letters*, 8:69.

28. Scott, *The Letters*, 8:183.

29. Donald, *Picturing Animals in Britain*, 139.

30. Scott, *The Talisman*, 23, 32. Several commentators have pointed out the pervasive connections between human characters and animals. Margaret Bruzelius, for example, sees the associations with Lionheart serving only to make King Richard "grotesquely bestial" ("The King of England,"

27). I would argue, however, that they function more broadly as a reflection of the taxonomic analogies that gained widespread currency at the end of the eighteenth century.

31. Scott, *The Talisman*, 107.
32. Scott, *The Talisman*, 107.
33. Scott, *The Talisman*, 108.
34. Scott, *The Talisman*, 123.
35. Scott, *The Talisman*, 75.
36. Scott, *The Talisman*, 75.
37. Scott, *The Talisman*, 134.
38. Scott, *The Talisman*, 134.
39. Scott, *The Talisman*, 134–35.
40. Scott, *The Talisman*, 135.
41. Scott, *The Talisman*, 269.
42. Scott, *The Talisman*, 136.
43. Scott, *The Talisman*, 136–37.
44. Scott, *The Talisman*, 188.
45. Scott, *The Talisman*, 189.
46. Scott, *The Talisman*, 188–90.
47. Scott, *The Talisman*, 197.
48. Scott, *The Talisman*, 198.
49. Scott, *The Talisman*, 222.
50. Scott, *The Talisman*, 225.
51. Derrida, "Economimesis," 15.
52. Derrida, "And Say the Animal Responded?," in *The Animal That Therefore I Am*, 130.
53. Shaw, *Narrating Reality*, 197.
54. Scott, *The Talisman*, 197.
55. Scott, *The Talisman*, 190.
56. Derrida, *The Politics of Friendship*, 92.
57. Derrida, *The Politics of Friendship*, 92.
58. Derrida, *The Politics of Friendship*, 93.
59. Derrida, *The Politics of Friendship*, 99.
60. Derrida, *The Politics of Friendship*, 100.
61. Scott, *The Talisman*, 222.
62. Scott, *Woodstock*, 546; the "ten lines of verse praising canine fidelity" are neither identified nor quoted by the editors of this edition.
63. See, for example, McCracken-Flesher, *Possible Scotlands*, 135–37.
64. Scott, *Woodstock*, 195.
65. Scott, *Woodstock*, 47.
66. Scott, *Woodstock*, 47.
67. Scott, *Woodstock*, 329.
68. Scott, *Woodstock*, 347.
69. Scott, *Woodstock*, 347–48.
70. Scott, *Woodstock*, 348.
71. Scott, *Woodstock*, 329.
72. Scott, *Woodstock*, 351.
73. Scott, *Woodstock*, 348.

74. Scott, *Woodstock*, 272.
75. Wilt, *Secret Leaves*, 176.
76. Scott, *Woodstock*, 415.
77. Scott, *Woodstock*, 417.
78. Reproduced in Scott, *The Waverley Novels*, 39:403–4.
79. Scott, *The Letters*, 10:90.
80. Scott, *The Letters*, 11:309, 320, 331.
81. Scott, *Woodstock*, 345.
82. Donald, *Picturing Animals in Britain*, 141.

CHAPTER 4. CYNICAL FRIENDSHIPS: ANTHRO-CANINE RELATIONS TODAY

1. Derrida and Nancy, "Eating Well," 108.
2. Oliver, *Animal Lessons*, 108.
3. Sinclair, *Lights Out for the Territory*, 58.
4. Throughout his book *Before the Law*, Cary Wolfe allows a hierarchy to orient his thinking by repeatedly differentiating nonhuman animals who resemble humans more than others. He says, for example, "that *at least some* nonhuman animals—elephants and great apes, for example—apparently grieve over the loss of those close to them"; and animal behavior and communication form "an exteriority . . . that enables *some animals more than others* to 'differentiate' and 'individuate' their existence" (18, 76; emphasis added in both cases). Such a differentiation based on obviously anthropocentric values seems due to inattentiveness on Wolfe's part, allowing the "principle of calculability" to determine how to think of animals, even in broad terms. Inattentiveness and habit can thus stymy the best efforts to open avenues of human-animal relations.
5. Kuzniar, *Melancholia's Dog*, 6.
6. Kuzniar, *Melancholia's Dog*, 6.
7. Kuzniar, *Melancholia's Dog*, 61.
8. Kuzniar, *Melancholia's Dog*, 65–66.
9. Calarco, *Zoographies*, 140.
10. Kuzniar, *Melancholia's Dog*, 10.
11. Kuzniar, *Melancholia's Dog*, 11.
12. Kuzniar, *Melancholia's Dog*, 36–37.
13. Kuzniar, *Melancholia's Dog*, 38.
14. Kuzniar, *Melancholia's Dog*, 37.
15. Derrida, "Envoi," 106.
16. Derrida, "Envoi," 107.
17. Derrida, "Envoi," 106.
18. Kuzniar, *Melancholia's Dog*, 40–41.
19. Kuzniar, *Melancholia's Dog*, 39.
20. Kuzniar, *Melancholia's Dog*, 40.
21. Kuzniar, *Melancholia's Dog*, 71.
22. Kuzniar, *Melancholia's Dog*, 72.
23. Kuzniar, *Melancholia's Dog*, 81.
24. Kuzniar, *Melancholia's Dog*, 83.

25. Kuzniar, *Melancholia's Dog*, 81.
26. Kant, *Critique of Judgement*, 141.
27. Derrida, "Economimesis," 22.
28. Kuzniar, *Melancholia's Dog*, 83, 82, 81.
29. Kuzniar, *Melancholia's Dog*, 83.
30. Kuzniar, *Melancholia's Dog*, 84.
31. Kuzniar, *Melancholia's Dog*, 84, 85.
32. Kuzniar, *Melancholia's Dog*, 91.
33. Kuzniar, *Melancholia's Dog*, 38, 37.
34. Haraway, *When Species Meet*, 73.
35. Haraway, *When Species Meet*, 80.
36. Haraway, *When Species Meet*, 237.
37. Haraway, *When Species Meet*, 67.
38. Haraway, *When Species Meet*, 223.
39. Haraway, *When Species Meet*, 208.
40. Haraway, *When Species Meet*, 208.
41. Haraway, *When Species Meet*, 226–27.
42. Haraway, *When Species Meet*, 66–67.
43. Haraway, *When Species Meet*, 97.
44. Haraway, *When Species Meet*, 99.
45. Haraway, *When Species Meet*, 105.
46. Haraway, *When Species Meet*, 105.
47. Haraway, *When Species Meet*, 98–99.
48. Haraway, *When Species Meet*, 102.
49. Haraway, *When Species Meet*, 103.
50. In an identical way, the Victorian sportswriter Charles Cook countered aspersions that the Dandie Dinmont terrier had been crossed with Dachshunds by interviewing surviving Scotsmen who claimed a direct involvement in breeding the Dandies, thus proving that the breed was indigenous to Britain (*The Dandie Dinmont Terrier*, 3–4). Like Haraway, Cook ties the primordial members of the breed to pastoral work, stating that "the requirements of the Border Country ultimately [produced] a terrier adapted for its special work" (4).
51. Haraway, *When Species Meet*, 96–97.
52. Haraway, *When Species Meet*, 96.
53. Haraway, *When Species Meet*, 96.
54. Haraway, *When Species Meet*, 96.
55. Haraway, *When Species Meet*, 96.
56. Haraway, *When Species Meet*, 71.
57. Haraway, *When Species Meet*, 58.
58. Haraway, *When Species Meet*, 59.
59. All references in this paragraph are to Sara Aldridge, "Dogs' Priceless Contribution."
60. Haraway, *When Species Meet*, 61; my emphasis.
61. Haraway, *When Species Meet*, 62.
62. Haraway, *When Species Meet*, 66.
63. Haraway, *When Species Meet*, 23.
64. Lawlor, "Auto-Affection and Becoming (Part 1)," 2. Lawlor presents much the same argument in another essay, "Following the Rats."

65. Lawlor, "Auto-Affection and Becoming (Part 1)," 2.
66. Derrida, "But as for Me, Who Am I (Following)?" in *The Animal That Therefore I Am*, 93. Since the chapters of this book work collectively toward a common aim, where the particular chapter does matter, I shall identify it by name.
67. Derrida, "But as for Me, Who Am I (Following)?" in *The Animal That Therefore I Am*, 160.
68. Derrida, "But as for Me, Who Am I (Following)?" in *The Animal That Therefore I Am*, 50.
69. In the 1800 "Preface" to *Lyrical Ballads*, Wordsworth assures his readers that they "will find no personification of abstract ideas" in his poems, since his aim is to keep his "reader in the company of flesh and blood"; his style, he says, can be summed up in the assertion that "I have at all times endeavoured to look steadily at my subject" (in Perkins, *English Romantic Writers*, 426).
70. Derrida, "But as for Me, Who Am I (Following)?" in *The Animal That Therefore I Am*, 43f.
71. Derrida, *The Politics of Friendship*, 293.
72. Derrida, "But as for Me, Who Am I (Following)?" in *The Animal That Therefore I Am*, 14; emphasis in the original.
73. Derrida, "But as for Me, Who Am I (Following)?" in *The Animal That Therefore I Am*, 13; emphasis in the original.
74. The antecedents of the "face-to-face" certainly go back much farther, as Jean-Paul Sartre opens his 1948 essay "Black Orpheus" with a radical version of this challenge, and the paradigm has fueled much modern poetry since the Romantic formation of Nature through the trope of prosopopoeia. For Sartre's versions, see *"What Is Literature?" and Other Essays*, 291.
75. Levinas, *Totality and Infinity*, 214.
76. Levinas, *Difficult Freedom*, 153.
77. Derrida, "But as for Me, Who Am I (Following)?" in *The Animal That Therefore I Am*, 107. David Clark presents a compelling critique of Levinas's anthropocentric ethics and its exclusions in "On Being."
78. Derrida, "But as for Me, Who Am I (Following)?" in *The Animal That Therefore I Am*, 107–8.
79. Derrida, "But as for Me, Who Am I (Following)?" in *The Animal That Therefore I Am*, 13.
80. Calarco, *Zoographies*, 63; emphasis in the original.
81. Derrida, "But as for Me, Who Am I (Following)?" in *The Animal That Therefore I Am*, 117.
82. Derrida, "But as for Me, Who Am I (Following)?" in *The Animal That Therefore I Am*, 102.
83. Derrida, "But as for Me, Who Am I (Following)?" in *The Animal That Therefore I Am*, 111.
84. Derrida, "But as for Me, Who Am I (Following)?" in *The Animal That Therefore I Am*, 112.
85. Derrida, "But as for Me, Who Am I (Following)?" in *The Animal That Therefore I Am*, 94.
86. Levinas, *Totality and Infinity*, 194.
87. Calarco, *Zoographies*, 69.
88. Calarco, *Zoographies*, 69.
89. Calarco, *Zoographies*, 70.
90. Derrida, "Envoi," 111.
91. Derrida, *The Beast and the Sovereign*, 1:161. In his early essay on Levinas, "Violence and Metaphysics," Derrida says, in regard to Levinas's ethics, "To neutralize space with the description of the other, in order thereby to liberate positive infinity—is this not to neutralize the essential finitude of a face (glance-speech) which *is a body*, and not, as Levinas continually insists, the corporeal metaphor of etherealized thought? Body: that is, *also* exteriority, locality in the fully spatial, literally spatial, meaning of the word; a zero point, the origin of space, certainly, but an origin which has no meaning before the *of*, an origin inseparable from genitivity and from the space that it engenders and orients; an *inscribed* origin. The *inscription* is the written origin: traced

and henceforth *inscribed in* a system, in a figure which it no longer governs" (115). In the case of modern dogs, the system in which we find them inscribed is breed, which in turn is inscribed in the landscape over which we enforce our privilege through the histories and romances we write to conceal the conditionality of similitude.

92. Derrida, "But as for Me, Who Am I (Following)?" in *The Animal That Therefore I Am*, 9.
93. Derrida, "But as for Me, Who Am I (Following)?" in *The Animal That Therefore I Am*, 63.
94. Derrida, "But as for Me, Who Am I (Following)?" in *The Animal That Therefore I Am*, 63.
95. Haraway, *When Species Meet*, 96.
96. Derrida, *The Politics of Friendship*, 29, 30.
97. Derrida and Nancy, "Eating Well," 108.
98. Derrida and Nancy, "Eating Well," 100.
99. Derrida, "But as for Me, Who Am I (Following)?" in *The Animal That Therefore I Am*, 157.
100. Derrida, *The Beast and the Sovereign*, 2:217, and n.
101. Kuzniar, *Melancholia's Dog*, 11.
102. Derrida, *The Politics of Friendship*, 178.
103. It is this frameless *Ungrund* that Laurie Shannon seems to have in mind when she expands Foucault's famous reading of the interlocking gazes in *Las Meninas* by focusing on the dog, whose eyes are closed, leading Foucault to dismiss him as "an object to be seen." Shannon comments, to the contrary, that "In the dog's 'not regarding' the sovereign, a prerogative is expressed," for the dog does not sleep. And in this "prerogative," Shannon continues, "Velasquez's dog declines to acknowledge the structures of sovereignty forming around him through the dynamics of human vision by *refusing to look*" (*The Accommodated Animal*, 120, 121; emphasis mine). While often referring to the late modern commentators like Foucault and Derrida, Shannon attends to the early modern understanding of animals, which is not yet determined by the post-Enlightenment drive to systemic totality. Though Shannon does not develop this key point further, she rightly draws attention to the inability of a modern thinker like Foucault to allow dogs anything more than objective status unless they offer up a gaze of recognition. Velasquez's dog has a noble status just by his size, but in refusing to participate in the "structure of sovereignty," he proves to be just as disruptive as the ignoble cur who refuses to acknowledge my sovereign subjectivity.
104. Derrida, *The Politics of Friendship*, 278.
105. Derrida, *The Politics of Friendship*, 220.
106. Derrida, *The Politics of Friendship*, 298.
107. Derrida, *The Politics of Friendship*, 66.
108. Derrida, "But as for Me, Who Am I (Following)?" in *The Animal That Therefore I Am*, 93.
109. Derrida, "But as for Me, Who Am I (Following)?" in *The Animal That Therefore I Am*, 27.
110. Derrida, "But as for Me, Who Am I (Following)?" in *The Animal That Therefore I Am*, 112.
111. Derrida, "But as for Me, Who Am I (Following)?" in *The Animal That Therefore I Am*, 106.
112. Derrida, *The Politics of Friendship*, 294.

Bibliography

Aldridge, Sara. "Dogs' Priceless Contribution to Hemophilia Research." *Hemaware: The Bleeding Disorders Magazine.* January 2009. Http://www.hemaware.org/story/dogs-priceless-contribution -hemophilia-research.

Ault, Norman. *New Light on Pope, with Some Additions to His Poetry Hitherto Unknown.* New York: Methuen, 1949.

Banton, Michael. *Racial Theories.* 2nd ed. Cambridge: Cambridge University Press, 1998.

Bardsley, Alyson. "In and around the Borders of the Nation in Scott's *Guy Mannering.*" *Nineteenth-Century Contexts* 24 (2002): 397–415.

Barrell, John. *The Political Theory of Painting from Reynolds to Hazlitt: "The Body of the Public."* New Haven, CT: Yale University Press, 1986.

———. "The Public Prospect and the Private View: The Politics of Taste in Eighteenth-Century Britain." In *Reading Landscape: Country—City—Capital,* edited by Simon Pugh, 19–40. Manchester: Manchester University Press, 1990.

Barry, Edward. *On the Necessity of Adopting Some Measures to Reduce the Present Number of Dogs, with a Short Account of Hydrophobia, and the Most Approved Remedies Against It.* London: Smart & Cowslade, 1796.

Beaufort, Henry Hugh Arthur FitzRoy Somerset. *Foxhunting.* London: David and Charles, 1980.

Beckford, Peter. *Thoughts on Hunting, in a Series of Familiar Letters to a Friend.* London: E. Easton, 1781.

Bede, Cuthbert. "Tally-ho Notes." *Fores's Sporting Notes and Sketches* 3 (1886–1887): 198–209.

Bernasconi, Robert, ed. *Race.* Oxford: Blackwell, 2001.

Bindman, David. *Ape to Apollo: Aesthetics and the Idea of Race in the 18th Century.* London: Reaktion Books, 2002.

Blackstone, William. *Commentaries on the Laws of England: A Facsimile of the First Edition of 1765–1769.* Chicago: University of Chicago Press, 1979.

Blaine, Delabere Pritchett. *An Encyclopædia of Rural Sports.* London: Longman, Orme, Brown, Green and Longmans, 1840.

Blaisdell, John D. "The Rise of Man's Best Friend: The Popularity of Dogs as Companion Animals in Late Eighteenth-Century London as Reflected in the Dog Tax of 1796." *Anthrozoös* 12 (1999): 76–87.

Blane, William. *Cynegetica, or Essays on Sporting, Consisting of Observations on Hare Hunting.* London: John Stockdale, 1788.

Blumenbach, Johann Friedrich. *On the Natural Varieties of Mankind.* Translated by Thomas Bendyshe. London: Longman, Green, Longman, Roberts & Green, 1865.

Boswell, James. *The Life of Samuel Johnson, LL.D.* 4 vols. London: H. Baldwin and Son, 1799.

Braunschneider, Theresa. "The Lady and the Lapdog: Mixed Ethnicity in Constantinople, Fashionable Pets in Britain." In *Humans and Other Animals in Eighteenth-Century British Culture,* edited by Frank Palmeri, 31–52. Burlington, VT: Ashgate, 2006.

Brindle. *The Dog's Plea: Or Reasons Most Humbly Submitted by the Barking Fraternity of Great Britain to the Men Their Masters, Shewing Why Dogs Ought to Be Exempted from Taxes.* London: R. Griffiths, 1753.

Brown, Laura. *Homeless Dogs and Melancholy Apes: Humans and Other Animals in the Modern Literary Imagination.* Ithaca, NY: Cornell University Press, 2010.

Bruzelius, Margaret. "'The King of England . . . Loved to Look upon a MAN': Melancholy and Masculinity in Scott's *The Talisman.*" *Modern Language Quarterly* 62 (2001): 19–41.

Buchanan-Jardine, John. *Hounds of the World.* Penrith, Cumbria: Grayling Books, 1937.

Buffon, Comte de (George Louis Leclerc). *Natural History, General and Particular.* Translated by William Smellie. 2nd ed. 9 vols. London, 1785.

Burns, Terence. *The Final Report of the Committee of Inquiry into Hunting with Dogs in England and Wales.* Norwich: Her Majesty's Stationary Office, 2000.

Caius, John. *Of Englishe Dogges.* Translated by Abraham Fleming. London, 1576.

Calarco, Matthew. *Zoographies: The Question of the Animal from Heidegger to Derrida.* New York: Columbia University Press, 2008.

Carr, Raymond. *English Fox Hunting: A History.* London: Weidenfeld and Nicolson, 1976.

Clark, David. "On Being 'The Last Kantian in Nazi Germany': Dwelling with Animals after Levinas." In *Animal Acts: Configuring the Human in Western History,* edited by Jennifer Ham and Matthew Senior, 165–98. New York: Routledge, 1997.

Clark, George. *An Address to Both Houses of Parliament: Containing Reasons for a Tax upon Dogs, and the Outlines of a Plan for That Purpose; and for Effectually Suppressing the Oppressive Practice of Impressing Seamen, and More Expeditiously Manning the Royal Navy.* London: Johnson, 1791.

Colcridge, Samuel Taylor. "On the Principles of Genial Criticism." In *English Romantic Writers,* edited by David Perkins, 557–63. New York: Harcourt Brace, 1995.

Cook, Charles. *The Dandie Dinmont Terrier: Its History and Characteristics, Compiled from the Most Authentic Sources.* Edinburgh: David Douglas, 1885.

Cruickshank, Eveline, and Howard Erskine-Hill. "The Waltham Black Act and Jacobitism." *Journal of British Studies* 24 (1985): 358–65.

Cummings, Robert. "*Windsor Forest* as a Silvan Poem." *English Literary History* 54 (1987): 63–79.

Dale, T. F. *The Eighth Duke of Beaufort and the Badminton Hunt.* Westminster: Archibald Constable, 1901.

———. *The History of the Belvoir Hunt.* Westminster: Archibald Constable, 1899.

Daniel, William B. *Rural Sports.* London: Longman, Hurst, Rees & Orme, 1801.

Dekker, George G. *The Fictions of Romantic Tourism: Radcliffe, Scott, and Mary Shelley.* Stanford, CA: Stanford University Press, 2005.

Derrida, Jacques. *The Animal That Therefore I Am.* Translated by David Wills. New York: Fordham University Press, 2008.

———. *The Beast and the Sovereign.* Translated by Geoffrey Bennington. 2 vols. University of Chicago Press, 2009–2010.

———. "Economimesis." Translated by Richard Klein. *Diacritics* 11 (1981): 3–25.

———. "Envoi." In *Psyche: Inventions of the Other,* vol. 1, edited by Peggy Kamuf and Elizabeth Rottenberg, 94–128. Stanford, CA: Stanford University Press, 2007.

———. "The Force of Law: The Mystical Foundation of Authority." In *Deconstruction and the Possibility of Justice,* edited by Drucilla Cornell, Michael Rosenfeld, and David Gray Carlson, 13–67. New York: Routledge, 1992.

———. *Of Grammatology*. Translated by Gayatri Chakravorty Spivak. Baltimore: Johns Hopkins University Press, 1976.

———. *Of Spirit*. Translated by Geoffrey Bennington and Rachel Bowlby. Chicago: University of Chicago Press, 1989.

———. *The Politics of Friendship*. Translated by George Collins. New York: Verso, 2005.

———. *The Truth in Painting*. Translated by Geoff Bennington and Ian McLeod. Chicago: University of Chicago Press, 1987.

———. "Violence and Metaphysics: An Essay on the Thought of Levinas." In *Writing and Difference*, translated by Alan Bass, 79–53. Chicago: University of Chicago Press, 1978.

Derrida, Jacques, and Jean-Luc Nancy. "Eating Well, or the Calculation of the Subject: An Interview with Jacques Derrida." In *Who Comes After the Subject?*, edited by Eduardo Cadava, Peter Connor, and Jean-Luc Nancy, 96–119. New York: Routledge, 1991.

Derry, Margaret E. *Bred for Perfection: Shorthorn Cattle, Collies, and Arabian Horses since 1800*. Baltimore: Johns Hopkins University Press, 2003.

Deuchar, Stephen. *Sporting Art in Eighteenth-Century England: A Social and Political History*. New Haven, CT: Yale University Press, 1988.

Donald, Diana. *Picturing Animals in Britain, 1750–1850*. New Haven, CT: Yale University Press, 2007.

Doody, Margaret Anne. *The Daring Muse: Augustan Poetry Reconsidered*. Cambridge: Cambridge University Press, 1985.

Drayton, Richard. *Nature's Government: Science, Imperial Britain, and the "Improvement of the World."* New Haven, CT: Yale University Press, 2000.

Duncan, Ian. *Modern Romance and Transformations of the Novel: The Gothic, Scott, Dickens*. Cambridge: Cambridge University Press, 1992.

Edwards, Sydenham. *Cynographia Britannica: Consisting of Coloured Engravings of the Various Breeds of Dogs Existing in Great Britain; Drawn from the Life, with Observations on Their Properties and Uses*. London: Whittingham, 1800–1805.

Ellis, Colin D. B. *Leicestershire and the Quorn Hunt*. Leicestershire: Edgar Backus, 1951.

Ellis, Markman. "Suffering Things: Lapdogs, Slaves, and Counter-Sensibility." In *The Secret Life of Things: Animals, Objects, and It-Narratives in Eighteenth-Century England*, edited by Mark Blackwell, 92–113. Lewisburg, PA: Bucknell University Press, 2007.

Fabricant, Carole. "Defining Self and Others: Pope and Eighteenth-Century Gender Ideology." *Criticism* 39 (1997): 503–29.

Fara, Patricia. *Sex, Botany, and Empire: The Story of Carl Linnaeus and Joseph Banks*. New York: Columbia University Press, 2003.

Fenves, Peter. "What 'Progresses' Has Race-Theory Made Since the Times of Leibniz and Wolff?" In *The German Invention of Race*, edited by Sara Eigen and Mark Larrimore, 11–22. Albany: State University of New York Press, 2006.

Ferris, Ina. *The Achievement of Literary Authority: Gender, History, and the Waverley Novels*. Ithaca, NY: Cornell University Press, 1991.

Festa, Lynn. "Person, Animal, Thing: The 1796 Dog Tax and the Right to Superfluous Things." *Eighteenth-Century Life* 33 (2009): 1–44.

Foucault, Michel. *The History of Sexuality: An Introduction*. Translated by Robert Hurley. New York: Random House, 1978.

Fountain, Robert, and Alfred Gates. *Stubbs' Dogs: The Hounds and Domestic Dogs of the Eighteenth Century as Seen through the Paintings of George Stubbs*. London: Ackermann, 1984.

Fram, Alan. "'Mutts Like Me' Shows Obama's Racial Comfort." *Associated Press*, November 8, 2008. Http://www.msnbc.msn.com/id/27606637/ns/politics-decision_08/.

Fudge, Erica. *Animal*. London: Reaktion Books, 2002.

Gasché, Rodolphe. *The Idea of Form: Rethinking Kant's Aesthetics*. Stanford, CA: Stanford University Press, 2003.

Gilbey, Sir Walter. *Hounds in Old Days*. London: Vinton, 1913.

Goldsmith, Oliver. *A History of the Earth and Animated Nature*. 4 vols. Philadelphia, 1795.

Gorkom, Joris van. "*What If?* On Respect, Secret, and Spectre." *Mosaic* 40 (2007): 117–32.

Haraway, Donna. *When Species Meet*. Minneapolis: University of Minnesota Press, 2008.

Hawkes, John. *The Meynellian Science, or, Fox-Hunting upon System*. London: W. Clowes & Sons, 1848.

Hay, Douglas. "Poaching and the Game Laws in Cannock Chase." In *Albion's Fatal Tree: Crime and Society in Eighteenth-Century England*, edited by Douglas Hay, Peter Linebaugh, John G. Rule, E. P. Thompson, and Cal Winslow, 214–17. New York: Pantheon, 1975.

Heidegger, Martin. *The Fundamental Concepts of Metaphysics*. Translated by William McNeill and Nicholas Walker. Bloomington: Indiana University Press, 1995.

———. *An Introduction to Metaphysics*. Translated by Ralph Mannheim. New Haven, CT: Yale University Press, 1959.

———. *The Question Concerning Technology and Other Essays*. Translated by William Lovitt. New York: Harper, 1977.

Helsinger, Elizabeth. "Land and National Representation in Britain." In *Prospects for the Nation: Recent Essays in British Landscape, 1750–1880*, edited by Michael Rosenthal, Christian Payne, and Scott Wilcox, 13–35. New Haven, CT: Yale University Press, 1997.

Hudson, Nicholas. "From 'Nation' to 'Race': The Origin of Racial Classification in Eighteenth-Century Thought." *Eighteenth-Century Studies* 29 (1996): 247–64.

Johnson, Edgar. *Sir Walter Scott: The Great Unknown*. 2 vols. New York: Macmillan, 1970.

Kalof, Linda. *Looking at Animals in Human History*. London: Reaktion Books, 2007.

Kant, Immanuel. *Critique of Judgement*. Translated by James Creed Meredith. Oxford: Oxford University Press, 2007.

———. *Critique of Pure Reason*. Translated by Marcus Weigelt. New York: Penguin Books, 2007.

———. "Of the Different Human Races." Translated by Jon Mark Mikkelsen. In *The Idea of Race*, edited by Robert Bernasconi and Tommy L. Lott, 8–22. Indianapolis: Hackett Publishing Company, 2000.

Kean, Hilda. *Animal Rights: Political and Social Change in Britain since 1800*. London: Reaktion Books, 1998.

King, William. *Reasons and Proposals for Laying a Tax upon Dogs: Humbly Addressed to the Honourable House of Commons; by a Lover of His Country*. Reading: D. Henry, 1740.

Kuzniar, Alice. *Melancholia's Dog: Reflections on Our Animal Kinship*. Chicago: University of Chicago Press, 2006.

Landry, Donna. *The Invention of the Countryside: Hunting, Walking and Ecology in English Literature, 1671–1831*. New York: Palgrave, 2001.

———. *Noble Brutes: How Eastern Horses Transformed English Culture*. Baltimore: Johns Hopkins University Press, 2009.

Lawlor, Leonard. "Auto-Affection and Becoming (Part 1): Who Are We?" *Environmental Philosophy* 6 (2009): 1–19.

———. "Becoming and Auto-Affection (Part 2): Who Are We?" *Graduate Faculty Philosophy Journal* 30 (2009): 219–37.

———. "Following the Rats: Becoming Animal in Deleuze and Guattari." *SubStance* 37 (2008): 169–87.

———. *This Is Not Sufficient: An Essay on Animality and Human Nature in Derrida.* New York: Columbia University Press, 2007.

Lee, Rawdon B. *A History and Description of the Modern Dogs of Great Britain and Ireland (The Terriers).* London: Horace Cox, 1894.

Lee, Yoon Sun. "A Divided Inheritance: Scott's Antiquarian Novel and the British Nation." *English Literary History* 64 (1997): 537–67.

Lemm, Vanessa. *Nietzsche's Animal Philosophy: Culture, Politics, and the Animality of the Human Being.* New York: Fordham University Press, 2009.

Levinas, Emmanuel. *Difficult Freedom: Essays on Judaism.* Translated by Seán Hand. Baltimore: Johns Hopkins University Press, 1990.

———. *Totality and Infinity: An Essay on Exteriority.* Translated by Alphonso Lingis. Pittsburgh: Duquesne University Press, 1969.

Lockhart, John Gibson. *Memoirs of the Life of Sir Walter Scott.* 5 vols. New York: Houghton Mifflin, 1901.

Longrigg, Roger. *The History of Foxhunting.* New York: Clarkson N. Potter, Inc., 1975.

Mack, Maynard. *Alexander Pope: A Life.* New Haven, CT: Yale University Press, 1985.

Mackay-Smith, Alexander. *The American Foxhound, 1747–1967.* Millwood, VA: American Foxhound Club, 1968.

Marvin, Garry. "A Passionate Pursuit: Foxhunting as Performance." In *Nature Performed: Environment, Culture and Performance*, edited by Bronislaw Szerszynski, Wallace Heim, and Claire Waterton, 46–60. Oxford: Blackwell, 2004.

Maxwell, Richard. "Inundations of Time: A Definition of Scott's Originality." *English Literary History* 68 (2001): 419–68.

McCracken-Flesher, Caroline. *Possible Scotlands: Walter Scott and the Story of Tomorrow.* Oxford: Oxford University Press, 2005.

McGann, Jerome. *The Poetics of Sensibility: A Revolution in Literary Style.* Oxford: Clarendon Press, 1996.

McNeill, William. "Life beyond the Organism: Animal Being in Heidegger's Freiburg Lectures, 1929–30." In *Animal Others: On Ethics, Ontology, and Animal Life*, edited by H. Peter Steeves, 197–248. Albany: State University of New York Press, 1999.

McWhorter, Ladell. "Sex, Race, and Biopower: A Foucauldian Genealogy." *Hypatia* 19 (2004): 38–62.

Moore, Daphne. *Foxhounds.* London: B. T. Batsford, 1981.

Munsche, P. B. *Gentlemen and Poachers: The English Game Laws, 1671–1831.* Cambridge: Cambridge University Press, 1981.

Nash, Richard. "Animal Nomenclature: Facing Other Animals." In *Humans and Other Animals in Eighteenth-Century British Culture*, edited by Frank Palmeri, 101–18. Burlington, VT: Ashgate, 2006.

Nietzsche, Friedrich. "On Truth and Lies in a Nonmoral Sense." In *Philosophy and Truth: Selections from Nietzsche's Notebooks of the Early 1870's*, translated by Daniel Breazeale. Atlantic Highlands, NJ: Humanities Press, 1979.

Oliver, Kelly. *Animal Lessons: How They Teach Us to Be Human.* New York: Columbia University Press, 2009.

Overton, Mark. *Agricultural Revolution in England: The Transformation of the Agrarian Economy, 1500–1850.* Cambridge: Cambridge University Press, 1996.

Paulson, Ronald. *Emblem and Expression: Meaning in English Art in the Eighteenth Century*. Cambridge, MA: Harvard University Press, 1975.

Pawson, Cecil. *Robert Bakewell: Pioneer, Livestock Breeder*. London: Crosby, Lockwood and Sons, 1957.

Perkins, David, ed. *English Romantic Writers*. 2nd ed. New York: Harcourt Brace, 1995.

Peterson, Christopher. *Bestial Traces: Race, Sexuality, Animality*. New York: Fordham University Press, 2013.

Pick, Anat. *Creaturely Poetics: Animality and Vulnerability in Literature and Film*. New York: Columbia University Press, 2011.

Pope, Alexander. *The Correspondence of Alexander Pope*. 5 vols. Edited by George Sherburn. Oxford: Clarendon Press, 1956.

———. *Minor Poems: The Twickenham Edition of the Poems of Alexander Pope*. 6 vols. Edited by John Butt. New Haven, CT: Yale University Press, 1954.

Popkin, Richard. "The Philosophical Basis of Eighteenth-Century Racism." In *Racism in the Eighteenth Century*, edited by Harold E. Pagliaro, 245–62. Cleveland, OH: Case Western Reserve University Press, 1973.

Reed, James. *Walter Scott: Landscape and Locality*. London: Athlone Press, 1980.

Rhee, Foon. "Chewing over Obama's 'Mutt' Reference." *Boston Globe*, November 10, 2008.

Ritchie, Carson I. A. *The British Dog: Its History from Earliest Times*. London: Robert Hale, 1981.

Ritvo, Harriet. *The Animal Estate: The English and Other Creatures in the Victorian Age*. Cambridge, MA: Harvard University Press, 1987.

———. "Barring the Cross: Miscegenation and Purity in Eighteenth and Nineteenth-Century Britain." In *Human, All Too Human*, edited by Diana Fuss, 37–57. New York: Routledge, 1996.

———. *Noble Cows and Hybrid Zebras: Essays on Animals and History*. Charlottesville: University of Virginia Press, 2010.

———. *The Platypus and the Mermaid, and Other Figments of the Classifying Imagination*. Cambridge, MA: Harvard University Press, 1997.

———. "Race, Breed, and Myths of Origin: Chillingham Cattle as Ancient Britons." *Representations* 39 (1992): 1–22.

Rogers, Pat. *Eighteenth-Century Encounters: Studies in Literature and Society in the Age of Walpole*. Totowa, NJ: Barnes and Noble, 1985.

Rohman, Carrie. *Stalking the Subject: Modernism and the Animal*. New York: Columbia University Press, 2009.

Rosenberg, Meisha. "Golden Retrievers Are White, Pit Bulls Are Black, and Chihuahuas Are Hispanic: Representations of Breeds of Dog and Issues of Race in Popular Culture." In *Making Animal Meaning*, edited by Linda Kalof and Georgina M. Montgomery, 112–25. East Lansing: Michigan State University Press, 2011.

Russell, Nicholas. *Like Engend'ring Like: Heredity and Animal Breeding in Early Modern England*. Cambridge: Cambridge University Press, 1986.

Sartre, Jean-Paul. "Black Orpheus." In *"What Is Literature?" and Other Essays*. Cambridge, MA: Harvard University Press, 1988.

Schelling, F. W. J. *Philosophical Inquiries into the Nature of Human Freedom*. Translated by James Gutmann. La Salle, IL: Open Court Press, 1936.

Scott, Janny. *A Singular Woman: The Untold Story of Barack Obama's Mother*. New York: Riverhead Books, 2011.

Scott, Walter. *Guy Mannering*. Edited by P. D. Garside. Edinburgh: Edinburgh University Press, 1999.

———. *Ivanhoe*. Edited by A. N. Wilson. New York: Penguin Books, 1986.

———. *The Letters of Sir Walter Scott*. Edited by H. J. C. Grierson. 12 vols. London: Constable and Company, 1932–37.

———. *The Talisman*. Edited by J. B. Ellis. Edinburgh: Edinburgh University Press, 2009.

———. *Waverley*. Edited by Andrew Hook. New York: Penguin Books, 1985.

———. *The Waverley Novels*. 48 vols. New York: Harper & Brothers, 1899.

———. *Woodstock or the Cavalier*. Edited by Tony Inglis. Edinburgh: Edinburgh University Press, 2009.

Secord, William. *A Breed Apart: The Art Collections of the American Kennel Club and the American Kennel Club Museum of the Dog*. New York: Antique Collectors' Club, 2001.

Seshadri, Kalpana Rahita. *HumAnimal: Race, Law, Language*. Minneapolis: University of Minnesota Press, 2012.

Shannon, Laurie. *The Accommodated Animal: Cosmopolity in Shakespearean Locales*. Chicago: University of Chicago Press, 2013.

Shaw, Harry. *Narrating Reality: Austen, Scott, Eliot*. Ithaca, NY: Cornell University Press, 1999.

Shaw, Vero. *The Illustrated Book of the Dog*. London: Cassell, 1890.

Shell, Susan. "Kant's Conception of a Human Race." In *The German Invention of Race*, edited by Sara Eigen and Mark Larrimore, 55–72. Albany: State University of New York Press, 2006.

Sinclair, Iain. *Lights Out for the Territory*. London: Granta Books, 1998.

Sloan, Phillip R. "The Idea of Racial Degeneracy in Buffon's *Histoire Naturelle*." In *Racism in the Eighteenth Century*, edited by Harold E. Pagliaro, 293–321. Cleveland, OH: Case Western Reserve University Press, 1973.

Tague, Ingrid H. "Eighteenth-Century English Debates on a Dog Tax." *Historical Journal* 51 (2008): 901–20.

Taplin, William. *The Sportsman's Cabinet, or a Correct Delineation of the Various Dogs Used in the Sports of the Field*. 2 vols. London: J. Cundee, 1803–4.

Thomas, Keith. *Man and the Natural World: A History of the Modern Sensibility*. New York: Pantheon, 1982.

Thompson, E. P. *Whigs and Hunters: The Origin of the Black Act*. New York: Pantheon, 1975.

Toadvine, Ted. "Life beyond Biologism." *Research in Phenomenology* 40 (2010): 243–66.

Vyner, Robert T. *Notitia Venatica: A Treatise on Fox-Hunting*. 2nd ed. London: Rudolph Ackermann, 1847.

Wall, Cynthia Sundberg. *The Prose of Things: Transformations of Description in the Eighteenth Century*. Chicago: Chicago University Press, 2006.

Wasserman, Earl R. *The Subtler Language: Critical Readings of Neoclassic and Romantic Poems*. Baltimore: Johns Hopkins University Press, 1959.

Weil, Kari. *Thinking Animals: Why Animal Studies Now?* New York: Columbia University Press, 2014.

Williamson, Tom, and Liz Bellamy. *Property and Landscape: A Social History of Land Ownership and the English Countryside*. London: George Philip, 1987.

Wilt, Judith. *Secret Leaves: The Novels of Walter Scott*. Chicago: University of Chicago Press, 1985.

Wolfe, Cary. *Before the Law: Humans and Other Animals in a Biopolitical Frame*. Chicago: University of Chicago Press, 2013.

———. *What Is Posthumanism?* Minneapolis: University of Minnesota Press, 2010.

Wood, David. "*Comment ne pas manger*—Deconstruction and Humanism." In *Animal Others: On Ethics, Ontology, and Animal Being*, edited by H. Peter Steeves, 15–35. Albany: State University of New York Press, 1999.

Woodfall, William. *An Impartial Report on the Debates That Occur in the Two Houses of Parliament.* 4 vols. London, 1796.

Wordsworth, William. "Preface" to *Lyrical Ballads.* In *English Romantic Writers*, 2nd ed., edited by David Perkins, 423–34. New York: Harcourt Brace, 1995.

Wyett, Jodi L. "The Lap of Luxury: Lapdogs, Literature, and Social Meaning in the 'Long' Eighteenth Century." *LIT: Literature Interpretation Theory* 10 (2000): 275–301.

Index